FOUR DAYS
OF NAPLES

FOUR DAYS
OF NAPLES

Aubrey Menen

Seaview Books

NEW YORK

Library of Congress Cataloging in Publication Data

Menen, Aubrey.
    Four days of Naples.

      1. World War, 1939–1945—Italy—Naples. 2. Naples
—History. 3. World War, 1939–1945—Children.
I. Title.
D763.I82N326   940.53'45'73   79-11799
ISBN 0–87223–531–9

FOR

Graham Hall
and I mean, for him

Contents

Acknowledgments
i x

Prologue
x i

PART ONE—THE DAYS BEFORE
I

PART TWO—THE REVOLT BEGINS
3 9

PART THREE—THE FIRST OF THE
FOUR GREAT DAYS
9 3

PART FOUR—THE SECOND DAY
I 9 9

PART FIVE—THE THIRD DAY
2 3 5

CONTENTS

PART SIX—THE FOURTH DAY

263

Notes

277

Acknowledgments

In addition to the sources mentioned in the Prologue, I am indebted to the following for information about the revolt and its background either published, or in manuscript, or in verbal communications:

Giacomo de Antonellis; Professor Giuseppe Maggi; Professor Amadeo Maiuri; Aldo de Jaco; Luigi Basto; Mario Schettini; Mario Orbitello; Giovanni Artieri; Alfredo Parente; Clemente Maglietta; Michele Prisco; Giuseppe Marotta; Antonino Tarsia in Curia; Edoardo Pansini; Antonio Russo; Francesco Penna; Alberto Agresti; Nino Aversa; Francesco Longo; Giovanni Abbate; Lord Maugham; William Merrills, MBE; Giuseppe Giordano; Stefano Fadda; Franco Cucci; Slim Aarons; Kurt Kramer; Domenico Soprano; Francesco Amicarelli; Lello Fontanella; Attilio Tamaro.

Some of my informants have asked to remain anonymous. These include German friends who, returning to Naples, were willing to describe their experiences but did not wish to be named, for reasons which are obvious.

Prologue

When I first saw Naples, in 1948, whole areas of it were rubble. Some of it was from Allied bombardments during the Second World War. But some of it was due to the deliberate attempt of a German colonel to destroy the city, piecemeal, as I shall tell.

It was then that I first heard of the extraordinary revolt of the Neapolitan street boys—the *scugnizzi*, as they are called. They are urchins, very poor, often dirty, but always intelligent and sharp. The boys themselves told me of what they had done.

But in 1948 the world was tired of war, so I did not write about it. Since then I have walked the streets of Naples and talked to its citizens for thirty years. During that time I have maintained contact with the boys, now grown-up fathers of families, and others who saw and took part in the rebellion.

With the aid of the Institute for the History of the Resistance, the Municipal Archives, the Biblioteca Nazionale, and the researches of previous investigators, I have established the historical truth of the events described in this book.

By a governmental decree, No. 518 of 21 August 1945, after a thorough investigation of the rebellion of Naples against the occupying German forces, medals were awarded. Two were of bronze, six of silver, and four of gold.

The gold medal (Medaglia d'Oro) is the Italian equivalent of the Congressional Medal of Honor of the United States of America, or the Victoria Cross of the United Kingdom.

The four gold medals were awarded, posthumously, to four boys who were, respectively, eighteen, seventeen, thirteen, and twelve years old.

PART ONE

The Days Before

CHAPTER ONE

It was a happy truckload of soldiers. Things had taken a sudden turn for the better, just at the time when everybody was expecting the worst. A week ago the soldiers had left Naples with their tails between their legs. And Naples was a good billet for the Germans. The climate was warm; the girls were pretty.

True, the girls were standoffish, at first go. But you could talk them up if you knew a few words of Italian. "Hitler, Mussolini, friends—*amici*. You, me, *amici*, yes?" And if the grand strategy of the world war did not work, chocolates, a bag of coffee beans, or some tinned meat would. Of course, nobody but a fool would trust the Neapolitans when their bellies were full. But they had not been full for some time. They were spectacularly empty. So it had been all right.

But in July 1943, things had begun to go wrong. The weather was still fine, the girls still pretty, and Hitler and Mussolini were still friends. Unfortunately, though, Mussolini had been kicked out of office by his own henchmen and arrested by his own king. The new government (if it really was new—nobody seemed to be sure) had sued for an armistice, and got it.

At first the Germans had received orders to withdraw to Rome, and it had been very humiliating. The Neapolitans had watched from their windows with those dark eyes that told you nothing. Some of the girls, bless them, had been in the streets and thrown flowers. But it had all been very glum.

Then, in a matter of days, new orders had come down from Rome: "Turn back, and hold the city." That was more like a soldier of the Reich's job—not running away like a lot of Italians. And there would be fighting to do. The enemy had landed some thirty miles down the coast, behind some mountains. When the wind was right, you could hear the thunder of the guns. The Germans were ready and waiting for them.

The officer in charge of the detachment in the truck checked his map. "Ottocalli." There were no street names—the Neapolitans were careless about such things as plaques—but there, and there, were the six roads leading to the piazza where he had parked the truck, according to orders. And, God in heaven, what a slum it was! But then it sometimes seemed that Naples was all slum. Up on the hill, where they had their headquarters, it was elegant enough— palaces, gardens, what you would expect of Italy—but the rest made one wonder how people could live in such hovels. Yet they did, and they had for centuries.

He twisted the map about on his knees. That must be the road that led to the airport of Capodichino. Orders were plain and pre- cise. They were to cut all telephone wires (he leaned out of the cabin and saw a soldier busy up a pole, so that was being done). They were also to stop and disarm any Italian soldier or airman coming from the airport. If he obeyed, he was to be treated as a friend and an ally. If he did not halt, he was to be shot on sight. The officer in command looked back to the window and saw that the machine gunner was duly at his post.

He waited. He surveyed the piazza, the narrow streets, and the houses. There was nobody to be seen. He frowned.

The corporal next to him said, "Anything worrying you, sir?"

"Yes. It's quiet."

"It is that, sir."

"Naples is never quiet."

"Come to think of it, no, sir. It isn't."

The officer in command watched the silent piazza with growing suspicion.

"Here comes someone," said the corporal.

There was the sound of a high treble voice singing a Neapolitan song. Then the singer came in view.

"It's only a boy, sir."

The small boy grinned cheerfully and waved to the soldiers.

"Pretty song," said the corporal, and waved back.

"And a pretty little thief," said the officer in command. "Those street boys are cunning little scoundrels, every one of them. They started a fight once in front of this truck. Drew knives on each other. I was fool enough to get down and try to stop it. Ugly sight, two small boys going for each other with nasty-looking blades. They stopped all right, after a bit of argument. Then I found that a gang of their friends had cleaned out the whole damned truck behind, while I was being a good Christian out in front."

"Put-up job, sir," said the corporal sagely. "Yes, I've heard about their tricks. What's the singing about, sir? You know a little of their lingo, don't you, and—"

"Just pillow Italian," said the lieutenant, and both young men laughed. "In any case, it doesn't help. The little devil's singing in Neapolitan and not a word of it can I ever understand."

The little devil sang very rapidly and loudly in his incomprehensible dialect, wiped his nose on the tattered sleeve of his shirt, and disappeared.

The soldier who had been cutting the telephone wires finished his task and climbed back into the truck, all amid the same unnatural silence.

Then it was broken by the sound of automobile engines. The corporal jumped onto the road and reported: "It's two trucks coming from the airport. Italian Air Force."

"Stop them," said the lieutenant, climbing down to stand beside the corporal. "And if they don't stop, use this. It's messy but more sure than shooting."

He gave him a hand grenade.

The two vans were coming at a fair pace down the road. As the first vehicle entered the piazza, the driver saw the German corporal and the grenade he held up high.

"*Alt!*"

The driver came to a screeching stop. But the driver of the van behind saw neither the corporal, the German truck, nor the raised grenade. With a quick twist of the wheel, he drove round the stopped truck and began to cross the piazza.

The corporal threw his bomb. It exploded in the rear of the vehicle, and three men were instantly killed. A fragment of the grenade went into the leg of the driver. He lost control, and the van crashed into the wall of a house.

The men in the first truck—the one that had stopped—came out, white-faced and trembling. At a word from the lieutenant, they threw their pistols and rifles into a heap on the road and then raised their hands.

When the echo of the explosion had died away, the great silence returned, the improbable, the impossible silence. Where were the shrieking Neapolitan women at the windows, the instant crowd of idlers, the turmoil of the smallest street incident?

The corporal looked at his lieutenant, so strangely slow to give his usual brisk rattle of commands, and he saw, with wonder, that his superior officer was afraid.

Then came a long, piercing blast on a whistle. Instantly faces appeared in all the windows, doors opened, and the streets were filled.

With boys. The lieutenant and the corporal stared about them in astonishment. Everywhere there were boys, eleven and twelve years old, adolescents, gangling lads, and all were armed. It was a most curious collection of weapons: hunting rifles, muskets from the First World War, pistols of all designs, and hand bombs. The whistle sounded again. A howl of rage broke from the hundreds of boys: "Assassins! Murderers! Out with you! Go! *Go!*" And the shooting began.

It was random, it was poorly aimed, but it made up the lieutenant's mind. For an instant he had thoughts of turning the machine gun on the howling boys, but the picture of young bodies lying in the streets deterred him. These boys' fathers had been Germany's allies and had fought side by side with his own countrymen.

"Back in the truck! Drive to HQ!" The orders now came crisply enough. "Sound your horn and drive like hell."

The horn blared. The boys, yelling with triumph, leaped aside to let the truck through.

The Germans had established their headquarters in the hotel with the best view in the city. It was on a hill that commanded the celebrated bay, the subject of millions of picture postcards.

The lieutenant, as he stood at attention in front of his commanding officer, had a less attractive panorama to look at. He was in a long, narrow room, with a table covered in green baize. Two oil paintings were the only decoration, old and no doubt worth money. The one on the left showed a lot of men sitting around a table, but was no help at all in what was turning out to be so unpleasant an interview that the lieutenant was sweating inside his too-thick uniform.

The lieutenant's view from west to east was singularly unbeautiful. The prefect of the city, until a few days ago its major civil authority, had a narrow face and a narrow pointed jaw, which he continuously thrust out in imitation of his ex-master, Mussolini. He sprawled a little in his boots and breeches, again in imitation of the stance of *Il Duce*, but he did not have his master's voice. Instead, his voice shot up from time to time, and, to make matters worse, his name was Soprano.

Next came the boss, Colonel Scholl, at the head of the table.* It was he who, at the orders of Rome, had returned to take over Naples. He had done so without the slightest change of expression on his broad peasant face. He did and said *everything* without the slightest change of expression. Perhaps, thought the lieutenant, he could not change if he wanted to. Only a violent tic in his left cheek sometimes set his face in motion. But it conveyed nothing.

Opposite the prefect sat Wessel, the interpreter. As a mere *Dolmetscher*, he was rather overdecorated, with braid and loops of cord, but that was the way with the army. Besides, he was a key man. Scholl spoke not a word of Italian. Wessel, however, was as fluent as a native. He not only changed his vocabulary when he did his duty, he changed the look in his eyes, the way he used his hands, the singsong of his voice. He claimed that he liked the Neapolitans, but nobody liked him.

"Let us go over the matter again. What precisely were your orders?" Scholl was addressing the lieutenant. "Let us go over them precisely." The cheek jumped as though it and not the lieutenant were being rebuked.

"To disarm Italian units, sir, coming from the airport. And to cut communication wires."

"Where?"

---

* The room has been preserved intact, and Soprano later wrote his memoirs, from which this portrait of Scholl is drawn. (See Notes.)

"At a junction called Ottocalli."

"Exactly where is that?" Scholl turned his blank face to a large map on a stand. The prefect rose briskly, making a lot of noise with the heels of his boots as was the fascist manner. Settling his little dagger more firmly into its sheath, he took up a thick pencil and drew a circle on the map.

The lieutenant suppressed a sigh. It was a striking gesture. It was done in all the training films. But the black circle always obliterated the names of half a dozen little Neapolitan alleys.

"You accordingly stopped a truck."

"Yes, sir."

"Another truck did not stop?"

"No, sir."

"You took action?"

"Yes, sir."

"The men on the first truck surrendered their arms?"

"Yes, sir. Immediately."

"What did you do with them?"

The lieutenant bit his lip.

"The arms, I mean," said Scholl.

"Quite, sir. I understood, sir."

Scholl looked down at the lieutenant's written report. "It would appear," said Scholl, "that you left them in the street."

"In the circumstances—"

"The circumstances were that you were opposed by a gang of ruffians."

"Boys, sir."

"*Boys!*" Scholl's voice echoed from the walls.

"*Scugnizzi*, sir."

Scholl looked at the prefect, who hesitated.

"*Scugnizzi*, Commandant," began the interpreter, "are—"

"I perfectly well understand," said Scholl sharply. "The word means 'students.' University louts. They always make trouble."

The interpreter glanced at the lieutenant and then at the prefect. He gave a slight shrug of his shoulders, very Neapolitan, very well done.

There was a long silence in the room. The lieutenant examined the picture on the right wall. It showed some sort of pagan goddess who was leaning forward, bare breasts thrust out. The lieutenant thought how splendid it would be to have his head cozily between those breasts.

"These students were armed?" It was Scholl again.

"Yes, sir."

Scholl's cheek twitched. He turned to the prefect, who had once more sat down. "My orders," said Scholl, "when I took command of the city, were that all arms be surrendered. Anybody who disobeyed was to be shot."

"And those orders were carried out, I assure you," said the prefect when the interpreter had finished translating.

"The prefect assures you that the arms were duly surrendered."

The prefect went on, thrusting out his inadequate jaw. The interpreter listened, and then explained. "The arms were thrown into the sea," he said. "At Santa Lucia." The interpreter looked back at the prefect, and both exchanged a long look. The interpreter gave a nod of understanding imperceptible to anybody but an Italian. The prefect returned the nod.

"I shall teach those students a lesson," said Scholl. Then, to the lieutenant, "You may go."

Outside Scholl's room, the interpreter and the lieutenant drank beer at a bar that had been set up in the adjoining salon.

"But they were *not* students," said the lieutenant. "At least, not most of them." He put down his glass. "Not unless your Neapolitan students are dwarfs."

"I never correct the commandant, when he pretends to know Italian," said the interpreter. "No. They were boys, all right." He shook his head with amused disapproval like a Neapolitan, then drank his beer like a German, banging down his glass. "Yes, *scugnizzi.*"

CHAPTER TWO

Santa Lucia is a fisherman's port, so pretty that it's hard to believe it's real. Brightly painted fishing boats rock in the small harbor on waves that never do much more than lap faintly underneath two charmingly rustic eating places with wooden balconies that give directly onto the water. The harbor is closed off on one side by an immense gray castle, built in the Middle Ages. The other side is open to one of the greatest views of Europe—that of the volcano Vesuvius, shaped like a great crouching lion.

Between the wars, and in the spacious days we know as Edwardian, Santa Lucia had been a favorite spot for tourists from all over the world. Four great hotels had been built nearby to accommodate them. For the further entertainment of the visitors, the *scugnizzi*, clad in small bathing suits or naked as they were born, would swim about in the harbor, then climb, dripping and glistening, to the rails of the restaurants which surrounded it, and importune the guests to throw coins into the water. The people would oblige, and the boys would plunge down like a shoal of dolphins. One boy would catch the coin. He would burst up out of the water, waving it triumphantly in the air. The visitors would applaud; the other boys would clamor for a chance to show off their own skills. More coins would be thrown, and as cleverly retrieved.

They were nearly always retrieved. The boys were very poor. If they did not collect enough money for a meal for their families at home, then, quite simply, the families did not eat that day. The boys began learning the art at the age of nine or ten. Naturally, these little ones did not always succeed in catching the coin underwater in time. But being *scugnizzi*—and there is no word in any language to describe their vivacity, their inventiveness, and their —well, the German lieutenant was harsh but not far wrong about them. For instance, the little boys who were not so good at catching coins would be instructed by older boys (thirteen- or fourteen-year-olds) to have a coin ready in their mouths and to dive only after coins of that denomination. If a youngster fumbled the job, he took the coin out of his mouth at the exact moment when he emerged from the water, and the thrower was delighted. In the case of a strange, foreign coin being tossed into Santa Lucia, only the expert boys dived. For all their apparent, and famous, waywardness, the *scugnizzi* knew and understood the value of organization.

Well before the real armistice, the boys had declared an armistice of their own. The restaurants had been closed because of the shortage of food, and the German troops distrusted the *scugnizzi* and were inclined to chase them rather than throw coins. So the boys gave up swimming.

It was at this point that a fourteen-year-old *scugnizzo*, Niello, gathered the other boys together to discuss the situation. The luxury hotels had been gutted by fire bombs during the Allied bombardments which had preceded the landing at Salerno. The boys met in one of the shattered ground-floor rooms of the hotel that had given the tourists the most spectacular view of Vesuvius. Niello was a slim boy with an excellent figure. His muscles had been strengthened by years of swimming since he was a boy of seven but smoothed into a classical harmony by his youth. A shock of black hair, rarely combed, surmounted a thin face, which—as was once said of Voltaire—when he smiled, seemed all mouth, and when he looked at you, seemed all eyes. His eyes were remarkable: brown to the point of being black, they were either veiled in a Neapolitan melancholy, or they would suddenly shine, be it with anger, or humor, or, most frequently, with an idea that had just flashed across his *scugnizzo* mind. Those who remember him remember above all his eyes. They could cajole, rebuke, and command without a spoken word.

"Niello" was a nickname given him by the boys because he was always talking of the Neapolitan hero Masaniello. Niello had had little schooling. His family was of the poorest—his father was an odd-job laborer, his mother worn with bringing up a large family of children. He helped his family with the money he made by diving, rounded out with stealing, or carrying trays of coffee from bars to shop assistants. Such straightforward jobs he rarely held for long, though, because he was sharp of tongue. The usual badinage of the barmen or customers, taken by most *scugnizzi* with a shrug and a cheerful obscenity, would produce from Niello a reply not easily forgotten. In all the vicissitudes of his boyhood he dreamed of Masaniello, whose story he, like all Neapolitans, had learned from his elders.

Masaniello's real name was Tommaso Aniello. Born in 1620, he was a *scugnizzo par excellence*. The son of a fishmonger, he soon asserted his authority over other boys. While they were merely ingenious and full of tricks, he was bold and daring. There was a traditional game at which he was extremely good. A wooden castle was built and the boys divided up into two "armies." One defended the castle, the other attacked it. Both sides were armed with sticks. Good, solid whacks were given on backs and backsides, arms, legs, and shoulders. The fight continued until either the attackers ran away or the defenders gave up the castle.

Niello, Masaniello's modern admirer, had tried to revive the game. The *scugnizzi* were enthusiastic, but, at the urgent requests of the boys' mothers, the carabinieri put an end to it.

In those tougher times, Naples was ruled by Spaniards, having fallen to that nation in the complex matings of Europe's royal families. It was ruled, and atrociously badly, by a Spaniard with the noble name of Roderigo Ponce de León. That, unfortunately, was the only noble thing about him. He taxed his subjects without mercy and finally, in 1646, enraged them by putting a tax on fruit, often the only luxury that was left to them.

Masaniello was by then a young man, but he was still a *scugnizzo* at heart, and still admired by the boys. He rallied them, and told them to arm themselves with the sticks they had used in their castle game. There were in all some two hundred of them and, with Masaniello at their head, they marched through the city, chanting slogans and singing songs against the viceroy. Any Spaniard they encountered was given a few expert blows with their sticks, and very soon the foreigners took refuge in their houses. This sudden eruption of howling boys alarmed even the soldiers, who made themselves scarce.

For four days the boys, their ranks swollen by hundreds of others, kept Naples in an uproar. They invaded the offices of the Spanish administration, drove out the occupants, and declared themselves the owners of the city. The adult inhabitants, urged on by the *scugnizzi* and ashamed to hold back where mere boys did not, joined in the rebellion. With thousands of boys on the rampage and the citizenry up in arms, Ponce de León acknowledged himself defeated. He asked Masaniello to come and see him.

The cheering people dressed Masaniello in a cloth of gold, and he went, escorted by his boys, to the castle in which the viceroy had taken shelter. Here Ponce de León received him in state and conferred on him the brand-new title of Captain of the People. The tax on fruit was repealed.

That was the story Niello turned over and over in his mind when the Germans took the place of the Spaniards in his native city. True, Masaniello's end had not been attractive; he'd got roaring drunk for nearly a week, been assassinated by the Spaniards, and his naked body had been thrown on a dung heap. But this only made Niello decide never to drink.

Niello was a natural leader; all the boys in Santa Lucia knew it. So when he told them, in very simple words, that it was up to them to do something against the Germans, they listened. He told them to stay together and he fixed a headquarters for what he hoped would one day be his troops, the bombed hotel in which they had forgathered.

Niello's first problem was to make the boys assemble on time. Time, in Naples, is not measured by clocks or watches. It is measured by one's belly. Niello's first stroke of genius was to have a gathering at suppertime. The boys would drift into the ruined HQ (which had a roof and four walls but nothing else) and those deputed to look after the commissariat would produce what food they had managed to steal. The other boys sat on packing cases, or on the floor. On Niello's order, the loot would be placed in a pile in the center. It was then surveyed by a boy whose father was a cook in a restaurant and who thus had acquired some experience in catering. At Niello's nod—the equivalent of "come and get it"—the boys would come up one by one and receive their rations. It was often a combination that only boys could digest—such as chocolate, sausage, and cold canned ravioli—but digest they did, and in continued silence. Then the food was cleared away, and stragglers were thus punished by getting none.

Niello's second problem was information, as it is with all commanders, so the meal was followed by situation reports. The boys who made them may not have looked like much to a sergeant major's eye—dirty shirts, ragged shorts, often made from camouflage cloth stolen from the army, or handed-down trousers—but each boy was the center of a vast nexus of relatives. Where a family could reach the number of fifteen brothers and sisters, with uncles, aunts, cousins, and their peculiar Italian relation, the nipote (the nephew or niece who was not actually a blood relation but had a place at the family table), information could pour in from all over the surrounding countryside and, most importantly, could cross enemy lines. An army must eat, and it eats off the country, at least for those variants of the staple diet such as fruit and chickens and other fresh meat. The daily market where that food was bought was often better informed of what had happened in the last hours than the White House or the chancellery of Berlin.

Pasquale, twelve years old, had a sister who married a man who owned farm property on the mountain overlooking Vietri-sul-Mare. This was the town on the other side of the mountain barrier that separates Naples from Salerno, except for a gap. From her farm she could see Salerno, where the Allied landing was taking place. Her farm was still—just—on the Italian side of the line. Each morning she would bring produce to Nocera Inferiore (on the plain on the Italian side) or, on Tuesdays, to Scafati, a little nearer to Naples. From there it would be bought by middlemen, put on trucks, and taken to the city. There (because this is Naples and not Utopia), it was sold on the black market.

On the day after the landing of the Allied forces, Niello called upon Pasquale to report.

Pasquale stood up. As a sign of respect, he pushed back his forelock, cleared his throat noisily, and sniffed.

Niello asked, "Have you seen Annunziata?" (Annunziata was the sister.)

"No."

"Then sit down."

Pasquale remained obstinately standing. "But my brother has."

The other boys groaned loudly. Pasquale had the misfortune of having a twenty-two-year-old brother who was one of those lads always bursting with news, and it was always false.

"Not Tatore, Mimmo," said Pasquale.

The groans stopped and the boys nodded in approval. Mimmo was thirty and serious.

Niello asked, "What does Annunziata say?"

"It's not going well."

This meant the Allied landing. The other boys looked worried. Pasquale, buoyed by the prestige that bad news gives the bearer, straightened his small shoulders and held his audience.

"Annunziata says that the American ships are firing big guns, and the shells come over Vietri and make a noise like a train going through a tunnel." He demonstrated the noise with brio.

"Where—" said Niello, "where—stop making that row, Pasquale—where are they firing at?"

"Salerno," said Pasquale, who did not know.

An older boy spoke up. "Cava de' Tirreni," he said. "My aunt just arrived from there at our place, scared to death."

"*Cava*," said Niello, with interest. "That means they intend to come over the mountains. To here."

There was a long silence. None of the boys was sure of what this would mean.

"Aldo," said Niello at last, "the newspaper."

Aldo, a tall boy of fifteen who had, on and off, been to school, got up. He took from the pocket of his trousers a copy of *Roma*, the principal local newspaper. It was strongly fascist (and still is, in spite of the fall of the regime, but so are all the other newspapers). Nobody trusted the radio; it had been under the thumb of censorship for too long. But to Niello, all news was valuable.

To get the newspaper into his pocket, Aldo had folded it repeatedly until it was a compact square. Now, very patiently—he was a methodical boy—he unfolded it. He was rated dull by the other *scugnizzi*, but he was given the grudging respect that kings and nobles once gave to priests—the "clerks"—because they could read fluently and the aristocracy not at all. The descendant of the "clerks" took a deep breath. The newspaper was now flat enough to read from.

"There's a lot of the usual," he said.

"Skip it," Niello ordered because Aldo had meant the editorials. "What's new?"

Most of the boys were leaning back and looking bored. Niello's passion for information could, at times, produce tedium.

"Something from Hitler."

"About Russia?" said Niello without enthusiasm. His strategic vision was not very wide, and he had heard too much propaganda about Russia.

"No," said Aldo. "It's about us."

Niello immediately sat upright. "Read it."

Following their leader, the other boys stopped lolling and yawning.

"He says Italy's surrender does not matter. He says the Germans will—will"—he read the text carefully—" 'continue to defend Italy.' "

"That's right," said little Pasquale, wishing to recapture his audience. "Annunziata says there are hundreds and thousands of them in the hills behind Salerno and they've got guns, millions of big guns."

"Shut up," said Niello. "Aldo, go on. Tell us exactly what he says—long words as well."

Pasquale subsided, but he was (except for his figures) right. The plan to land at Salerno was one of the worst-kept secrets of the war. The Germans had advance news of it and moved a large body of troops to oppose it. So fierce was the resistance that at one stage the generals in command of the Allied forces held a conference in which it was proposed to withdraw. The proposal was, however, in the end, rejected. The fighting went on. Ninety percent of the town of Salerno was destroyed.

Aldo continued, reading slowly in the high voice that he had learned to use on the occasions he had actually gone to school.

" '. . . will continue to defend Italy, free from every brake and' —what's 'ritegno' mean?"

"Same thing as brake," said Niello briskly. "Go on. Go on."

Aldo cleared his throat again. " 'The measures adopted for safeguarding German interests subsequent to events in Italy are very severe.' "

The boys were very silent, very still.

"There's more, but a lot of long words and—"

"The measures," said Niello impatiently. "What are they?"

"Doesn't say. Just—well—" He smoothed the paper.

"Just *what*, you donkey? Read it."

" 'The fate of Italy'—this bit's easy—'the fate of Italy must be a lesson to all.' That's the end." Aldo sat down, wiping his upper lip, which had a moustache of beads of sweat.

The boys all looked to Niello. Suddenly their shirts felt thinner than ever. They felt cold and wished that the autumn had not begun.

"Niello, what's it mean?" Other voices took it up. "Yes, what's it mean? What's it mean?"

Niello, his eyes at their darkest, looked not at the boys but out of a window with its jagged fragments of glass.

"I think I know." It was a rather fat and sleepy boy of thirteen who had broken the silence.

Niello looked at him and pointed. "Go ahead, Gi-gin."

Gi-gin was sure he would be listened to if it was gossip or news. He had an uncle in the Customs Guard. These men lived by rumors and hints: tip-offs as to who will be landing contraband and when and where, information which might lead to promotion; tip-offs, too, equally important, as to which head smuggler is ready to pay adequately for them to look the other way.

Gi-gin, lazily, in slurring dialect of the richest sort, said, "My uncle knows an officer who translates for that son-of-a-priest-and-a-carabiniere Scholl, and he says Scholl's going around saying in German that he has orders, real orders, to turn Naples into mud and ashes."

The order, and in those precise words, was in fact given to Scholl from the highest quarters, both in Rome and Berlin.

Niello looked once more out of the shattered window.

"Then we must fight," he said, very quietly.

"Listen to our Masaniello," said an older boy derisively. "Fight, he says."

"What with, sticks?" said another boy.

"No," said Niello. "With guns."

There were cries of protest from all over headquarters.

"Where will you get them? . . . Where have you been, don't you know what the Germans . . . ? It's forbidden. . . . They're stopping people in the street and searching them. . . . They're threatening to shoot anybody who has . . ."

"Shut up, everybody," said Niello, and there was silence. "I already know what you're trying to say. Peppino told me this morning. Peppino, report."

Peppino, a squarish, short boy of fourteen, got to his feet. He spoke clearly, using none of the swear words that customarily peppered the boys' conversation.

"I saw it in Piazza Dante," he said, without emotion. "There was a patrol of Germans. They were stopping all the men. They banged their hands all down the men's bodies, looking for guns. 'All you *guappi* carry guns and you're all of you *guappi*,' I heard one of them say in a sort of Italian."

(A *guappo* is a tough, a bully, possibly a criminal. The word gave rise to the English slang for an Italian, "wop." "Wop" is *guappo* without the initial "g.")

"Did they find a gun?" said a voice.

"No," said Peppino stolidly, "but I'll tell you what they did find."

"What?"

"What they were looking for."

"Well, spit it out, spit it out."

"A watch."

Niello intervened. "Peppino, you'll have us here all night. How many watches did you see them steal?"

"About six. And wallets. They said, 'Papers, papers,' and when the men produced their wallets, they laughed and put them in their pockets. Then they went on to rob the jeweler's shop."

"Which?" said Niello, like a defense counsel encouraging his key witness.

"The one next to the church. They went in, pointed a weapon at him, and said, 'Gun, gun.' He said, '*Nicht* gun, *nicht* gun.' But he had one."

"All jewelers have," said Niello. "They must have known it. Go on."

"So they hauled him off by the arms and his balls."

"Balls?" said a voice, and some boys giggled.

"They put him in a truck and it drove off with him. Then they looted the shop." He seemed suddenly to lose his calm. "The bastards, the bastards, the bastards," he said, and sat down abruptly.

The boys whistled. This was Peppino talking, the boy who never swore.

Niello turned to another boy, a small, wiry child of eleven with thin, agile legs.

"Did you watch from the castle, as I told you to?"

"Yes, Niello."

"Did they see you?"

"No. At least I think they didn't, because when they looked my way, I ran."

Niello took over. "I saw for myself. They were taking the arms they had got from us and throwing them into the sea just a bit beyond the castle. I was too conspicuous," Niello went on. "They drove me away. So I asked little Francesco here to keep watch. How many did they throw in?"

"Dozens. Shotguns mostly. But some pistols. And a lot of rifles, the sort the police use sometimes."

"Well," said Niello, standing up. "We don't fight with sticks. We fight with guns. And how are we going to get them?" he asked with the touch of rhetoric necessary in every leader. "You, my friends, are going to dive for them."

There was complete silence. Niello broke it. "You boys, I take it, can swim," he said ironically.

"But they'll see us," said the boy with the sister Annunziata.

"Not at half-past four in the morning. The sun rises at five. There will be just enough light for us, and not too much."

"And a patrol," a boy grumbled.

"That is why you—and you—and you," Niello said, appointing his team, "when you see a patrol, will run out to them from the other side of the road, screaming your heads off. They will be Italians. I've watched. The Germans leave the road by the rocks to us. It has no military value. You'll scream, 'Quick, quick, father's trying to kill mother. He says she's been fucked by a German.' Then you'll lead them to a place that I'll show you where they will have to run up steps to follow you. When you've got them climbing up, disappear into an alley and run for your lives. We'll hear your screams, and that will be the signal for us to disappear too, till the coast is clear. Do you understand me? Good. Now, the boys who'll dive will be me, you, you, you . . ."

The boys were now all on their feet, excited by the prospect of action. Those who had been appointed were pleased at being chosen, while others, with that perpetual worry of boyhood—the fear of being passed over—were anxious to draw attention to themselves.

"Sit down, everybody," ordered Niello, rising himself.

He was obeyed. By the light in his eyes all could see that he had thought of something that they, mere followers, would not have thought of for themselves.

"We have forgotten something," said Niello. The royal "we" had its usual effect. There was a respectful quiet.

"Some of the patrols are our regular soldiers. But some are the carabinieri." Niello paused dramatically. "The carabinieri are not fools."

There was a murmur of assent. The carabinieri are soldiers in uniform, under military discipline, but they are really the super-police of Italy. They have distinguished themselves in many war-time battles, but it is not this that has won them the peculiar respect in which the Italians hold them. Their training is severe; they are not corrupt; and, as Niello said, they are not fools, by which he meant that they understand their own countrymen to perfection.

Niello continued: "If it's the carabinieri, it's no good spinning them a yarn—no good for *my* plan, at any rate. They may believe that crap about father and mamma, but they will take you by the arm and say, 'Where's the trouble? Lead us to it.' And they'll keep hold of your arm till they find it. Or don't find it because there isn't any."

The silence went so deep that some boys even stopped shuffling their feet.

"'Sright," said an anonymous voice. "They did that to me when—"

"Quiet," said Niello, cutting short a story they had all heard a dozen times. For a long moment he said nothing more. He had that essential to all leaders of men: he allowed time for the others to see that they had not an idea in their heads. All eyes were upon him.

"The boys who will watch for the patrols, stand up."

They stood, chin up, very military.

"Stand up, Maurizio."

Maurizio was eleven. He had a snub nose, long eyelashes, liquid eyes—in a word, he was a very good-looking boy.

"Maurizio, do you know where the commendatore keeps his hunting guns?"

"Of course."

(*Commendatore* is an honorific title scattered as freely as knight-hoods in Britain or *Légions d'Honneur* in France, but it carries weight. In Naples, as one rises in the world, it is fashionable to show that one has not lost touch with the common folk. The *scugnizzi* know how to profit from this admirable trait. Some of them get themselves "adopted" by the rich, not in a legal sense but in an af-fectionate way, running in and out of the rich man's house and his rooms like—as they say—"a cat." Sometimes the relation has some-thing of pederasty in it, but mostly not. In Maurizio's case, pretty boy though he was, it had not.)

"Maurizio," Niello went on, "can you steal one of those guns?"

"Of course."

"And ammunition?"

"Of course."

"In that case, steal them. Will it be noticed?"

"No, the hunting season's over."

"Good. Then you will station yourself at the *top* of the steps that lead down to where those two boys are keeping watch. You will have the gun with you. They will have a flashlight. If it is the carabinieri who are on patrol, they will flash it once. Get ready. As the patrol passes, they will flash it twice. Fire the shotgun. Both barrels. See that you're in some place where it'll make a big echo. The noise of the gun will bring those carabinieri up the steps at full pelt. Then *all* of you *disappear*. Am I understood?"

There was an appreciative sound from all.

"Very well. We begin at half-past four tomorrow morning."

The next day, the boys, shivering in the morning chill, dived and dived again, bringing up hunting guns, pistols, World War I rifles, even old muskets of generations ago. They worked without inter-ruption until an immense clamor of shrill boys' voices from the shore showed that a patrol, fortunately of Italian soldiers, had been duly lured away. The patrol did not return for a precious half-hour.

The master touch to the whole operation was added by Niello. He was in a fisherman's rowboat. Another boy was rowing him slowly back and forth some short distance from the diving boys. He had a blazing acetylene light shining down from the stern onto the water. Another boy beat rhythmically on the sides of the boat with a stick. This was the time-honored practice of fishermen out for a haul of small fish at nighttime. The light attracts the shoal; the beating noise confuses them. They are brought aboard in a silver cascade.

Niello went through these motions, but caught no fish in his net. Instead, at the right moment, he turned off the light. He was rowed silently to the rocks. The arms, which had been pushed into crevices, were loaded into the boat, which was then rowed swiftly round the castle and into the little harbor of Santa Lucia.

CHAPTER THREE

Scholl was not content with relieving the citizens of such dangerous possessions as guns, watches, and folding money. He began to disarm soldiers and sailors on leave while they were walking the streets.

Servicemen on a few hours' liberty are generally in good humor, out to enjoy themselves and look at the girls. Surrounded by Germans armed to the teeth, they usually yielded up their weapons without protest. They were thoroughly tired of them, anyway, and besides, a man longing to get back to civilian life after years of weary war is not going to risk a bullet in his head for the sake of what very soon would become a rusting souvenir.

But while Scholl was disarming the Neapolitans, the *scugnizzi* were arming them. The thing spread from Santa Lucia all over the city. Just as had happened with Masaniello, hundreds of street boys wanted part of the action that Niello had set rolling. The word passed from young mouth to young ear:

"We're going to fight. Get guns."

Niello's tactics were to be the order of the day when trouble came: "Fight and *run*." This is not, perhaps, the sort of command a beribboned general would willingly give his men, but it was a stroke of genius in dealing with lithe boys who knew every alley and turn of the ancient city.

As was inevitable after years of war, there were deposits of arms all over Naples, quite unknown to the occupying Germans. When the surrender came, many Italian units had abandoned their barracks. The soldiers quietly deserted and went back, in civilian clothes and on foot, to their villages. The boys, climbing through narrow windows, looted the arms. Others, expert thieves, stole rifles and munitions under the noses of tired and perplexed Italian soldiers while still others distracted the soldiers' attention by staging sham fights in the way that had so annoyed the German lieutenant. The boys took the stolen arms home and gave them to elder brothers, uncles, and other relatives, who hid them, but who were fearful of where it would all lead.

It was Scholl's passion for collecting firearms which led to the first shot fired in the rebellion of the boys, the first David to go out against Goliath.

The shot was fired in one of the most crowded areas of the city. Piazza Garibaldi is a vast square, so big that it takes five minutes to cross on foot at a brisk pace. On one side is the principal railway station—or rather, at this stage of the war, *was* the railway station, for it had been mercilessly bombed by the Allies. On the other side is a gigantic bronze statue of Garibaldi, a hero who, in the nineteenth century, had also led the fight against a conquering enemy, this time the Austrians. All around the square were shops, stalls, and dealers on the pavements who made up the black market by which Naples survived the war. The bronze Garibaldi looked down serenely on all this illegality, as he still does today.

Immediately next to this piazza is the Piazza Umberto, equally full of people at all hours. It is an undistinguished muddle of buildings, not at all like the setting for the statue of the hero in the adjacent square, but it, in its turn, has had a hero, Giacomo Lettieri, a fifteen-year-old boy.

Two German soldiers stood at one corner of this piazza, armed, determined, and having a fine time carrying out Scholl's orders. Not only were they searching the citizens for arms (and watches), they were disarming any passing Italian member of the armed forces. One of these uniformed passersby was unlucky. Perhaps it was because he could not believe that such a thing could happen in such a familiar place, perhaps because he did not understand German. At any rate, he ignored the order and walked away.

The Germans opened fire.

The soldier fell to the ground, and in a moment a pool of blood formed round his body. He had been shot stone dead. Had his spirit, leaving his corpse, looked about, it might have had food for thought. In an instant the square, previously so full of people, had emptied.

Except for Giacomo Lettieri. The boy looked around him, first at the bleeding body, and then at the empty piazza. He was quite alone. Heads peered from windows or out of sheltering doorways, and meeting his gaze, or that of the two Germans, were hastily withdrawn to safety. So much for the adults.

The Germans studied Giacomo. Giacomo looked at the Germans. The Germans pointed their automatic weapons at him and, with that gesture of the barrel the world is familiar with, motioned him to clear out.

Suddenly a fierce, young, southern rage seized the boy. If that was all his elders could do in the face of the obscene spectacle of the dead soldier lying in his blood, he, Giacomo, would do better. "Fight" was the word running among the boys in the city. Giacomo, hot and sweating with an uncontrollable anger, decided to fight.

There was a rifle lying on the pavement, one of those that the two Germans had taken from the soldiers. Giacomo doubled down to make himself less of a target. He ran, stooping, toward the gun. He picked it up, aimed, and shot one of the German soldiers dead.

"Fight, and run, run, run." The second soldier had already opened fire, spraying the piazza with bullets. Giacomo ran down a narrow street, crossed in great stride the wider one, then plunged into a warren of alleys next to the great bulk of one of the ancient gateways of Naples. He turned left, left again, then right. He stopped at the Via Tribunale, his lungs heaving. He was not being followed. There were no Germans about. He was safe.

He was safe for just two weeks. His home was in the Via Tribunale and he hid there for a while, protected by his family, who maintained to everybody that they had no idea where that scamp of a son of theirs had got to.

"After some girl, I'll be bound," said his father, and, chuckling, added, "He takes after me when I was young."

But soon the confinement, and the tense nerves of his father and mother, began to oppress Giacomo's spirits. He was an active boy, with a great love of dashing about on his motorbike. Finally, in the dead of night, with the consent of his parents, he left his home for a place where he could at least stretch his legs after nightfall. Walking, he went to a relative's house outside Naples in the countryside.

One day another relative came on Giacomo's own bike to bring him some fresh clothes. Seeing his beloved motorbike leaning against the wall of the house, Giacomo slipped out into the open. Although he had given his word that he would not do so during the daytime, the sight of his motorbike, gleaming still from the loving care he had always given it, put his promise out of his head.

He wheeled the bike away from the wall. He fiddled with the controls. It was irresistible; he had to start up the motor and hear its roar once again.

The noise brought his cousin running out of the house just as Giacomo was moving off. The cousin jumped into his path. "Where the hell are you going?" he shouted.

"Just for a spin."

"But I've got to get back to Naples straightaway!"

"Back in five minutes," said Giacomo.

"Five—but *make* it five," shouted the cousin as Giacomo rode off.

Giacomo exulted in the feel of the bike between his legs. He let out the motor and, swaying expertly from side to side, careered down the winding country lane. He came out onto a broad road. He said to himself, "Well, say ten minutes." Then later, the bike working beautifully, he said, "Well, say fifteen minutes. Who keeps appointments in Naples?"

So it would be fifteen minutes before he gave back the bike to his cousin, then half an hour, then one hour, then two hours.

And then, never.

Automatically he headed for Naples, and soon he was in the center of the city, enjoying the freedom, feeling muscles working again that had been idle for long, wearisome days. He pulled up at a crossroads to let a horse and carriage pass. A boy hailed him from the other side of the street.

"*Ciao*, Giacomo. How are you? Long time no see."

Giacomo waved cheerily and drove on.

But the boy who had greeted him was with an adult. The adult said, "Giacomo who?"

"Lettieri."

"I see."

Now this man was a Fascist, and a very sincere one. When the armistice had been declared, the prefect, Soprano, had instructed the population to treat the Germans with every politeness. This man did so willingly. The Germans returned the courtesy by making him a spy.

His job was to be a jolly good fellow, mix with his fellow citizens, and get them to talk. He was then to point out the agitators, the crypto-Communists, and, of course, those of them who were maybe spying for the Allies. The Germans told him which people they particularly wanted and to let them know when he saw them. He was quite good at his job, because he had been doing it for years for the sake of the Party, smelling out the tiny handful of anti-Fascists that precariously existed in Naples.

One of the people the Germans wanted, and wanted badly, was Giacomo. So the spy immediately stopped a passing German car, and in a few minutes was at the hotel that was the German headquarters. He told them breathlessly that the criminal boy had returned to Naples. He was sure it was the boy who had shot the soldier, because he had been in the piazza when it happened and had had an excellent view of his face. The boy's name was Lettieri. He had further information: The Lettieri family lived in the Via Tribunale, and he was quite certain of one thing—Lettieri would try to see his mother. He was, after all, a Neapolitan.

In Naples, even today, when the carabinieri want to find a suspect who is in hiding, they put on civilian clothes and keep a watch on the family house. Sometime or other most lawbreakers return, not to the scene of the crime as they are reputed to do elsewhere, but to their mothers' embrace.

Giacomo was no exception. It was a few minutes before midday; he had spent an hour or two drinking coffee, eating cakes, and just looking at the view of the bay, which he had not seen for so many days. Then, cautiously, he hid his motorbike in a courtyard to which few people ever went, some distance away from where he lived, and ran swiftly to a deserted alley that ran by his house. There was a back wall over which he had often climbed when he had ignored his mother's warnings not to stay out into the small hours. He smiled to himself now as he saw the familiar curtained window. He thought it would be a happy surprise if he came in the way his mother so disapproved of, this time to meet no rebukes, but only welcoming arms.

He lifted the window and jumped inside.

His mother was in the room, but she was unable to embrace him because she was flattened against a wall, staring terror-stricken at a pistol pointed at her head by a German soldier. Against the other wall were Giacomo's little brothers and sisters, covered by the automatic weapon of another German soldier.

Giacomo's mother shrieked when she saw her son, and at once two other soldiers rushed into the room and seized the boy. By twelve noon he was in a truck which tore through the streets until it was outside the city. Here Giacomo was bundled out with kicks and blows.

It was a very beautiful place, the site of the Arco Felice, the Happy Arch, a tall arch of bricks built in Roman times to carry an aqueduct. Its proportions are so elegant, and the surroundings so romantic, that the Neapolitans have taken it to their hearts; hence its name. It was the last of Naples that Giacomo saw.

He was taken to a temporary encampment, where he found eleven other Neapolitans, prisoners like himself. Some were young men, others old. The Germans divided them into two groups, the younger on one side, the elders on the other. It happened that among the prisoners were two brothers named Colucci. The older one asked to join his younger brother, and this boon was granted.

The soldiers gave Giacomo a spade. They told him to dig an oblong ditch. Giacomo obeyed. It was a long task, and the soldiers watched in silence. At one point he stopped and, wiping his forehead, he asked, "What's this for?"

Whether he received an answer to his question is not remembered by the witnesses. A few moments later, as he leaned on his spade, a soldier shot him in the small of his back. In terrible agony, Giacomo fell into the ditch. As he lay there, the soldier shot him in the head, and thus he died.

There were five others in the group of younger persons. These were pushed and shoved to a nearby stone quarry, lined up, and killed one by one.

Then the soldiers returned. They beat the older men with rifle butts until they lay motionless under the blows on the ground. They were then kicked into activity. They were forced to drag the bodies of the five young men to the grave where Giacomo lay. They were made to throw the bodies into the grave, and then to fill it in.

So Giacomo lay near the Happy Arch, to be honored years later (if only he could have known it) with a silver medal for valor.

The day that Giacomo fired his shot, the boys went into action. Niello's sense of terrain told him that the flat part of Naples by the sea around Santa Lucia was no place for a battle. There were too many wide streets with no shelter, and the narrow ones were too far away to be used as escape holes. He decided to fight in the hills that rise behind the town. There was a wide choice. Capodimonte, with its park, its shubbery, and woods, was admirably suitable, but the Germans had noticed its advantages, too, and had planted cannon there, with which they were later to shell the city.

Besides, Niello insisted on another factor—the alleys.

When the Germans had left Naples by the Via Foria, they had rumbled past a huge structure known, when it was built in the eighteenth century, as the Hotel of the Poor; subsequently it was called by the less brutal name of the College of the Sons of the People. When the Germans returned, they passed the same vast structure. On any map of Naples it is the biggest building of all, twice as big as the Royal Palace. Its facade is three hundred and fifty-four meters long—an indication of the size of the poor population of Naples in the eighteenth century, or, for that matter, in the twentieth. It is still an orphanage.

Maurizio, the pretty boy whose friend was the commendatore, had a brother there. Maurizio was a fancy-free *scugnizzo*, but his brother, Emilio, was "in college." To be "in college" in Naples is to be a boy of a large, poor family who is considered too wild to be allowed to wander on the streets. Such a boy is put in an orphanage, with no shame either to his parents or to the boy.

Maurizio would often visit his brother. That is why, young as he was, he was able to solve Niello's tactical problem.

"Ottocalli," he had said, as Niello bent over a tourist's map stolen from a bookstall.

"Shut up," said Niello irritably. He found maps difficult to understand, a failing which, in the checkered history of modern warfare, seems to have been shared by many other commanding officers.

"Ottocalli," persisted Maurizio. "It's just the place. I've seen it when I go to see Emilio."

When the German lieutenant had reported the action which later took place there, both the prefect and the interpreter had leaped to their feet to point out to Scholl where Ottocalli was. The prefect had drawn the neat circle around it which had so irritated the lieutenant.

With Niello and Maurizio, the thing took more time. There was much stubbing with fingers and painful spelling out of names, but at last Niello finally located the large oblong of the College of the Sons of the People, and there behind it was the slum area of Ottocalli, stretching up a hill with a maze of alleys. In the middle of it was Piazza Ottocalli, with no less than six lanes converging on it. The surrounding alleys were so very slumlike that the tourist map had disdained to mark all of them. But Niello knew them. Punching Maurizio affectionately on his back, he said, "You're right. All of us—to Ottocalli."

Most of Niello's band had relatives who lived in the area and they went willingly, because whatever it was that they were going to do, they would have the sympathy, if not the help, of the inhabitants. They made their way up the Via Foria on foot and on bicycles, for there was now no other form of transport.

No sooner had they arrived than other boys and youths crowded around them. Niello quickly checked who had guns and who not. There was to be no shooting till Niello gave a signal, which would be a long blast on a whistle. Meantime, they would make a reconnaissance. He told those boys who lived in Ottocalli to return to their homes and keep watch from their windows, but very discreetly. His own boys he disposed in various alleys, hiding them in doorways and around corners so that they could not be seen from the piazza.

Francesco, the thin boy, was deputed to be the Signal Corps. Some minutes after the boys had scattered to their positions, a truckful of German soldiers arrived.

"Watch them," said Niello to Francesco, "and tell us what they're up to."

"How, Niello? Shall I wave, or just come back and tell you, or—"

"Sing, you little donkey. What songs do you know?"

" 'Io Te Vurria Vasa.' " This was, and still is, a very popular song in dialect.

"Sing it, and make up the words. The Germans won't understand. Sing loud. Sing happy."

Little Francesco strolled around the piazza. He kicked a can about and grinned at the soldiers, one of whom waved back; another, with the shoulder tabs of an officer, gave him a very suspicious look. The truck was parked on the corner of the road that led to the airport of Naples, Capodichino.

Francesco began to sing in the loud Neapolitan way: "I would like to kiss you, two men are cutting the telephone wires, there is a machine gun in the truck, to kiss you, to kiss you. They are fiddling with it. They're up to something na-a-a-sty."

They were. They were out to commandeer the next passing vehicle.

"They're blocking the road," sang Francesco in a piercing treble. Then he ducked for safety down an alley.

Two trucks of the Italian Air Force came down the road from the airport, and Niello and the boys saw the Germans signal the trucks to stop. They watched one obey, and the other skid to disaster. They saw the red blaze of the hand bomb. Little Maurizio, crouching in his alley, was almost sick, for, as the smoke cleared, he saw for the first time in his life three dead men, one with half his head blown away.

Niello gave his signal. Immediately the boys poured into the alleys, while others flung open the windows of their houses. All the boys were armed, but those in the back of the groups had only guns and muskets fished from the sea, which did not as yet function reliably. Boys emerged from all the six surrounding roads. All the boys were pointing weapons in the direction of the Germans, of which one or two were actually firing. The boys were shouting a war cry, "Out with the strangers!" a line from a song that had been sung against the Austrians in Garibaldi's time. A variety of other shouts, less poetic, mixed with the din.

Niello stood ready with his whistle to give the signal for retreat. It was not necessary. The Germans in the truck set their vehicle in motion and, driving straight at one group of boys (who all jumped safely aside), fled down the road that led directly to the Via Foria.

The boys cheered wildly. They had seen their elders running from the Germans. Now they had seen the Germans running from them. They surrounded Niello, shaking his hand, banging him on the back. He should have been flushed with victory. Instead, he was ashen. He put his pistol away in his shirt and said, "The wounded. Look to the wounded."

A wounded man was helped out of his truck. The firing, the war cries, and the cheers had brought the adults to their windows and doorways. Now the women took over, carrying the man into a house and tending him.

Niello stood staring at the three dead men; one had his head split open from his forehead to his throat. The other boys stood around their leader, half horrified, but, boylike, half fascinated by the gruesome spectacle. Niello looked about him. He pointed to an automobile parked in an adjacent street. It was very old and very battered.

"Who owns that?"

A man who had come out of a house when the brief battle was over said, "I do."

Niello looked at it for a moment. It was a hardtop sedan with some boxes inside. "Is there any gas in it?" he asked.

"No," said the man. "It hasn't even got an engine. I took that out and hid it."

"Will it roll if we pull it?"

"Yes," the man said.

"Good. I want to borrow that car. Can I?"

"Yes," said the owner. "Anything you like."

Niello gave more orders. The body of the soldier with the split-open head was taken out of the truck, and one of the large bed-covers for double beds was produced. They are the pride of Neapolitan housewives. On occasions of rejoicing the family wash is taken down from the balconies, and bedspreads hung in its place. The body of the dead man was laid on the bedspread. Since he was still bleeding, it was a sacrifice on the part of some unidentified woman. Six boys then carried the body, slung in the bedcover as if in a hammock, to the sedan. Rope was commandeered and the corpse was fixed to the roof.

The boys were now detailed off. Some were to push the sedan from behind, others to haul it in front. On either side were two files of boys. When all was ready, Niello gave the order for the macabre funeral car to move forward.

As the car rolled onward, the boys set up a mighty shout: "Look what the German murderers have done! To arms! To arms! Fight! Fight! Look! Look! Look! This could happen to your own sons, to your husbands. To arms!"

Windows were flung open. People poured out into the street. Women threw shawls over their heads and set up the high piercing cry that hired mourners in southern Italy use when accompanying the dead on their last journey. Men exploded in oaths and blasphemies.

The procession moved slowly through narrow streets and alleys, avoiding the wide highways where the Germans might be. The city police stood aghast, not knowing what to do. After the procession had gone on for ten minutes, a huge crowd, as is the custom at funerals in Naples, followed on foot. No policeman, no carabiniere, dared interfere. Had one done so, he would have been torn to pieces.

Crossing the Via Foria, where scouts had been sent ahead to see that the way was clear, the procession moved into Spaccanapoli, the poorest section, and the oldest, of the city. Here the boys' cry of "To arms, to arms!" echoed from the facades of centuries-old churches and convents. Shopkeepers slammed their wooden shutters as a sign of respect. Priests and nuns ran out onto the street, crossing themselves and murmuring prayers for the dead. "To arms, to arms!" chanted the boys, and women wept.

When news of the procession was brought to Scholl, he issued a proclamation. He ordered it to be plastered on the walls everywhere in the city. It was designed to bring the Neapolitans to their senses, and to justify anything Scholl would do, or had done.

1. With immediate effect I have assumed absolute command with full powers over the City of Naples and its environs.

2. All citizens who behave in a calm and disciplined manner will have my protection. On the other hand, whoever acts

*either openly or in an underhand way against the German
Armed Forces will be shot. Every German soldier wounded
or assassinated will be revenged a hundred times.*

Citizens! Stay calm and be reasonable.

SCHOLL
Colonel

It was sternly worded, but Scholl was truly shocked. The Italians, though unfortunately not Aryans like the Germans, were held to be a civilized people. After all, they and that very Italian man, Mussolini, had invented fascism, and Hitler himself had approved of a lot of it. So why were they behaving like this?

Scholl stared at the map of Naples, then out of the window into the street below, and finally at the humped shape of the island of Capri on the horizon of the bay. The action made him raise his head. Raising his head made him square his shoulders. What was he brooding about? Had he not—he, Scholl, in peacetime a manufacturer of electric light bulbs, now a full colonel (such were the fortunes of war) with a whole city given over to him—had not he, Scholl, colonel, already explained everything in this very room?

It was the students. Had he not put his finger on it? Students always make trouble. Why? Because they read books. He would teach them a lesson.

He sat down at the head of the table, eyed the two pictures, and decided one was indecent; very indecent. He brought his mind back with an effort.

He had not been a student himself, thank God, but he could be fair. Books had their points. Students read books at all hours, even at night. Reading books after dark was, without question, a useful thing, because it called for electric light bulbs. On the other hand, reading some books could be very dangerous to law and order. In the Thirties in Germany there had been a great burning of books, and everybody had felt much healthier in mind and spirit for it. Scholl would teach these Neapolitans a lesson in civilized living, a way of life they seemed to have forgotten. He would burn some books.

Where does one find books? Scholl knew. Some might consider him just an ignorant factory manager, but he knew where you found books even though he had not had time to read them. People might think that making electric light bulbs was an easy affair—a bit of glass, a bit of tungsten, and there you are. But no; what with one thing and another, it took up all one's time and one went home to the wife and family too tired to read books. But tired Scholl knew where books could be found.

In the university. Scholl had never set foot inside a university, but he knew all about them. There was Heidelberg, where the students, in between reading books, had duels with sabers which left marks on their cheeks for life. Many of the top brass who gave Scholl his orders had marks on their cheeks to this day to show that they had been to a university. Scholl did not have a mark on his cheek. It just twitched. But he knew where books could be found, didn't he? He gave some orders. He was content.

The University of Naples is one of the oldest in the Western world. It was founded by the emperor Frederick II in 1224, thus beating the founding of the Sorbonne (1253) and Oxford (1249) by a short head. Old it was, and so was its library. Saint Thomas Aquinas had taught there. So had Giambattista Vico, the Neapolitan whose philosophy so impressed James Joyce. Vico held that men had first begun to think clearly and thus be civilized when they heard a thunderbolt. Scholl prepared a thunderbolt of his own —to teach the Neapolitans what civilization really meant. Now he, Scholl, would teach them; not Vico or Saint Thomas Aquinas.

The university is housed in a building constructed in various ages, from the sixteenth century onward. Its facade is in the classical style beloved in the Victorian age by banks and stock exchanges. It is approached by a long flight of steps, and the entrance is barred by heavy portcullises of bronze. It lies toward the end of a long street that leads from the Piazza Garibaldi (where Giacomo won his silver medal) to the Castel Nuovo, where Ponce de León took refuge from Masaniello. The street is named after a forgotten monarch, but the Neapolitans call it the Rettifilo, which translates as the Street Called Straight. Beside the university runs a narrow road, Via Mezzacannone, the meaning of which name is lost in antiquity.

Armored cars roared and rattled into the Street Called Straight, blocking it off completely from the Castel Nuovo and the Piazza Garibaldi. Those citizens who were caught remained caught, a captive audience for the show.

German soldiers leaped out and began firing wildly at the houses in Via Mezzacannone. Nobody knew why. Then they smashed down some doors, stormed into one or two apartments, and explained themselves. Somebody had shot at a German soldier going (in Scholl's language) about his lawful affairs. The shot had come either from the university or the apartments in Mezzacannone, inhabited, in part, by employees of the institution.*

The soldiers demanded that the students responsible be produced. There were no students because it was Sunday, a detail Scholl had overlooked. This was frustrating, so the soldiers threw furniture out of the windows and set fire to an apartment or two. Employees of the university were carted off in vans.

Meanwhile, a detachment had entered the university proper. Their entrance was facilitated by a couple of mortar bombs that blew holes in the bronze gates. Once more they found a lot of things to steal, much more valuable than watches. There were microscopes, telescopes, spectroscopes, scopes-for-I-wonder-what, all glittering and obviously expensive. These the soldiers reverently took, and loaded them on the same trucks in which they had put the employees. The instruments, they said, would be useful in the war effort of the Reich.

Pulling themselves together and remembering their orders, they turned their attention to the library. Julius Caesar had burned down the library of Alexandria, but, a writer himself, he had not meant to do it. These soldiers, like their master, were not writers. They sprinkled the shelves with gasoline, withdrew, and threw hand grenades into the midst. The place burned satisfactorily, and so did a good part of the rest of the university.

While the library burned merrily, a military operation was being carried out in the Street Called Straight. Some seven thousand people were rounded up, from the sidewalks or chased out of their houses. For no apparent reason except, perhaps, a Teutonic sense of tidiness, they were divided into two columns: men in the first;

---

* The most minute investigation has not discovered any such shot.

women and children in the second. They were marched, under the heavy machine guns of a number of armored cars, to the area in front of the university.

The assembly completed and the audience ready, the principal actor of the show was dragged onto the stage. He was a sailor, a merchant seaman, a "strapping young man" as those who saw him remember him. As the soldiers tugged and pushed him, he shouted desperately at the crowd: "I didn't do anything! I didn't do anything! I swear I never shot anybody. On the bones of my dead mother I swear I didn't!"

It was the most serious oath an Italian can swear. We can believe him.

The crowd, however, was to be fully informed of the plot of the play. A Fascist functionary got up on the base of a monument and made a speech. He was elegantly dressed, with a neat beard. The sailor, he told his listeners, had dared to draw a gun on a member of the forces of Italy's allies, the Germans. He had shot the soldier dead.

The sailor was being pushed up the steps of the university with rifle butts, but he found breath to scream: "I didn't! I didn't!"

The audience was also a part of the cast of the play. A movie camera, mounted on a light tank, filmed them as they listened, filmed the orator, and panned slowly along the facade of the university, from which flames were now pouring.

In addition to the mortar bombs, a tank had fired a cannon shot into the bronze gates, tearing a great hole in one of them. Inside the gates was a hallway, now fully ablaze. The sailor was pushed toward this oven, but the officer in charge changed his mind. It would be a salutary lesson to burn the sailor alive, but the act would necessarily take place offstage, from the audience's point of view. He therefore ordered the sailor to be dragged back and tied to one of the other gates. The sailor's cry of agony as the hot metal burned his back was all but drowned by the voice of the orator.

"Kneel," he said to the crowd. "Kneel out of respect for this act of justice."

The crowd, under the machine guns of the armored cars, knelt.

The janitor of the university was in the crowd, and has put down his observations in writing. Three soldiers, according to him, stood at the foot of the steps and fired at the sailor with automatic weapons. The shots tore open the sailor's belly and, as he fell, he screamed, "Mamma, mamma, I didn't do it."

The officer in charge stepped forward and shot him with a pistol in the back of the neck, after which he lay still and silent, for he was dead.

"Clap," said the orator. "Applaud this well-merited punishment of an enemy of the great Italian people."

And the kneeling people clapped.

PART TWO

The Revolt Begins

CHAPTER FOUR

The boys of Santa Lucia gathered the day after in a glum silence.
The food was distributed and eaten in the same unnatural quiet.
Then Niello, his dark eyes at their darkest, said, "Well, what
news?"

There were more boys than usual, some who did not belong to
the swimming clan but were *scugnizzi* of the street. They had come
because of the procession with the corpse. Many had joined it. All
wanted to know whether it had roused the people. Niello ignored
the newcomers and called, one by one, upon his faithful.

He looked to Peppino, the boy who never swore. Peppino
stood, reluctantly.

"Any news?" Niello repeated.

"Nothing we don't all know."

Through the minds of all the boys passed the vivid pictures of
Scholl's reprisals—the burning of the university, four sailors shot
on the steps of the Stock Exchange, and random killings of other
members of the armed forces.

"Gi-gin?"

He with the uncle in the Customs did not even trouble to rise.
"I saw the bodies of the sailors. They left them on the steps."

"Everybody saw them," said Niello impatiently. "And everybody saw our procession. What did they say?"

Again a silence.

"What did they *do?*" Niello repeated. "Your brothers. Your
fathers. Are they going to fight?"

One by one the boys said no, but none by opening their lips.
Some gave a slight shake of the head, imperceptible to anyone who

did not know the Neapolitan well. Others accompanied the shake with a little deprecatory noise made with the tongue against the teeth: "Tsk." Others lifted a forefinger and moved it slowly to and fro, the Naples gesture for "Nothing doing." In a city where so much fails, so many hopes are dashed, one does not make a great display of announcing failure.

Little Maurizio, the friend of the commendatore, got up. He threw back his small shoulders. He pushed out his chin. He had often seen the commendatore address political meetings, and he faithfully copied, in miniature, the big man's way of getting up to speak. He looked at the ceiling. He joined his hands behind his back. Then, in his childish treble, he said:

"The commendatore says we have only made things worse for everybody."

There was a murmur of agreement. A quick smile of satisfaction flashed across Maurizio's face, to be instantly suppressed.

"Why?" said Niello.

"Well, why, *because*," said Maurizio.

"Because what?"

"Because, because," said Maurizio, who had forgotten all the reasons the commendatore had given him as he sat on his friend's knee. His thoughts had been elsewhere. He had been estimating, as usual, the size of the tip he would be given.

"Anyway," he went on with a touch of stubbornness, "anyway —" He unclasped his hands and, not knowing what to do with them, doubled his fists and thrust them into the pockets of his shorts. "Anyway, he's missed that gun you told me to take, because he's given up all his guns to the Germans and he thinks it's the butler, and the butler's a thief, God knows, so it might have been."

He sat down abruptly, feeling he had made a fool of himself in some inexplicable way. But he had got the ball rolling. Boy after boy confirmed the commendatore's opinion.

After the first deep emotion of seeing the corpse on the car had passed, brothers, fathers, uncles, male relatives of every age had gone about their business as usual. When questioned, they had angrily dismissed the thing as a boyish prank in bad taste. "Poor devil, why drag him through the streets like that?" "Did you think of what his mother might have felt?" And so on. They were excuses, and they did not last. The procession had its effect, but it was to be a delayed one; just then, Scholl's reprisals were much in their terrified minds.

Then one of the street *scugnizzi*, a new boy to the group, rose. "My mother says I shouldn't have been in the procession. It won't do any good. She wants me to go and say *Avemariagratiaplena* fifty times and go and pray to San Gennaro." He rattled off the invocation, then still said in Latin, as one word.

There was a general murmur of agreement, and a voice in the uncertain timbre of an adolescent added, "That's what monsignore the cardinal says—my mother says, that is, that that's what he says." Untwisting his tongue he added, "He does, too."

Niello smiled his broad smile that illuminated his whole face. He looked at the boy who first brought religion into his plans. "Do what your mother tells you to do," he said.

There was general approval of this wise advice, but the meeting was suddenly cut short. A boy, breathless and wide-eyed, burst into the room. He had been deputed to stroll around Santa Lucia and keep alert to any move on the part of the Germans, for Niello suspected that, after the procession, the boys might be identified and his headquarters raided before he had time to find a new one.

The sentinel, tumbling over his words, told Niello that a group of Germans had come to blow up the whole of the pretty little port.

"Scatter!" ordered Niello. "Leave one by one, walking slowly."

Naples cannot be understood without understanding San Gennaro. He was, and is, the most important person in the city. It does not matter that a pope, his cardinals, and the pope's most learned historian of Christianity have declared in solemn Latin and a dozen other tongues that San Gennaro never existed. For Naples, he does. They have a little vial of his blood to prove it. And although the cardinal in whose care the souls of Naples are entrusted believes the pope is infallible, he never denies that this is really the blood of San Gennaro, while at the same time (since the pope cannot be wrong) he must privately hold that there is no such person. He has learned that in Naples it is true, and not true.

San Gennaro's real name (although of course he had no real name because he was not real himself) was Januarius. He was the bishop of Benevento, a town to the north of Naples. He lived in the time of Constantine the Great and he was martyred for his faith. He had his head cut off in Pozzuoli, a suburb of Naples on the northern arm of the bay. A man, once blind, whose sight Januarius had miraculously restored, piously gathered up some of his blood in a bottle.

In 1387 Januarius worked another miracle, although he had been dead a thousand years. His blood in its bottle had turned to powder, but suddenly it liquefied, then it returned to being powder. In the same year it liquefied again, and once more went back to its dry state. San Gennaro was plainly a bishop of orderly habits, for he arranged that his blood should liquefy twice a year, and always in the same months—May and September. Most times, the blood lique-fies. That signifies that all will be well with the city. When it does not, there will be trouble for all.

September, it will be recalled, was the month in which Scholl took over the city.

The faithful turned to "Monsignore" (the Neapolitan way of referring to His Eminence the cardinal) for advice. What should they do? They crowded outside his residence. They flocked round him in the cathedral. "Monsignore, what shall we do? The *scugnizzi* say we should fight. Monsignore, how can we fight the Germans? Monsignore, Monsignore, what shall we do?"

Cardinal Ascalsi knew his flock. He was, after all, the bishop of Naples and not of another and different city. He passed among the suppliants, benign, calm, smiling reassuringly. He listened, finger-ing his great gold pectoral cross.

"Wait for the miracle of San Gennaro," he said. "Then we shall know."

With that he would extend his hand. Bobbing down, the faithful kissed the jewel of his ring, and were calmed.

That was why Niello was wise to tell the boy to obey his mother. He, too, was of Naples and no other city. But Niello had no trust in San Gennaro at all.

Niello was the last to leave the headquarters. As he prepared to do so, he heard a shot. Thinking it had been fired by the Germans, who invariably fired warning shots in the air when they began an operation, Niello shrugged his shoulders.

But at that moment one of the boys burst into the room. "They're firing!" he shouted.

"I know. I heard," said Niello. "They always do."

"Not *them. Us.* We're firing back."

"Gesù-Maria!" said Niello and, crouching low, went out. A rattle of gunfire greeted him and, amazingly, it was coming not from the Germans but from the Castel dell'Ovo.

The Castle of the Egg is so called because of its shape. It juts out to sea in a stone oval, founded securely on the rocks of a small promontory. It is a medieval castle and has very thick walls. Also, like all other castles of that period, it has rooms large or small deep in its bowels and beneath ground level, such as storerooms and dungeons.

With the Allied bombing, a great number of Neapolitans were left without homes. Many migrated to the countryside, where they had relatives. Others, not so lucky, lived in any sort of shelter they could find—caves in the hills, road tunnels, railway arches, or what remained of bombed-out warehouses and factories. Two hundred citizens—men, women, and children—took possession of the basement rooms of the Castel dell'Ovo. It had been a military post, but with the fall of Mussolini and fascism, most of the troops had been withdrawn. A handful—some twenty men—remained to man an antiaircraft battery and a radio.

Very soon the castle became a sort of village. In the daytime the residents foraged for food. In the evenings they gathered to eat, talk, and make their own amusements. The tiny armed force willingly joined them.

The most popular member of the community after nightfall was Pulcinella. That was not his real name; nobody, not even himself, ever used that. To be Pulcinella was much more honorific. It went back for more than three centuries, to the time, that is, Shakespeare saw a Pulcinella in an Italian troupe of players who visited London and picked up hints from his clowning and his humor. Pulcinella always wears a white smock with large black buttons down the front, wide trousers, pointed shoes, and a pointed hat—in a word, the costume of Pierrot, a character derived from him. He also wears a black mask across the top of his face.

Pulcinellas, whole generations of them, had their years of glory on the Italian stage. Now they had fallen on hard times, but they were still, in these years of war, a fixed part of the Neapolitan scene. They were still professionals, as they had been in Shakespeare's time.

The Pulcinella of the nights in the Castel dell'Ovo was an experienced man of some forty years. In better times he would parade through the alleys of Naples, dressed in his costume and followed by a man who beat on a drum. With him was a *scugnizzo* who went round with a hat to collect offerings from the crowd that always gathered. Pulcinella sang songs; he told jokes; he made wisecracks about the current news, much in the manner of a stand-up comedian of today. Every so often he would break off to do a little advertising: So-and-so has a particularly fine delivery of clothing from Milan; such-and-such has cut his prices; a famous film actor would appear for six nights running at the principal theater; and so on. But it was his wry and cheerful comments on the events and scandals of the day that brought in the coins. He was a licensed jester; he could, with caution, even make fun of the Fascists when they were the rulers of the country.

On the night the news spread that Scholl was going to blow up Santa Lucia, he performed as usual, but his jokes fell flat. He changed his repertoire. He picked up a mandolin from a family's pile of household goods and, strumming, began to sing the famous songs of Naples. He chose one to suit the mood (as he thought) of his audience, a song about Santa Lucia itself.

"When the moon rises," he sang, "wherever I am in the world, I know I cannot stay away from Santa Lucia."

"Well, you'd better," said a rude youth, "or you'll get your ass blown off."

Pulcinella, his artistic soul wounded, stopped singing. There were a few titters, quickly suppressed. Through the holes in his black mask, Pulcinella's eyes gleamed with anger.

"And you, young gentleman," he said to the lad who had interrupted, "what are you going to do about *your* ass? Run to mamma?"

The company looked at one another awkwardly.

"We sit here," said a woman, "and do nothing. And they're going to blow up Santa Lucia. Why?"

"Why did the Americans drop bombs on us?" said an elderly man, full of philosophy. "It's war. What can we do?"

"Shoot the Germans when they come," said the rude youth. "Those over there," he said, pointing to the soldiers. "They've got guns. They've got ammunition."

"Uh-oh, no," said one of the soldiers hastily. "I'm not here to shoot down German soldiers. I shoot down airplanes."

"You shoot *at* them," said his companion with a soldier's ironic wit.

"All right, all right," said the first soldier hotly. "So I haven't hit any of them. You try and do better with that rusty old iron of an antiaircraft gun. It's a bloody disgrace, the guns they give us. Where's the money we pay in taxes all gone to?"

Pulcinella touched a chord on his mandolin. He sang a few couplets of his own invention. They dealt with one of the principal topics of the whole war—the corruption which surrounded *Il Duce* and which he tolerated. *Il Duce* reviewed the troops in one place, sang Pulcinella, and while he slept, the officers rushed the troops' new uniforms and equipment to the next reviewing place. It was an underground story, heard many times before in bars and cafés, but made more piquant by Pulcinella's neat rhymes and tripping tune. When he had finished, there was loud laughter and applause.

Just as the clapping died away, a young woman came into the room. Everybody looked at her, for she had the astonishing beauty that is sometimes found among the poor of Naples. Her face was oval, and her eyes, widely spaced, were deep, dark wells. Her mouth needed no makeup. Her black hair, usually her pride, was dank with sweat and in disarray, but this only added to her attraction. She walked with a heavy, tired step, leading a little boy of nine by the hand, then sat down wearily on a chair that a man had hastily made available.

"Rosa," he said, "you look tired."

She held up a bag, but said nothing.

"What did you get?"

"Flour."

"Flour!" said several people. It was a rare commodity.

"I stood in line for five hours," she said. She took off her shoes and rubbed her toes. She had no stockings.

"Where?"

"The barracks." There were stores of food in the military buildings of Naples, but Scholl had commandeered it.

The antiaircraft gunner said, "Did the Germans let you?"

"Yes and no. They made us stand in line to keep us in order. They had guns. Then a van drove up. The Nazis jumped out. They opened the doors of the barracks. We all broke the line, but they fired shots in the air and made us stand in line again. Then the soldiers began carrying out bags of flour—quite small bags. Then—" She stopped.

"Go on," said several people.

"Then a little boy, just a bit older than my Giacomo here—" She stroked his hair. Giacomo began to cry, silently. "Don't cry," said his mother. "It won't do any good. It won't bring him back."

Giacomo sniffed and wiped his face with the back of a grubby hand.

"Something happened?" said the gunner quietly.

Rosa stared at him with her great eyes. "Yes. A little boy saw a bag they had dropped. He ran to pick it up. They shouted at him to stop. But he wouldn't. He picked up the bag and ran. Then they shot him. He just lay there, bleeding. The bag had burst and there was flour all over the road. A workman who was passing by went and picked him up. He stood there with the boy in his arms. 'He's dead,' he said. And then, 'Who is going to tell his mother?' "

The gunner swore. "Christ!" he said. "Jesus Christ!"

Rosa looked at her son. "It might have been Giacomo," she said in a flat voice, emptied of all emotion.

"It might have been anybody, any of us," said the rude lad. "It's just as the *scugnizzi* said. So now you see what I mean."

A narrow bridge, two hundred meters long, joins the shore to the castle. (It is this bridge which, today, tourists must cross to reach the restaurants of Santa Lucia, and watch a new generation of *scugnizzi* diving in its waters.) The Germans had occupied this bridge. The detachment was small; there were some soldiers and some members of the Sturmpionier, the Pioneer Corps. This latter group had busily set about mining the bridge when, to their utter astonishment, they were fired on from the Castel dell'Ovo. They immediately flung themselves flat on the ground and wriggled to safety behind the wall that runs around the port.

It was in this undignified position that Niello's boys found them when, at Niello's orders, they had scattered. They hid themselves behind the same rocks as those in which they had temporarily cached the arms they had brought up from the sea. It was a glorious moment for all of them. Their procession, it would seem, had not been in vain. The adults, at last, were fighting back.

There was a pause while both sides studied the situation. The Germans peeped over their low wall and examined the sheer stone flanks of the castle. There was nobody on the roof. The shooting, they therefore decided, was coming from the narrow slits of windows that made an irregular pattern in the ancient stones. This made things difficult. The slits were designed so that bowmen outside would have found it a hard problem to get an arrow inside. It was much the same with bullets. Unless somebody stuck his head out, he was safe, except for the actual moment in which he emerged to aim and fire.

Inside the castle, the civilians and soldiers who had, after a night of discussion, finally decided to fight began to wonder exactly what they had done, and how they were to go on doing it. The slits were scattered: Medieval bowmen, they presumed, had merely twanged away without coordination or leadership. Facing modern automatic arms was a different matter.

Crouching with the Germans was a middle-aged Fascist, who was acting as a guide. He suggested that Neapolitans usually would listen to reason if it was told them in their own dialect. Neapolitans, he said, were apt to be silly when they lost their tempers, but the silliness did not last. He proposed that he should talk to them.

The soldiers in the party were inclined to agree. But the Sturmpionier had come to blow up the bridge, and it was their habit to blow things up as told and to leave it to others to settle what followed. The box with its plunger was on the sidewalk of the bridge. The fuse trailed from it as the charge of dynamite was securely strapped in place.

"Cover me with fire to distract their attention," said the chief pioneer, and rose. A soldier got up with him, and together they walked boldly to the bridge. They set foot on it. The soldier played a burst of bullets against the castle from his automatic gun, not aiming at anything in particular since there was nothing but a wall and slits as a target. The pioneer walked toward the detonator.

There was no sign from the castle. The boys behind the rocks clenched their fists, digging their nails into their palms.

The pioneer bent over the detonator. A shot rang out from the castle and the soldier pitched forward on his face, flinging his gun wide. He lay so very still, the boys knew he was dead. Only by a great effort of will did they refrain from raising a cheer.

The pioneer ducked and ran for shelter behind the low wall. Pioneers were not fighting men. Shooting broke out from the castle, but he escaped, zigzagging in the approved fashion. It died down when he was no longer visible.

"Bring him in," ordered a sergeant, and two soldiers ran out to fetch the body of their comrade. Again the marksman behind a slit took aim. Two bodies now joined the first on the bridge.

The boys jumped up and down, but the Germans were too busy to notice them.

The pioneers carry walkie-talkies to use when warning their comrades in the vicinity of an impending explosion. The sergeant took this and began to try to make contact with headquarters—a long business as it turned out. Meanwhile, hundreds of shots were exchanged between the Germans and the castle. When the sergeant got through, he described the situation and asked for orders. He got them, but, with due deference, he pointed out that a handful of men could scarcely storm an enormous medieval castle that had probably withstood thousands of besiegers and survived weeks of cannonades. Headquarters said it would send reinforcements. The firing went on.

To the boys' disappointment, no further Germans were hit; it was not at all like the movies. But the shots, even though they missed their target, were still a delight.

Then, with a roar, two tanks came pounding up the Via Partenope, which Niello had rightly divined was much too broad for the boys to fight in. Their long cannons were trained on the castle. The Fascist interpreter climbed on one of the tanks, and, safely out of range of fire from the castle, spoke through a loudspeaker.

"Please be reasonable," the loudspeaker blared. "You have no hope. They mean to shell the entrance to the castle, and then bury the lot of you alive."

There was silence from the castle. There was no more firing, for the good reason that, in this first great spree of resistance, the soldiers and the civilians had exhausted all their ammunition.

The Germans, watching through binoculars, saw men moving

on the ramparts. Things were being thrown into the sea. They were the breechblocks of the antiaircraft guns, and were soon followed by listening devices and a radio. The Germans withheld their fire, for here was an obvious sign that they had won.

Soon, soldiers, airmen, and some sailors who had deserted came out of the castle entrance, their hands raised. Civilian men followed them, then women and children, fluttering white handkerchiefs.

From the rocks the boys peered out at the procession, and were heartbroken.

The defeated were dragooned into an orderly column and marched away in the direction of Vesuvius, toward the main port. A long road, Via Cesare Console, leads up to the heart of the city. The boys followed at a long distance, keeping the Germans in sight. There was hope among them that the prisoners would be taken to some barracks and then—the women and children at least —be sent home.

Halfway up the road the Germans halted the column. Eight of the men in uniform were called out. The civilian men, the women, and the children were herded onto a patch of grass to watch. The men in uniform were lined up facing a wall. A machine gun from one of the tanks was pointed at them.

"Why are those men standing like that?" little Giacomo asked his mother. "Are they going to do peepee?"

His mother put her hand over his eyes. It was hot and trembling. "You mustn't look," she said.

Giacomo pulled her hand away. "Why?" he said. "It's nothing I haven't seen before. Men doing peepee against the wall."

Firmly she covered his eyes.

An order was given. The machine gun spoke. Amid the terrified screams of the women and children, the eight men were mowed down. They fell to the ground in twisted attitudes, some staring up at the sky as though a thunderbolt from the clouds had struck them.

An old woman next to Giacomo's mother said to the little boy, "Why shouldn't you see what your mother's done? She and her tongue! If it hadn't been for her, this wouldn't have happened. You and your tongue and your stories and your flour!" she went on in a hysterical gabble. "Bitch!" she shouted. "Bitch!"

"Silence!" said a man in the tank. "Get in line!" The soldiers, using the butts of their rifles, pushed the crowd into a semblance of order. A command was rapped out and the crowd moved forward. The same tank that had killed the men now ground and rattled close at their heels.

They were held for a day, then released. The bodies of the men lay in the road for three days, as a warning to the rest of the population.

They are buried today in the military cemetery of Poggioreale. Their names are Sergeant Major Alfonso Cappuccio, Soldier Salvatore Spiridiozzi and Soldier Ludovico Papini, Sailor Guglielmo Bertazzoni and Sailor Bruno Zambretti. Three of the bodies have never been identified. They were apparently twenty-five-year-olds: an airman, a sailor, and—an antiaircraft gunner.

Scholl had been instructed to "reduce Naples to mud and ashes." We may ignore the rhetoric and say, in defense of the German high command, that this was a legitimate act of war. A little less grandiloquently (but only a little), it was known as the "scorched earth policy," and it was adopted by the Russians. The aim was to retreat leaving nothing of value behind which could be useful to the enemy—food, growing crops, bridges, factories, machinery, and so forth.

Scholl began in a manner that was almost comic. He issued solemn orders for the immediate surrender by the owners of the appropriate shops ("on pain of being immediately shot") of one thousand watches, to go, this time, not on his soldiers' wrists, but to be transported to Germany. One thousand radios and one thousand cameras were also required on the same terms. Further—and here is the touch of the absurd—he also sequestered one thousand accordions. Neapolitans are well known to be musically inclined, and perhaps Scholl had been infected. One wonders why he did not order one thousand experts at dancing the tarantella to be rounded up and sent to accompany this curious gift to embattled Germany.

Naturally, the German Army, locked in combat at Salerno, had not much transport to spare for such things as accordions. Scholl solved this problem. He issued an order that all automobiles and trucks should be instantly commandeered.

And here the air of Naples seems to have affected his soldiers. As well as being fond of music, the Neapolitan takes delight in recounting the doings of clever tricksters, even though he may be an honest man himself. The word "imbroglio" has even passed into the English language for a contrived muddle in which the trickster emerges triumphant.

The trick in this case is still recalled with wry amusement by the Neapolitans. It went this way:

The means of transport were to be seized whether on the roads or in garages. A German soldier would duly present himself and his written order. The soldier chosen as the lure or bait would always be able to speak a little Italian. The owner of the car or truck would read the requisition order and begin to tear his hair.

"But for the love of God, how can I earn my living if you take away my truck? I'm a poor man!"

The bait would be sympathetic. "Me poor man, too. Me understand. Me poor soldier. Soldier must obey, or me shoot."

"No, no, don't shoot, don't shoot!"

"No, no, *me* shoot. Them. Officers. *Me* shoot. *Me* got wife and children."

"*Mondo cane, mondo cane,*" says the owner of the truck, an Italian phrase meaning it's a world only fit for dogs.

"Me got dog. Wife, two children, big dog. In Hamburg."

Then, in the fashion of all soldiers, he would pull out his wallet to show snapshots to prove his point. The owner would do the same.

"Beautiful, beautiful," the bait would say, tears in his eyes as he saw the victim's pictures. "Italians, good people. I love Italians. Naples very beautiful. I love Naples." He would eye the money in the truck owner's wallet. There would be no words between the two for a few moments. "Italians very clever people. Know how to do things."

The money from the owner's wallet would rapidly change hands.

The bait would stuff it into his pocket. He would warmly pump the other's arm. "*Arrivederci.* Italians very clever people. Me, poor man. *Mille grazie* [a thousand thanks]." And he would disappear.

Round the corner he would rejoin his accomplice, a soldier who could speak not a word of Italian. He would show him the loot. A few minutes later this second soldier would accost the owner and, pointing a gun at his head, duly, honestly, and formally requisition the truck, which would then be delivered to Scholl.

These and other tricks of the same nature drew forth in Scholl a curious sense of right and wrong. He posted a proclamation on the walls of the city which said that German soldiers who took property without the proper authorization did so at the risk of being punished. The proclamation was in German, and not in Italian.

His moral duty done, Scholl set about the further destruction of the city. He organized demolition squads, one of which the boys had seen at Santa Lucia. That pretty little port was soon laid in ruins. What was left of the hotel that had been the boys' headquarters was gutted by flamethrowers. Niello's army, as he had foreseen, was temporarily homeless. But a good commander is always ready to shift his headquarters; and Niello was already searching for a site. It led, as I shall describe, to one of their most useful and humane actions.

The demolition squads next moved on to the main port. Nature had not made this a very good one. The Greeks and the Romans had used Miseno, far out on the northern arm of the bay, or Pozzuoli, where Saint Paul had once landed on his way to Rome and martyrdom. But the foreign rulers of Naples had wanted easy sea communications with their native countries, and, by man-made works, they had greatly improved Naples' inadequate harbor. Moles had been built out into the sea, within which the Mediterranean was always tranquil. They made it such a good harbor that Horatio Nelson kept his British men-of-war there for a long time, finding security, and a mistress, Lady Hamilton.

All this the squads industriously destroyed. A good deal of the demolition was carried out at night, a piece of what was then called psychological warfare, because it kept the inhabitants awake. It is not easy to sleep when you can hear your native city being systematically reduced to ruins. During an aerial bombardment, one at least went to a shelter where there were your neighbors, songs, and jokes to keep up your spirits. Now you just lay in bed, quite safe, but wide awake, wondering what sort of desolation would greet you when you got up in the morning.

There was plenty to see. Santa Lucia went down to gelignite and flamethrowers. The main port was too solidly built for that treatment, but there were ships in it, and they were sunk. The port buildings were blown up, and so were the adjacent houses. Both ports were mined with booby traps. These, in fact, were Scholl's visiting card which he left behind him when he finally fled. They exploded long after the Four Days had driven him out and Naples was in the hands of the Allies. He booby-trapped the main post office. The mines went off seven days after the arrival of the Americans (October 1) when the post office was packed with people sending the good news to their relatives in various parts of Italy, communications having been restored. Fifty people were killed and one hundred injured. Twenty days later, when the boys and the fishermen had begun putting Santa Lucia together again, more mines went off, killing five and injuring twenty-five.

But the booby traps were more in the nature of a joke on Scholl's part, or a parting insult. The serious business was the destruction of Naples' means of livelihood. Naples had never been a great manufacturing center, but there were some substantial plants, giving employment to thousands. More importantly, there were tens of thousands of small workshops, where artisans made numberless articles, including those carved boxes and statuettes that are still made in family concerns and are still eagerly bought by tourists. Both categories of plants were destroyed by Scholl—the factories completely, the small workshops as far as time would allow.

The motorcar works of Alfa-Romeo went up in smoke; the factory of the famous beer Peroni suffered likewise, although it was very many months since it had made any beer. Ansaldo, the shipbuilders, followed, together with (and this was right and proper according to the rules of war) an armaments factory, a branch of Armstrong's, one of the most prosperous firms in the world just at this juncture. It made torpedoes for both sides.

Niello's headquarters were no more. He needed a safe place to which to retreat. Ottocalli would not do; it had been excellent for guerrilla warfare, but the Germans had searched every house in order to find him. He chose Camaldoli.

The hill of Camaldoli is over four hundred meters high and it has a view often described as the finest in Italy. It overlooks all the city and both arms of the bay. The islands of Ischia and Capri stand sentinel on either side of this stupendous panorama. Behind lie the mountains of the Apennines, while on the side to the north lie the plains that are bisected by the road to Rome. The hill is approached by a rural road that winds repeatedly between orchards and vineyards. Near the top is a village with an irregular little piazza and an old gray church, and at the very top is a monastery with a chapel that has a solemn facade, known locally as the Hermitage. Running down from this is a cliff, its rocks overgrown with vegetation. The hill is hived with caverns.

In the village was a deserted house with a square tower. Niello forced open the wrought-iron gate and climbed the rotten wooden stairs. He came out on the top of the tower. He had with him a pair of magnificent Zeiss binoculars (stolen, naturally, by one of his gang). He saw that, from this tower, all Naples, with its entrances and exits, could be kept under view.

This was Camaldoli's great advantage.

He cautiously weighed its disadvantages. The winding road was long and wearisome to climb. It would be an obstacle for tanks, which would get stuck in the hairpin bends, but not for motorcyclists, who could race up it with ease. The Germans were well equipped with this means of transport, and had daredevil riders who knew how to use it. As a headquarters, it could be taken by assault, but not before the enemy's move was well advertised. And in that case, there were the caves. Many were deep, all hidden by thick, semitropical vegetation. If the boys hid in there, it would take weeks to winkle them out.

Camaldoli was, Niello decided, too far from Naples and had too difficult a communication road for it to be used as a fighting headquarters. But as a redoubt, a place of last refuge for his men, it was ideal. Hitler, later, was to think the same of his house, the "Eagle's Nest," in the Bavarian Alps over Berchtesgaden.

Niello had taken a detachment of boys to reconnoiter. He sent them now on an expedition among the cliffs to find a suitable place where provisions and arms could be stored for any final desperate stand. Meanwhile, he enjoyed himself with his huge binoculars on the tower, imagining how he woud dispose his troops if he had an army to take the city.

He focused on a path that wound in and out of the face of the declivity in which were the caves. One of his boys was scrambling up it, with an expression of sheer terror on his face. He was Eduardo, a thirteen-year-old *scugnizzo* and one noted more for the nimbleness of his legs than his courage. Niello, studying the boy's face, was tempted to leave his observation post and run to meet him. But he restrained himself: Having to wait for news to be brought to one was the bane, and the essential art, of being in command. He compromised by going down the stairs and waiting by the rusty iron gate to the tower.

Eduardo, breathing painfully, his clothes torn by brambles and his bare knees covered with soil from where he had stumbled, finally arrived at the gate. He collapsed on a stone seat. Niello waited till he could speak.

"Well," he said at last, "have you seen a ghost?"

"Worse," said Eduardo. "Much worse. The black men are here."

"Come inside," said Niello.

Inside the tower, Niello made Eduardo sit down on the stone floor. He obeyed. His eyes were dark with fear. Niello searched in a haversack and brought out a bottle of red wine. He offered it to Eduardo.

"Thanks, I need it," the boy said. He pulled out the cork with his teeth and tipped up the bottle between his lips. He ran the wine about in his mouth for a while, then spat it out onto the floor.

"Better," he said, his tongue loosened. "The blacks are just down there. . . ."

"Drink," said Niello.

"Thanks," said Eduardo again. He put the bottle to his lips and drank deeply.

He stopped drinking and wiped his mouth with the back of his hand. "Good," he said.

"It should be. Andrea pinched it from Gambrinus."

That was the name of Naples' smartest restaurant, right opposite the Royal Palace.

"Now report," said Niello, and sat down beside him.

"I was looking for a cave when—"

"Where?"

"Down by the path that runs beneath the Hermitage. I was going along—"

"Which way?"

"That," said Eduardo, pointing to the north. "I saw a cave— well, just the top of it; the rest was all covered with bushes and things. There was a sort of trampled path through them, so I knew it had been used. Lovers, I thought. You know. That sort of thing. They often come up here to—" Eduardo broke off with a knowing smile that the wine had helped.

"Stop gossiping," said Niello sternly.

"Yessir," Eduardo replied. Gossiping is the vice of the city. Once launched on it, a citizen is hard to stop. Niello took the bottle of wine away.

"Now report properly. You saw a cave. You were frightened. Why?"

"I went inside to see if it would do for us. Then two enormous black men pounced on me, yelling like mad. I fought them off me. I hit one of them clean on the jaw. He fell over. Then the other man made for me, but I tripped him up—"

"How could he have made for you if he had already pounced on you?" said Niello, without any due emphasis to his question, and in a quiet voice.

"Well, I mean . . ."

"Now stop lying and tell the truth," said Niello.

"Yessir," said Eduardo.

"Two black men," Niello prompted.

"Well, not exactly black. Brown more like."

"Were they in uniform?"

"Not exactly in uniform. Bits of uniform like."

"Were they armed?"

"No."

"Then why were you frightened?"

Eduardo fell silent. He hung his head.

"You were frightened because of the stories from Sicily of black men raping women and children. Am I right?"

"Yes." Eduardo nodded eagerly.

"So being a child, you were raped," said Niello. "Where did they put it? Up your bottom?"

"Cut it out," said Eduardo, sulkily begging off any more sarcasm.

Niello, smiling, cut it out. He handed back the bottle and Eduardo took a grateful swig.

"Tell me, did they have beards?"

"Yes. Big black beards. And big teeth."

"So they were smiling at you."

"Maybe. I was scared anyway."

"Come with me. Show me the cave."

"But, Niello—"

"You needn't come in. Just take me there and then come back here. There's bread and salami in the satchel. Get moving."

Eduardo hesitated. "You'd better take a gun."

"I don't think so," said Niello. "Forward march, and quick about it."

Eduardo led him there. Then, leaving Eduardo to go back to his salami, Niello went alone into the cave. Two shadows rose in front of him. They advanced from the gloom into the light coming from the mouth of the cave. They held their hands in the air.

"*Kaputt*," they said. "Good men. Not bad men," they said in a language Niello did not really understand, but which, from the sound of it, he knew to be English. "Good boy," the tourists had cried at him in Santa Lucia when he had emerged from the water holding triumphantly aloft the coin they had thrown into the harbor.

Niello nodded. He had assessed Eduardo's report correctly.

"Prisoners of war?" he asked. The two bearded men looked blankly at each other. Then Niello crossed his wrists dramatically in front of him. "Prisoners," he repeated. "*Kaputt.*"

Both men broke into broad smiles. They had indeed, Niello reflected, large teeth, and very white they were in their brown faces. They both crossed their wrists in imitation of Niello's gesture, nodding vigorously.

"You escaped?" Again the blank look. Niello made the swift gesture, very like a karate chop, which unmistakably suggests running swiftly away.

The men nodded. "We," they said, pointing to each other, "Indians." "Indians," they repeated. "Indiani," said one of them, obviously the brighter of the two, for he had picked up the Italian plural. Then he seized his companion and swung him around.

Niello, who had felt till then that he had done very well in the circumstance, was dumbfounded to see that the man had his jet-black hair done up in a bun like a woman. Niello began to have doubts about his analysis of the situation. "Indians, eh? I wonder. No turbans?" East Indians figured abundantly in the stories of Sandokan, a swashbuckler in Malay and very popular reading for boys then and now. Niello made an expressive gesture, circling his head with his hand.

Meekly, both men pulled up a leg of their trousers. There were the turbans, bloodstained, and used as bandages for the scratches and wounds gathered in their escape.

Niello nodded. "Good boy," he said in English. "Good boy."

Both men heaved a great sigh of relief. Then one of the Indians patted his stomach, and then put his hand to his mouth in a gesture of eating. Next he put his hands together in the Indian form of greeting and bowed low before the *scugnizzo*.

"Please," he said in English. "Please."

"Wait," said Niello. He smiled reassuringly at them, and left abruptly.

He clambered up the cliff face by means of the goat track by which he had come. When he reached the top, he went to the deserted house he had selected as an observation post. A little weary in the legs, he climbed the rickety stairs. At the top Eduardo, seated on the floor, his back against the parapet, was preparing to eat the bread and salami that he had found in the satchel. The two-thirds-empty bottle of wine showed Niello how he had happily spent the intervening period.

He was carefully slicing the salami with his clasp knife when Niello emerged. The long, torpedo-shaped loaf he had already sliced neatly along its middle. He looked up.

"Glad you're back safe. I was right, wasn't I? They're the blacks we've been warned about."

Niello did not answer. He picked up the satchel, then the bottle. Putting the strap of the satchel over his shoulder, he recorked the bottle and put it beside the open loaf of bread. Then he took the salami out of Eduardo's hand.

"Give," he said, indicating the knife.

Obediently, Eduardo gave it to him. "I was just going to eat," he said. "You said I should eat, and one must eat."

"So must the blacks," said Niello. "They've got to get up their strength. Do you know why?"

"No, why?"

"To rape you," said Niello. "Get the boys here in twenty minutes."

"Yessir," said Eduardo, eyeing the satchel hungrily as Niello disappeared down the stairs.

The two men in the cave were Indian soldiers, captured during the fighting in North Africa and transported to Italy as prisoners of war. By a quirk of the history of the war, the British transported a great number of Italian prisoners to India.

The two men were Sikhs, a fighting sect of Indians. The bun of hair that had disconcerted Niello was a symbol of their faith. They do not cut their hair or their beards, which is the reason they wear turbans. These two men had put their turbans to a practical use. In the confusion following the armistice, it was an easy matter to escape from the prisoner-of-war camps. But it was then that the trouble began, for they had to make their way south to where the Allies were. They chose the route through the Apennine Mountains, which run like a spine down the peninsula.

Just now, Niello had the problem of what to do with his two Sikhs. They could not live in the cave; autumn had begun, and in Naples that can be damp and cold with a good deal of rain. They could not be smuggled, as they hoped, to the Allied lines; the Germans were too well established around Salerno for that to be possible. They had to be put somewhere safe until, as Niello trusted, the Allies arrived.

Niello assembled his boys, and, as always happened in Naples, one of them had a relative—a female cousin—who lived in the countryside nearby. She was Emilia Scivolini, one of the most remarkable characters in the whole story of Naples' resistance to Scholl.

CHAPTER FIVE

Emilia was a mature woman when Niello met her. She had married young, to a peasant-proprietor of Camaldoli, but, what with war in Ethiopia (which her husband had fought and survived) and this one, her married life had consisted largely of sex on leave to produce the usual brood of children. Finally, her husband had been sent to the Russian front. He had never been heard from again.

Husband and wife owned a prosperous farm on the slopes of the hill of Camaldoli. It was run from a large and rambling farmstead, built a century ago for a family even larger than those customary in modern times. There was an abundance of rooms nobody used, except visiting relatives who, in this time of disruptions, came rarely.

Emilia ran the farm in her husband's absence. Some of the fields she had to leave fallow due to a lack of farmhands. The others, with a vineyard and an olive grove, gave her a surplus over her needs. So Emilia still lived comfortably. There was food for her children, an invalid father, a nondescript mother who was always complaining, and herself. There was also some money kept in a tin box under her matrimonial bed. She had gotten used to sleeping alone in this bed, what with one war and another. In any case, it was said of her, in the Neapolitan phrase, that she was "married to her stove." She liked cooking and she was a good cook.

She had a Junoesque figure—not fat, but ample—and had been quite a beauty in her youth with those slightly slanted eyes, common to women of these parts, which Sophia Loren has made world-famous. She habitually wore black, which she had put on in mourning for some aunt or uncle and had found, like so many Neapolitan women, that it became her. It showed she had seen life and death, something rather deeper than procreation, which was the limited lot of younger women.

On Sundays Emilia went to the old gray church, a black lace shawl over her head, and muttered prayers for her husband at the elevation of the Host. There was a crucifix in a side chapel, with a man-size Christ hanging from the cross. He was made of plaster, and ample quantities of plaster blood were to be seen as if flowing from several wounds. Emilia thought the crucifixion was a pity. She had not read the Bible because she could not read at all, but, from what she had heard about Jesus of Nazareth, she knew him as a good man who did not harm anyone. Nazareth she knew very well. It is the name of a village next to Camaldoli, and she always imagined him and his mother walking its roads. We may fairly sum up Emilia's religion by saying that she did not really like anybody being crucified.

Niello went with the boy who was her distant cousin to the large and now rather dilapidated farmhouse. For an hour he was quite unable to get his message across, because it was nearing lunch-time and Emilia insisted that the two boys join her at the family table. This settled, she disappeared into the kitchen, saying, just as Eduardo had done (and it is a saying in the city), "Tell me afterward. You must eat."

It had been a long time since the two young city boys had eaten their fill, so the message duly waited. Then, over a table still littered with plates and glasses, Niello said he had found two Indian prisoners of war in a cave.

"They were hungry and—" He did not finish the sentence, because Emilia had immediately got up and gone to her kitchen. Niello and the boy cousin exchanged glances and shrugs. She came back with a basket.

"Take that to them," she said. Then, feeling more at ease, she sat down at the table again.

"What did you say they were?" she asked. "*Inglese?*"

"No," said Niello. "Indians. But they are on the English side. That is why they got captured."

"Indians?" said Emilia, looking very blank. The word conveyed to her red men with tomahawks, living in wigwams.

Niello patiently explained that these were not red Indians but brown ones. Emilia still looked puzzled.

"Like Gandhi—he with no trousers," Niello said.

Emilia clapped her hands. "Like that sweet little man," she said.

Gandhi, for reasons never made clear, had visited Mussolini. The Fascists had made much of the visit. Pictures of him had been displayed everywhere.

"What can I do for them?" asked Emilia.

"Hide them," said Niello. "And, of course, feed them."

"What do that sort of Indians eat?"

"Rice, I think. Yes, rice. I read it in Sandokan."

"I haven't got any left. Mamma here gobbled it all up."

"Then they'll have to make do with your spaghetti."

"Lucky fellows," said the boy cousin, reminiscently licking his lips.

"All right," said Emilia, getting up. "You boys help me clear the table. You can bring your Indians here. As long," she said, her hands full of a pile of plates, "as long as you're sure they're not red Indians. I wouldn't like to be scalped," she said, and laughed.

"You won't be scalped," said a thin, querulous voice. "You'll be shot."

It was *la mamma*, nettled by being called greedy, and, as always, ready to find fault.

"Shot?" said Emilia uncertainly. She went into the kitchen. There was a rattle of plates in the sink and a clatter of knives. Then came the noise of a squeaking pump being operated as she drew up the water from a well beneath the farmhouse. "Who says I'll be shot?" shouted Emilia.

"The Germans," said *la mamma*, also raising her voice till it cracked.

The noise of the pump stopped. Emilia came out of the kitchen, wiping her hands on a cloth. "What do you mean, 'the Germans'?" she said to her mother. She sat down slowly at the table.

"When I say Germans, I mean Germans," her mother said, shaking a finger at her. "If you hide those savages, the Germans will shoot you. Up against a wall. They shoot everybody who hides prisoners of war. They've said so."

Emilia took a grape from the bare wooden table on which it had fallen from its bunch. She ate it slowly, pursing her lips. She spat out the skin.

"The wine will need keeping," she said. "Too much rain."

"If anybody needs keeping, it's you," said her mother. "In

Nocera Inferiore." This was the little town in which there was a lunatic asylum.

Emilia looked straight at Niello. The boy returned her look steadily.

"Is this true, Niello? About shooting, I mean."

"Of course it's true," shouted her mother. "Everybody says so."

"There's a poster outside the carabiniere's post down the road," said Niello.

"Ah, yes, yes, of course. I read it," said Emilia. Her father silently raised both hands in a gesture of despair. It was Emilia's fixed habit when embarrassed by being illiterate to claim she could read.

"It says," said her boy cousin, "that anybody giving shelter to prisoners of war will be"—he paused and grew specific—"*'passed under arms,'* " he quoted.

"What's that mean?" asked Emilia.

"*Shot*," said her mother, biting off the word.

All at the table watched Emilia. She picked up the dish of grapes, rose, and made once more for the kitchen. At the door, she turned. "Well," she said, smiling, "it'll be quick. And I won't have to listen to any more of your grumbling, mamma." She nodded to Niello. "Bring them here. Rice, you said. I'll see if they've got any up at the Hermitage. They've been hoarding like mad ever since the war began." She went into the kitchen. The pumping began again. Niello and the boy cousin collected the plates. Other members of the household got up and helped them.

"Pigheaded," said Emilia's mother, above the clatter. "Pigheaded, that's what she is. Always was, from a little girl. Remember when she wanted that pink dress? 'Too short,' I said, 'you're a growing girl.' 'Too short,' said Don Mario. 'Don't come to Mass in it.' "

Her father performed a complicated gesture with his head, an acquiescing nod that by subtle stages turned into a worried shake of the head. He reached into the breast pocket of his jacket and took out one of the long, dark Italian cigars that are made from tobacco grown in the hills overlooking Salerno, and are known as *Toscani*. He examined it carefully for faults.

"But she wore it. She wore it," said Emilia's mother. "Didn't she, Arturo? Arturo, I'm talking to you."

Emilia's father looked up from his cigar. "Eh?" he said. "What?

I suppose so. You're always right. There's a hole in this cigar," he went on. "It won't draw. I bet it won't draw."

He lit it, and it did not draw. Emilia's mother watched the operation, as she had done a thousand times before. "You should choose better when you put down our good money for it," she said, again a statement from her as ritualistic as the Mass to which Emilia had gone in her pink dress.

Arturo took another cigar from his pocket.

"Well," said *la mamma*. "If she wants to get herself shot, let her, I say, let her."

"Now, mamma," said Arturo, lighting up a second cigar. "You don't mean that," he said in a contented voice between puffs. "She's a good girl."

The cigar drew well.

An hour later, Niello and little Maurizio sat on the low wall that runs along part of the road that leads from the church to the Hermitage. Niello seemed deep in thought. Maurizio held his peace. He swung his bare brown legs for a while, then caught sight of a lizard. He scratched out a piece of the crumbling stone and threw it accurately. It hit the lizard, who rolled over, recovered, and scuttled for safety. Maurizio yawned.

"Niello," he said, "what's wrong?"

"You wouldn't understand. You're too young."

"You always say that. Then you talk to me nineteen to the dozen."

"That's because you've learned manners from your friend the commendatore. The other boys haven't got any."

Maurizio's pretty face lit up with the compliment. "The commendatore says I'm a bright boy—the brightest *scugnizzo* he knows. He says," Maurizio rattled on, "one day I'll be a famous—a famous . . ." He paused.

"Famous what?"

"Never mind."

"Criminal?"

Maurizio tossed his heels into the air with a loud laugh, almost falling off the wall. "How did you guess?"

"You told me. One day when you were imitating the way he talked. Do it now. It takes my mind off things."

Maurizio put his hands behind his back, pushed out his small chest, and, as far as he was able, deepened his voice.

" 'My dear good friend signor Niello,' " he said, laying a hand on Niello's shoulder. " 'You look very worried on this bright September morning. These are bad, bad days. No,' " he said, holding up a warning finger. " 'Don't tell me just *now*.' " His voice broke into a treble, but he recovered. " 'Let me offer you a coffee at Vivo's bar, laced with just a little of his excellent brandy, if he has any left. Then we shall both feel better.' "

Niello smiled. "Thank you, Commendatore. Let us do just that."

Maurizio slid off the wall and waddled importantly to a bar a few yards away. Still clowning, he entered.

"A coffee with brandy, I think you said, Commendatore?" said Niello. "Boy," he went on to the young man behind the bar, "the commendatore would like your best coffee with just a dash of brandy."

The young man polished a glass. He joined in the game.

"I am deeply distressed," he said in an unctuous voice, "but I have no coffee and no brandy. The Germans took the lot yesterday. Perhaps the commendatore would like a glass of soda?"

" 'These are bad times, bad times,' " said Maurizio again, then broke down into giggles. He resumed his normal voice. "I haven't any money for a soda. Have you, Niello?"

Niello felt in his pockets and shook his head.

Two sodas were served. "They are the last two we've got. The factory is closed," said the young man. "You're Niello, aren't you?" the young man went on. "We've heard of you. It's on the house."

The boys drank. Niello frowned into his glass. He turned to the barman. "You say the Germans were up here? Right up here?"

The barman nodded.

"How many?"

"Just two. On a motorcycle and sidecar. They took all the coffee and the good liquor." He pointed to a gap in the shelves.

"Thanks for the drink," said Niello.

The barman murmured that it was nothing and that he was glad to have met . . . but Niello was propelling Maurizio toward the door. The boys sat on the wall again.

"This is the trouble," Niello said, and he told Maurizio about Emilia. "You see," he said finally, "if the Germans come up here, it may happen."

"What?"

"I told you. She could be shot."

Maurizio sat completely still.

"Because of me," said Niello.

Maurizio put his hand on his friend's arm. "The Indians could run for it," he said. "They could hide in the bushes. That time I stole the camera from the car, a man spotted me and chased me. That's what *I* did. I hid in the bushes. He never found me. He passed right by me. Swearing something wicked, he was. The names he called me! But he never found me."

Niello put his arm around Maurizio's shoulders, but his look was far away.

"If they had time. Time . . ." he said. Then, "I must have a plan."

"You will," said Maurizio. "You always do."

The lizard cautiously crept out of hiding, but, seeing Maurizio back again, fled precipitously.

Maurizio watched it. "You know," he said thoughtfully, "I don't think I'll ever be a famous anything. I'm too fond of fooling around. But you will."

"Time," said Niello, almost to himself. Then: "Thanks for the compliment—Commendatore. Let's go."

Niello and Maurizio went to the abandoned tower. Eduardo was nowhere to be seen.

"*Marronne*," said Niello, swearing part of an oath which refers to the mother of God in none too polite terms. "I'd quite forgotten him."

"Who?" asked Maurizio, panting slightly, for he had found the steep steps trying for his short legs.

"Eduardo. He must have gotten hungry and gone home."

"Eduardo is always hungry," said Maurizio critically.

"Especially today. I borrowed his lunch and gave it to the Indians."

"*Mannaggia la Marronne*," swore Maurizio, rounding out the oath of the elder boy. "He'll never forgive you."

Niello had not heard the old saying that an army marches on

its belly, but he felt guilty about Emilia's spaghetti. It increased his feeling that he was slipping in his leadership.

Emilia's boy cousin joined them on the tower.

"How did it go?" asked Niello.

"Fine," said the boy cousin. "I took the food basket to them. While they ate, I told them we would come for them when it was dark."

"That was clever of you. While I was sitting on the wall with Maurizio, it suddenly hit me that those two don't speak Italian. It was quite a sweat talking to them. I was waving my hands about like a marionette. How did you manage it?"

"You'd told me about their not understanding anything much, so I borrowed Aunt Emilia's old wristwatch and twiddled the hands about. One of them's as stupid as an ox, but the other's quite bright. He caught on. He gabbed away to his friend, then they nodded to me. Here's the watch." He took it from the pocket of his trousers and looked thoughtfully at it. "I must remember to give it back," he muttered to himself. Then, aloud to Niello, "You know," he said, "it's true. Aunt Emilia might get put against a wall. The Germans have been up here once already."

"I know," said Niello.

"Don't worry," said Maurizio brightly. "Niello's got a plan."

"Only half of one, worse luck," said Niello.

"Well, let's hear the half of it, at least," the boy cousin urged. "I'm scared."

Niello picked up the binoculars and gave them to the cousin. "Down there, at the foot of the hill, is where the road begins. Anybody who wants to come up *here* must start *there*, unless he's going to clamber up the cliffside like a monkey. Now just take a look at that group of houses where the road begins. Through the glasses."

"Can't see a thing," said the cousin.

"Twiddle the knob, you thickhead."

The boy obeyed. "Yes. I can see the houses. Well?"

"Do you know anyone who lives in them?"

"Of course I do. The pink one belongs to Paolo. Paolo Longobardi," he explained. "He's my godfather."

"Good, we're getting somewhere," said Niello, his self-confidence returning a little. "We'll put a lookout here, who'll keep watch. The boys can do it in turns."

"It'll be a bore," protested Maurizio. "Up here all alone."

"Make it *two* boys," said Niello impatiently.

" 'Sright," said Maurizio, glad to have his finger in the pie. "They can play seven-and-a-half"—the most popular of card games among boys; the suits—swords, cups, money, maces—are of antique design.

"But it's no good unless it's played for money," said Maurizio, now well launched as a committee member. "And who's got any money?"

"I'll offer a prize," said Niello.

"What?" Maurizio asked.

"How do I know until you steal it?"

"I see," said Maurizio calmly. "I'll try for one of the black-mar-keteer's wallets in Piazza Garibaldi."

"Then that's settled. Now, how's your godfather about the Germans?"

"They took away his Fiat," said the boy cousin. "He loved that car."

"Then he'll help. What he's got to do is watch out for the Germans—him and the family. If he sees them—they come on motor-cycles, I'm told—he's to hang out something red on that clothes-line you can see. That'll warn the boys up here."

"If they're not busy bashing each other because one of them's cheated," said Maurizio.

"There's that," said Niello, taking back the binoculars. "But there's another problem. How are we going to stop the Germans just roaring up the road even when . . ." He surveyed the coun-tryside around them through the lenses without finishing the sentence.

Maurizio finished it for him. "Even when we *know* they're roar-ing up," he said sagely.

"To shoot my aunt," said the boy cousin.

Niello, intent on his survey, made no answer.

Since the chairman of the committee was silent, Maurizio felt that he had the attention of the meeting once more. "We've got to delay them. Time," he said solemnly, quoting Niello without acknowledgment, "time is what we need."

Neither Niello nor the boy cousin said anything.

"One thing we could do is to put a cart across the road as though it's broken its axle or something," Maurizio went on.

The boy cousin said, without heat, "You can go around carts, you donkey."

"Two carts," said Maurizio stubbornly. "The drivers can be having a quarrel. They can be bashing each other."

"Bashing again," said Niello. "You can't get your mind off bashing." But he still looked through the binoculars.

"Besides," said the boy cousin, "they'll suspect a trap, wave their guns—"

"And the drivers will run like hell," said Maurizio in a resigned voice. "Well, *I'm* not the great brain, *he* is," said Maurizio, pointing to Niello.

Niello put the binoculars down on the parapet of the tower. "Who owns that field over there?" he asked. "The one with the flock of sheep."

"My aunt," said the boy cousin. "She rents it out for grazing."

"And that boy who's looking after the sheep, who's he?"

The cousin shrugged. "Shepherd boy. Don't know his name. Lives in Camaldoli."

"Maurizio," said Niello, "shout something rude to that boy."

"You're crazy," said Maurizio.

"Do as I say."

The *scugnizzi* have leather lungs when they need them. Maurizio cupped his hands around his mouth and shouted, "Hey, you! You there with the sheep!"

The boy, raggedly dressed and totally bored, looked up eagerly. He, too, put his hands to his mouth to make a trumpet. "What do you want?" he shouted, his voice echoing across the fields.

Maurizio turned. "What *do* I want, Niello?"

"Ask him when he last got up one of those ewes."

Maurizio, grinning, obliged.

The shepherd boy, after an interval for thought, replied, "Just after that whore who is your mother was had by a soldier in a ditch."

"Say 'Thanks,'" ordered Niello.

Maurizio did so. The shepherd boy stuck out his arm, clenched his fist, and struck his biceps, the classic gesture meaning "Bugger you," but he was laughing.

"Wonderful," said Niello. "Wonderful. Your aunt won't be shot."

Nor was she.

Two days later, a truck with six German soldiers stopped at the foot of the winding road that led up to Camaldoli. The driver took out a map and bent over it. A man was leaning over a low wall.

"Camal*d*oli?" said the German with the map to the man by the wall.

The man drew himself up smartly. He gave the fascist salute.

The German replied with a casually bent arm. "Camal*d*oli?" he repeated.

The man frowned and looked very puzzled. He came around the wall and approached the truck. The soldier with the map punched at it with a forefinger, which he then pointed to the winding road. "Camal*d*oli?" he shouted.

The man looked at the map. A great light shone on his face; a vast smile accompanied it. "Ah, *Cam*al*d*oli," he said, stressing the word as it should be. The German, like most people who are not Neapolitan, had stressed the one before the last, which, indeed, makes the word sound very Italian.

The man and the soldier exchanged the word several times. Then, at last, the man agreed that the winding road led there. But, good-humoredly, he made the German pronounce it correctly before he would let him go on his way. Out of the corner of his eye the man saw his wife come out of his house into the garden, carrying a wet blouse. It was red and she was singing merrily. She pegged the blouse on the clothesline and went indoors.

A moment later she came out with a plate of apples, which she offered smilingly to the soldiers as the truck was moving off. The driver stopped the truck. The soldiers took the apples. Far up in the hills a boy shouted. Munching the apples, the soldiers waved their thanks and the truck drove off.

It twisted and turned up the hill, growling in low gear. Halfway up, the soldiers encountered a flock of sheep that was pouring over the right-hand bank of the country road. The truck stopped, and the sheep filled the road from side to side.

The driver hooted. The shepherd boy who was conducting the flock nodded eagerly to show that he understood. He gave sharp commands to his four dogs and they, barking furiously, ran hither and thither, snapping at the legs of the sheep. The soldiers relaxed, aware that the boy was doing his best to clear the road for them.

The dogs bounced about, making a tremendous din, for the boy was giving them a stream of contrary orders, which he had never done before. The dogs enjoyed it hugely and, obeying dutifully, in a minute had the sheep in an inextricable confusion, pointing in all directions, colliding, stumbling, and bleating loudly.

The soldiers enjoyed this bucolic scene for a minute . . . two minutes . . . five minutes. The driver, growing a little impatient, sounded his horn, but the German beside him shook his head and the driver stopped. It was only alarming the sheep and making things worse. There was nothing to do but wait, and wait the soldiers did.

It was a charming interlude in a pleasant country trip. They arrived at the top of the hill and, doing their duty, looked into a cave or two, and found nothing. Then a woman who introduced herself as Emilia insisted that they come into her farmhouse. There she gave them thick slices of ham and onions which she had pickled herself. She put bottles of wine beside the plates and saw to it that the soldiers made good use of them. The Germans drove back to Naples in a happy mood. There they reported to their superiors that in Camaldoli (pronouncing the name correctly if in a rather blurred way) there was nothing untoward, and the inhabitants were friendly.

There were a lot of other people in the mountain villages of the Apennines who also wanted to help prisoners of war but who were reluctant to be shot. The word soon passed that the boys had organized a safe refuge, so, giving the escapees a hasty chunk of bread and something to drink, they put them on the road to Camaldoli.

At first Emilia kept the escapees in her capacious farmhouse. But soon there were too many of them, so she kept them in the many caves of the hill, giving them blankets against the cold, and food, food, always food. The boys were not as bored as Maurizio had feared, for they, too, shared Emilia's excellent cooking. The trick with the exasperated flock of sheep worked perfectly, as did Emilia's glowing hospitality to such Germans who finally made it to the top of the hill. The Germans were convinced that in Camaldoli at least there were Italians who regretted the fall of Mussolini and believed in the invincibility of the führer.

There were not only Indians, there were French and British and Australians, and even Russians. Emilia cooked happily for them. Neapolitan legend has it that she looked after over a hundred of them. The figure need not be taken literally, but certainly she cared for a score and more.

Niello and the boys wisely did not let the escapees bunch up on the top of the hill. At night they conducted them to the suburbs of Naples and housed them with friendly families. Tucked away in the back rooms of the winding lanes of the city, they were fairly safe.

But not entirely so. There were Fascist spies, and prisoners of war need a breath of fresh air, however quick. Scholl had been told that something of the sort was going on. He issued a proclamation that anybody giving information about people harboring escaped prisoners would be given a thousand lire (a large sum in those days) and, unconsciously taking a leaf out of Emilia's book, ample provisions. Legend again says that nobody swallowed the bait. Unfortunately, that is not true. One man, at least, did, and his betrayal ended in horror, unbelievable horror if it were not so well attested.

Behind the hill of Capodimonte, the countryside began. San Rocco was a small village, inhabited entirely by peasants who tilled the fields. Behind their farms rose the mountains, with the roads and paths by which the escapees made their way toward Naples and, hopefully, the Allied lines. Some, the lucky ones, were directed to Camaldoli. Others, hungry, weary, and desperate for help, stumbled into San Rocco.

The boys could not be everywhere. It was true that their numbers were swelling each day; every *scugnizzo* of Naples wanted to be a member of the band that at least was doing something and not lying inert like their elders. But communications were by word of mouth. Telephones had long ceased to function. Trucks and automobiles had been commandeered. There remained only slow carts, bicycles, and strong young legs to carry messages.

A loyal Fascist, inspired by Scholl's offer of reward, relayed information that the villagers of San Rocco were harboring fugitives.

A platoon of German soldiers was ordered to investigate, and to make reprisals if the rumor should prove true.

They set out. This time there were no boys to warn San Rocco, and there was no plan for signals. Word had reached the boys that the village was about to be inspected, because the Fascist spy had boasted of his contacts with the Germans and had let the name of the village slip, but it was too late. All that could be done in a short time was to send a lad on an old and inefficient bicycle just ahead of the soldiers. He arrived, sweating and out of breath, only a few minutes before the German trucks.

The soldiers leaped out of the trucks. The villagers watched behind closed doors. The soldiers went from house to house, demanding entry. When a door was not opened, they smashed it down with the butts of their rifles.

The terrified peasants denied giving shelter, but there had been no time to do more than send the escapees running full pelt into the woods, and they had left evidence behind them—a pair of trousers from a foreign uniform a woman had been mending; a military button on the floor; plates with food on them in the loft of a house.

The spy named five households which he was sure had harbored the refugees. The male head of each house was dragged outside. One of them was sick in bed. His wife pleaded frantically for him, but the soldiers upset the bed and the sick man fell on the floor. He was kicked and pushed to join the others.

A sergeant shouted out a German version of Scholl's orders that such an act as sheltering prisoners was to be punished by death. The men were not lined up. They were taken one by one to the small village square, and there they were shot down. The bodies lay about in grotesque attitudes.

The villagers did not react with the screams and wails of the city dwellers. They watched the executions in dumb fear.

The stolid peasantry infuriated the soldiers. They went to one of the plowed fields and, borrowing spades, dug holes in the earth. Then they dragged the bodies of the dead men to the field and planted them, feetfirst, in the holes, dropping them in until the earth reached their chests. The dead men were upright, their heads lolling, their eyes open and staring, blood soaking the earth from their wounds.

The soldiers surveyed the macabre scene and retired a few paces.

The villagers watched. Then the soldiers cocked their weapons and fired repeatedly at the dead bodies. Ultimately they tired of their sport at this unique rifle range, and left.

Niello and his boys were now the most-talked-about citizens in the town; there were, after all, very few people to be proud of. But the rescuing of prisoners of war was women's work. Niello had given the word "Fight," but, apart from a skirmish or two and the brief uprising in Castel dell'Ovo, nobody fought.

Niello brooded. He knew his fellow citizens. There were those who waited for a miracle—and a miracle might just possibly be forming over the mountains where the Allies were. The Americans and British did not seem to be making much progress, but the tide of war might turn any day. These Neapolitans said, "Wait."

Then there were those who took everything in their stride. These said, "One arranges oneself," and busied themselves doing it. These called the boys—well, boys: naturally impulsive, naturally hotheaded, naturally wrong.

There were some who shook their heads in sorrow at what was happening to some of their less lucky fellow citizens—those who had been shot, and whose dead bodies had been half buried and shot at. But, as has been remarked by a cynical Frenchman, "Nothing is so easy to bear as the misfortunes of our friends."

There were also those—and these are always the hardest to put up with in a disaster—who said, "Keep smiling. Happy days will soon be here again."

Niello thought of his hero, Masaniello. But Masaniello had, in his way, been lucky. The Spaniards had made a mistake. They had put a tax on fruit.

Scholl had made no mistake. True, he was destroying the city, but this was war. True, he had burned the university, but books were books and could be reprinted. True, his soldiers had robbed the citizenry without mercy, but when ever had there been a war without looting? Scholl was a monster, but he had not made the mistake that Niello was looking for.

Then, on September 22, he made it.

CHAPTER SIX

By the next day, Scholl's mistake was plastered over the walls of Naples.

In a way, the posters were familiar. Each year, young men, then and now, read gloomily an ill-printed notice calling them up for military service—the draft. It refers to them as a "class"—the "class" of such-and-such a date, being the year in which they were born.

The air on that Sunday morning was humid; there was a threat of rain. The boys, hugging themselves in their summer clothes which, for lack of any others in the shops, many of them still wore, read the notice in the early-morning light—those of them, that is, who could read.

It was instantly clear to Niello and his band of followers that here was no usual call-up notice. It was signed by the prefect, Soprano, but the hand was clearly that of Scholl.

"*Notice*," it said, and then went on to inform the astonished boys and their elders who stood reading it over their shoulders that all males of the classes between 1910 and 1925 were called to do "obligatory service in the national work force." That meant everybody between the ages of eighteen and thirty-three. A list of recruiting centers followed, with instructions as to which class should report where. Then came the threat: those who did not obey would be recruited by force and subjected to the "sanctions foreseen by the laws of war."

There was no such thing as a national work force. There were no laws of war that applied to it. Niello spoke to the boys who were gathered around him.

"You remember that other notice? The free trip to glorious Germany?"

They nodded. This had been another poster, but one which Naples had treated as a huge joke. It had come from no less an authority than the German high command and it invited any and all of the workers to come to the Fatherland and work for the final victory in its factories and on the defenses of the Reich. For this trip, said the notice, "no passport will be necessary."

Not a single Neapolitan had taken up the offer.

"This is the same thing," said Niello. "It means your fathers and brothers will be taken to Germany."

"Will they come back?" said one of the boys.

"Who knows?" said Niello. "Warn your mothers. Tell them to let none of the men or lads report."

"But it says here," said another boy, stubbing a finger on the poster, "they'll be *forced* to. What's that mean?"

"Shooting," said a lad succinctly.

"Yes," said Niello. "If they can find them."

The boys looked at him in bewilderment.

"What have we done with the prisoners of war?" he went on.

There was a babble of voices. "We've hidden them . . . Emilia . . . the caves . . ."

Niello nodded. "What we've done for foreigners, surely we can do for our own kith and kin. Right?"

"Right," said the boys.

"But," objected one of them, "we can't hide *everybody* in Camaldoli."

"No, but we boys know a hundred places in which to hide. Right?"

"Right."

"I hid in a catacomb once," said Aldo. "Eerie. Skulls and bones."

Two of the catacombs of Naples are famous tourist sights, but there are a dozen other cemeteries of early Christians, less spectacular, rarely visited, but excellent places for concealment.

"I hid in the crypt of our parish church," said another boy, grinning. "It was when the cops were after me for contraband. The black beetle found me"—by which he meant the priest—"but he was quite decent about it. He let me stay there till it all blew over."

Niello said, "We'll make a list and spread it around. I want to know of every place that *you* know."

A small three-wheeled carrier drove up. The boys fell silent. A lad got out and dumped a pile of newspapers on the pavement by a newsstand not yet open. The newspaper was *Roma*, the only one that Scholl now allowed to be published. Niello glanced at the headline. It announced, as usual, German victories on the Salerno front.

"Who's going to buy that trash?" asked a boy.

"The Fascists," answered Niello. "They carry it under their arms to avoid getting pushed around. Today, you'll be the newspaper. Scatter, and tell everybody what to do. Join the food lines, talk to the women. We'll meet again at midday."

"Where?"

"Where I live. Now, off you go."

Niello lived in Montecalvario, one of the poorest quarters of Naples, and it was there, on that same day, that the uprising of the people began.

Niello's house was in the Vico Giardinetto—the Alley of the Little Garden. It is a slum, spectacularly so, and one which is still gazed on with wonder by tourists. It leads straight off from the principal road of the city, the Toledo, with its expensive shops, then rises steadily up a hill whose incline is so sharp that a funicular railway was installed long ago very near it, for those whose legs could not stand the climb. The alley is narrow. An active boy could leap across it with ease if there were room for a brief run up to the jump, but there is not. There is also no little garden. The only greenery to be found is in some window boxes, mostly hidden all day long by the display of the family wash. It is these innumerable festoons of clothing that still attract the tourist today. The tall houses are divided into apartments; the apartments into dwellings for two or three families; and the rooms of the dwellings, in Niello's house, were sometimes divided again by a curtain to make two residences. Several alleys, exactly the same, run parallel to the Vico Giardinetto. The whole area is the national home of the real, true-blue Neapolitan *scugnizzo*.

Niello's family lived in two rooms on the third floor of a house halfway up the hill. A number of people lived in these two rooms: mother, father, two elder brothers, and younger children of which the number is imprecise, the neighbors' memories being various in their estimates. Niello rarely spoke of his home, because the two rooms were not his home in any real sense of that word. He had no corner to himself. He did not even have a bed of his own; he shared one, when he slept at home, which was not always. His visits, however, were regular. He brought food when he could find or steal any; he brought money from the temporary jobs he would take up when the rent was due. But he mostly came to see his elder brother, Renato. Renato was just over eighteen years old, a finely built lad with broad shoulders, a handsome face, usually illuminated by an engaging smile, and no brains whatsoever. Niello was exceedingly fond of him.

On September 23, Niello climbed the narrow street, his legs aching. He would willingly have taken the funicular to the top of the hill and walked down instead of up, if he had had any money, which he did not, and if the funicular had been working. So he put one foot before the other, gritting his teeth. He had been, for hours, walking over Naples, placing the escapees, and he was dead tired. He walked with his gaze on the broken ground of the alleyway.

Near his home, he suddenly heard his mother's voice.

"Niello! Thank God you've come!"

He looked up. She was shouting, or rather screaming, from their window. Other faces, drawn and anxious like hers, were at all the other windows.

"What is it?" said Niello in a tired voice.

"They've taken Renato!"

"Who?"

"The Germans. Do something! There, look! *Do* something."

Niello looked in the direction in which his mother was frantically pointing. Just beyond his house was a truck. German soldiers were pushing men and boys toward it and making them mount. A dozen were already in it. Among them, near the open end, Niello, his heart sinking, saw Renato. The lad, his face white with terror, made a despairing gesture toward his brother, then let his hands fall despondently. Around the truck stood a small crowd, all silent. Among them Niello saw some of the boys he had summoned to the meeting.

For a few long moments Niello's brain failed to work in his tired body. He stared at the sight before him, his face blank. Then an old man on the sidewalk said, "They are taking them off. It's the poster. They ought to have reported. They didn't. So they're being fetched. They ought to have reported. . . ." The old man's wavering voice faded.

Slowly Niello took in what was happening. There were just two soldiers mustering the men into the truck. A third sat at the wheel. The two soldiers were pointing long-barreled pistols at the deportees, but in an uncertain manner. Every so often they looked nervously around them.

With reason: Every one of the hundreds of windows was packed with persons—men, women, children—staring at the truck. A line of inhabitants of the alley surrounded it completely. The cry of Niello's mother had cut through a threatening silence. It was so quiet in the alley that, as each man and lad mounted the truck, the creak of its springs could be heard.

Niello's elder brother once more looked at him. There were tears in his eyes. Then, as Niello made no sign, he raised one hand in the gesture of "goodbye," the palm upward, the fingers closing gently once or twice. It was the way that children are taught to say "ciao." Then Niello's brother turned away his face.

Suddenly there was a shout. It was a boy's voice. Whose voice, history never can be sure, for every boy, except Niello, who was in that street claimed afterward that it was his.

"Look!" the high voice cried. "Look what they're doing to your sons, your husbands. Look!"

It was the cry of the boys who had taken the dead body of the man who had been shot in Ottocalli and paraded it through Naples. This time there was no solemn shaking of heads, no prayers. The Madonna, God, and Jesus were mentioned in the angry roar that suddenly burst from the windows and the alley, but with blasphemies that would have made nuns faint.

Strength suddenly flooded back through Niello's body. He found his voice. "They're taking them away," he shouted. "You'll never see them again. To arms! To arms!"

The other boys in the crowd took up the cry that had had so little effect when first it was raised.

"To arms! To arms!"

The two Germans went white. A howling, growling, swearing Neapolitan crowd in a narrow slum is a frightening thing. The driver started his engine, but, looking back, saw that the pistols in the hands of his companions were shaking. The noise of the engine raised such a roar of execration from the crowd that he hastily shut it off again.

Niello flung wide his arms. With a broad gesture he invited everybody in the houses to come into the street.

They poured out of the narrow doorways. Men were clutching hatchets, hammers, and thick sticks. The women waved brooms and metal pots and pans. Some men had hunting guns, others old-fashioned army muskets, gathered when the first raid for arms had taken place. Soon the crowd packed the street.

It was like the sheep. But would the Germans be more willing to shoot men and women than dumb animals?

The shouting, the obscenities, died down with that suddenness characteristic of a Neapolitan crowd. The people watched the soldiers. The soldiers watched the people.

Then a shot rang out, echoing from the houses so that it sounded like a fusillade. It came from the back of the crowd. One of the soldiers waved his pistol at the men and boys on the truck. The crowd once more roared, but this time much more menacingly. A great fear came into the Germans' eyes, and well it might, for if they could shoot a few of those who blocked their way, they would surely be torn to pieces when their pistols were emptied.

"*Aus! Aus! Aus!*"

"He says, 'Get out!' " said a voice. "Run for it."

In a wild scramble, those on the truck leaped or fell into the alley. The driver started his engine. The crowd stood solid in front of the truck. Not till the last man and boy was safe and away inside the sheltering houses did it part to let the truck through.

Nobody read the newspaper; nobody trusted the radio—those who had a radio left after the looting. But news traveled fast all the same. The very fact that one had no information made one doubly eager to ask and to listen and, above all, believe. The *scugnizzi*, until now regarded as fluent liars, became oracles. Soon everybody knew that the Germans had been frightened in the Alley of the Little Garden. Everybody knew that the men and the lads had been let go. Everybody knew that if they wished to see their sons and husbands again, they must hide them immediately. Everybody knew, in a word, it was now or never.

"To arms!"

Scholl had disarmed the civilians, but he had forgotten the military; or perhaps it is more fair to him to say they presented him with a dilemma. Legally, the Italian Army was still an ally. But the fact was that, as the fighting on the Salerno front grew nearer and nearer, hundreds of Italian soldiers had quietly left their barracks, bundled up their uniforms, and put on such mufti as they could find. Some barracks stood empty. While Scholl's patrols would take away the gun of a soldier or sailor in uniform who did not instantly obey orders, Scholl knew nothing of the arms that the deserters, now mingling with the population, had left behind them.

The hunt for arms by the civilians began that same morning. The deserted barracks were closed, bolted, and barred. To break down the doors would have alerted the Germans to what was going on. The barracks had to be entered quietly as by thieves in the night, and who could be better at doing that than the *scugnizzi?*

Small, active boys shinned up drainpipes to reach narrow attic windows. They wriggled between bars on the ground floors, slipped and scrambled down the wide and unused chimneys of barracks built two hundred years ago. They found gratings that could be pried open to let them drop into cellars. There was many a store they had robbed in this way in the past. For that they had been considered criminals. Now they were heroes.

Once inside, it was a moment's work to unbar the doors, their elders and betters waiting, hidden, outside. Then Naples rearmed. Boys, youths, and men formed chains. The guns were taken from the cellars or the armories and passed silently from hand to hand until they reached the door. There men and youths hastily hid them under their jackets or shirts and walked slowly and nonchalantly away.

The *scugnizzi* took their share. And in their choice of arms, the boys' friends among the prisoners of war that they had led to safety gave invaluable advice.

Niello's boys in Camaldoli would bring them their food. Then, when the escapees had eaten, the boys would sit down as boys do, to hear tales of the war. There were Italo-Americans, speaking a strange, old-fashioned Italian they had learned from their immigrant grandmothers in the States. There were British sons of Italian restaurant keepers in England, knowing enough Italian to communicate. There were even university students who had studied the language, and if the boys found their way of speaking stilted and too like that of the radio announcers in Rome, they eagerly grasped at what they had to tell.

It was one such, a British commando, trained to a hair in sudden assault against heavy odds, who gave them the hint that was to bring some of the boys victory against Goliath, and some of them death.

"Guns are fine in the movies," he told them. "Bang, bang, and you're dead. Well, so he might be if you creep up behind him and his mates don't see you doing it and get you first. Firing from behind pillars or from windows, that looks pretty, too. But while you're firing, they can fire, too, and the machine-gun spray covers a lot of area very quickly. Besides, you'll be fighting—if you're really going to fight—not men but tanks. I've fought tanks, and there's only one way to do it."

The boys gathered closer, listening intently.

"The hand grenade," the commando said. "And don't aim at the openings, unless you're champion throwers. Aim at the tracks. Even that isn't much good if the tank is standing still. But if it's moving toward you, and you hit the tracks, it slews around and is unmanageable. Then go at it with—look, hand me that empty wine bottle. . . ."

And thus, in the caves of Camaldoli, in cellars in the city and attics where the prisoners were hiding, the *scugnizzi* learned the art of making that instrument of guerrilla warfare which was to survive the conflict—the Molotov cocktail.

They also learned to throw the hand grenades: how to pull out the pin, if necessary, with their teeth; how to throw the grenade with a wide, circular motion of the arm, and how—an art that made the boys tingle, half with fear and half with excitement—to hold it back until it was sure to explode at the exact moment when it hit the tank.

Scholl's mistake brought the *scugnizzi* what they desperately needed—allies, and, what is equally important, allies with their own youthful dash and enterprise.

These allies were the students, the lads who went to high school and to the university Scholl had burned. They were not *scugnizzi* and never had been. In those days a street boy could not aspire to higher education, while the student customarily looked down on boys who went barefoot, as many of the *scugnizzi* did. But suddenly the well-shod young realized that at any moment they might be carried away to Germany and a labor camp, perhaps never to return. It was no use looking to their parents for help. These, well shod too, merely wrung their hands, invoked San Gennaro, or just stayed dumb with fright. Moreover, those very same expensive shoes they all wore had been bought with money gained in toeing the fascist line. They did not know (as so often happens in a crisis with the well-to-do) what to say.

The *scugnizzi* did. They were here, there, and everywhere. They had information. They knew places to hide. They would say, "Quick, quick, the Germans are coming up the road! Follow me!" and the students followed most willingly.

They found themselves in strange places—the caves of Camaldoli, deserted warehouses, peasant cottages where they lay down, in Biblical style, in cattle stalls among asses and oxen, but with no magi to bring them gold, frankincense, and myrrh. They were lucky if they were brought food and drink, but mostly they were, and that was because of the women and, again, the *scugnizzi*.

This great mob of hungry refugees quite overwhelmed Emilia and the other women who had followed her example with the prisoners of war. It was left to the lads' mothers and sisters to provision them with such food as remained in the city.

But here was a problem: To be seen going with a food basket through the city to some unusual place would raise suspicion, particularly among those Fascist spies anxious to earn Scholl's reward.

The women quickly adopted the ways of the *scugnizzi*. To go by night, as the street boys did for their robberies, had its perils: the streets of Naples had been unlit for weeks; to be seen out with a flashlight held the risk of being challenged since there was a curfew order, not fully enforced, but enforceable. But one of the devices of the *scugnizzi* had always been to form a religious procession. Holding candles and singing a hymn at the tops of their voices, they would follow a holy statue. While the bystanders gaped, or crossed themselves, or shut their eyes in prayer, a boy would hand his candle to a companion, slip away, and pick a pocket, steal fruit from a stall, or, neatly, with practiced fingers as light as the touch of a butterfly's wing, relieve a devotee of his wristwatch.

Naples, on that Thursday, was boiling with anger. Everybody was now on the side of the *scugnizzi*, even the priests and the nuns. Some of their favorite good boys—holy boys, good students, candidates maybe for the priesthood itself—were hungry and thirsty in all sort of corners. They willingly lent a hand. Before curfew time, in the fall of the evening, little religious processions were organized, the women with shawls over their heads, the *scugnizzi* carrying the platform on which stood the colored plaster statue of a saint or of the Madonna. In front went some boys with candles, leading the way, one or two hastily dressed in choirboys' surplices lent for the occasion. Behind, more boys and among them the women, carrying shopping baskets, as though they had joined the holy parade on the spur of the moment.

Thus, singing, praying, they passed the sentinels and deceived the spies. At some dark angle, the procession would suddenly dissolve, a priest or a nun would carry the holy statue back to the church or nunnery from which it came. The women, following whispered instructions, would be led by *scugnizzi* who knew the way. After much stumbling in the dark, they would arrive, some of them footsore if their sons were in the caves in the hills, to be greeted as angels of mercy when they arrived with the food.

These processions wound their way to the sound of thudding mines, as Scholl's demolition squads went about their work. It had become a grimly familiar sound, but, to the boys, it had its uses. Under cover of all this destructive noise, the *scugnizzi* were practicing under the eyes of their friends, the prisoners of war. In fields in the periphery, in bombed-out factories, they were learning to throw hand grenades. It took only an evening, and they were experts. Above all, they learned the exact stretch and swing of the arm that must be used if the bomb is to reach its target at the moment when it will explode. They practiced with hand grenades and without them. They learned how to look as though they were throwing a bomb, even if they didn't have one. It proved to be one of the most useful tricks the *scugnizzi* had ever learned.

The German soldier leaned on his rifle. The close September warmth was most unlike the bracing air of his mountain village in Steinach. As he put it to himself, in this damned place you are always randy.

A young girl, neatly dressed, with stockings and a straw hat, loitered past him.

"You," said the soldier. "*Alt.*"

The girl halted, her dark eyes wide under their long lashes.

The soldier said, "Come here."

She approached him.

He chucked her under the chin. "*Sei bella. Bella.*"

She hung her head and giggled.

He put his hand on her dress to feel if her breasts were developed. She stood still. Suddenly she pointed warningly to her left. A nun came shuffling up, bent with the burden of a heavy basket. "No, no," she said. "*Nein, nein,*" shaking her head reprovingly at the soldier.

The soldier withdrew his hand and blushed.

"Come," said the nun severely to the girl, and with that the two went on their way.

Fifteen minutes later, on the outskirts of the city, nun and girl disappeared within the walls of a bombed house. The girl lifted her dress and pulled it over her head with a sigh of relief. She bent and, kicking off her shoes, stripped off her stockings. She stood up in shorts and shirt, a *scugnizzo*.

"*Marronne,*" said the boy, rolling hat and dress into a bundle. "I thought he'd seen through me."

"Don't swear," said the nun automatically.

"He stopped me twice this afternoon and searched me when I was dressed like this. He's suspicious of all us *scugnizzi*."

"Where did you get the dress? It's nice."

"It's my sister's. Thanks for the help."

"It's nothing. Here's the basket. Leave your dress here. I'll give it back to her."

The boy took the basket. "Thanks again," he said.

"*Ciao.* God go with you. And don't swear."

"No."

Suddenly, on this crucial Thursday, thousands of Neapolitans found themselves in just the same position as the prisoners of war. They urgently needed a roof over their heads. Scholl turned thousands out of house and home.

Naples is by no means the land of "O Sole Mio" in spite of the loud proclamations of interminable tenors down to this day. It rains a lot, and the rain is just as wet as it is anywhere else. In the spring and autumn the rain can be accompanied by a bone-chilling wind. Naples, instead of lying baked in the sun, is a humid place. Elsewhere people sing that on a clear day you can see forever. In Naples they say that when you can see the houses on the island of Capri, it is going to rain soon, and it always does.

The reason for Scholl's drastic move was this. In a way, the optimistic reports in *Roma* about the Salerno front had some truth in them. The Allied advance northward to the city by land was making very slow progress. "It does not matter," said the newspaper to the people who did not read it, "if a square yard of soil is lost or gained here or there. What matters is the creed of the German soldier, from the highest official to the most humble soldier, to fulfill their mission, which they recite with the same faith as a Catholic says his prayers."

There are agnostic Catholics and, it appears, agnostic German officers, one of whom, as we have seen before, was Scholl. It was true that the Allies were doing none too brilliantly on land. But at sea, with the huge fleet of American warships, they had unquestioned superiority. What could be more logical, therefore, than a sea attack on Naples, taking the Germans, however devoted, on the flank? Ischia and Capri, the two islands standing sentinel to the bay, were virtually undefended, as Scholl knew. An assault in force, and they would fall. The bay would then be at the Allies' mercy. Landing craft, of which the Allies had a great number, could drive up to the shores and to the jetties of the harbor, which had proved indestructible. The city, albeit with the prospect of bitter fighting in the hills, could be breached from the bay.

Faced with this critical situation, Scholl decided on a Napoleonic gesture: he ordered the immediate and total evacuation of every building and residence on the seafront, and for a depth of some three hundred meters going inland.

Napoleon, however, was a soldier, and Scholl was not. Napoleon, though he lost in the end, was never a silly Billy. Scholl was. The moment that the Allies would have begun their preliminary bombardment of the shoreline, the inhabitants would have fled of their own accord. They always had, in the whole history of modern warfare. If Scholl saw himself valorously defending the city from Santa Lucia or the Castel dell'Ovo, he was an idiot. As soon as their landing craft had ground up on the beaches and the men were deployed, the Allies would have been in a trap. They could have been decimated by cannon placed on the hills of Capo- dimonte, Camaldoli, and other ideal sites for artillery. They would have been sitting ducks.

They were not so foolish. There never was an invasion of Naples by sea.

The exodus caused by Scholl's evacuation order is still recalled in Naples, and with a touch of irony, especially among the poor. Obviously, the apartments on the curve of the bay are among the most desirable in Europe; from Posilipo, on the northern arm, to the harbor in the south, they enjoy the whole splendid panorama of the islands, the bay, and Vesuvius. They were therefore expen- sive, and still are. For this reason, the Via Chiaia, a central artery of the area, and Via Poerio are lined with expensive shops to serve the refined needs in clothes, antiques, and such of the rich in- habitants. The latter, on this blackest of black days, were faced with piling their possessions on handcarts, horse-drawn carriages, or even wheelbarrows, and begging shelter from all and sundry.

An abiding memory of those who have written about the evac- uation is the way one took the wrong things. Having servants at their beck and call all their lives, they had no idea of what was es- sential and what was not. They were suddenly plunged into the different priorities of the poor, and were lost.

The kids, the thoroughbred dog, and the Persian cat went first aboard, but got there by themselves. Blankets next because Naples has known its earthquakes. But then the favorite picture by the famous artist, irreplaceable portraits of grandpapa and grandmama, crucifixes, statues of the Madonna, favorite books, and fur coats took up the space instead of pots and pans and tins of food. The slum dwellers watched the procession with sympathy—and humor. These were the people who had the money to buy on the black market in Piazza Garibaldi and Porta Capuana. These were the people who had grown fat in years of fascism. These, indeed, might even be the people behind the black market itself. They were also, of course, the parents of the students whose very existence now de- pended on the barefoot boys.

It was the poor who had the handcarts, the horse-drawn victorias, the only means of transport. The motorcars of the rich had been commandeered, or artfully driven away into the country and hidden in barns. The price of any form of wheeled vehicle, it is ruefully remembered by the rich, shot up to the skies. It was an ill wind that blew over Naples in those days, but it blew somebody some good.

As for the students, they still remember the conversations that took place in their refuges. One memory shall suffice. A group of teen-agers from eighteen to twenty spent the night of the twenty-third and five nights following in a cave at Camaldoli. They spent it in the dark, for to light even a candle might have aroused suspicion. They lay in the darkness upon straw, with a single blanket or overcoat for covering. They spoke to one another like boys in a boarding school after lights-out, in mutters and whispers. They were anonymous voices, because their owners had been gathered by chance.

"What shall we do if they find us?"

"Fight."

"Fight."

"If you fight, they run."

"Has anybody got a gun?"

"Yes."

"Yes."

"Yes. But I've never fired one. I wouldn't know how to use it."

"You point it at the bugger, press the trigger," said a sarcastic voice, "and it goes 'bang.'"

"Where did you get your gun?"

"The *scugnizzi*. They're giving them away."

"Sure. Till the *scugnizzi* start using them on us," said a cultivated voice. "Holding us up. Like Chicago."

"No they won't. It's for the revolution."

"Lenin said—"

Loud groans echoed through the cavern.

"Politics be damned. Look where your politicians have got us. Sleeping on straw like pigs in a sty."

"No, but I agree with the boys," protested the voice that supported Lenin. "There's got to be a revolution. But first we've got to persuade the proletariat to join us. Lenin—shut up, I *will* have my say—Lenin said that was the only way."

"Quiet, everybody." An authoritative voice came through the darkness. "Listen."

In the silence could be heard a scratching and a scampering.

"What is it?"

"Rats."

"My God! What'll we do?"

"Ask Lenin."

"Keep your toes inside the blanket. Goodnight, all."

Sunday, 26 September. Scholl himself announced, after his fashion, the first great victory of the *scugnizzi*. It was raining, and the sky was heavy with dark clouds. It was the sort of day that, in other times, lowers the spirit of the Neapolitans. Today, for the first time since the bombardments, their spirits rose. They read this poster:

"Only 115 persons have presented themselves in the various quarters of the city for enrollment for obligatory labor, whereas 3,000 persons should have presented themselves."

Three thousand? Only *three*? Scholl, who must have drafted the notice, was clearly a shaken man. Even the devoted Fascists among the citizens said so. The correct number, as they had been told, was thirty thousand. A slip, but a significant one. The poster went on:

"This is sabotage against the Armed Forces of Germany. . . . Beginning tomorrow, the military patrols will arrest all those who have so far failed to report. Those not presenting themselves are in contravention of published orders and will be shot by the patrols without delay."

In the little courtyard outside the Church of Santa Chiara, Niello met the boy who had asked to wait before fighting, because his mother believed in San Gennaro.

"Well?" said Niello.

"Mamma is in tears, but she told me to find you and . . ."

"And?"

"Fight, if you say so."

"And San Gennaro?"

"He agrees. The miracle took place just as mother was asking him about me in her prayers."

"We're meeting in Montecalvario in an hour."

"I'll be there. *Ciao*."

"*Ciao*," said Niello. Then he smiled. "San Gennaro never says no," he said. It is the Neapolitan phrase of the skeptics, the non-believers, and the young who do not wish to upset *la mamma*.

Scholl did not intend to transport all the able men and lads of Naples to Germany; slave labor, as it was later to be called, was plentiful in 1943. But the high command was well aware that an attack on Germany itself was planned by the Allies. Against that, the Germans were fortifying the areas in which it was expected—particularly the coast of the English Channel. These fortifications went by the name of the man who had planned them, Todt. Germany now had need of skilled persons. During the whole of the fascist era, the Italians had been famous for their expertise in construction work. They had built dams and irrigation works of all sorts in many countries. It was these skilled artisans that Scholl wished to export, together with such workmen who had gained experience under them. Hence the order to report, so that their qualifications could be checked.

Students, architects, engineers of all stages of experience were thus in great danger. It was these who went into hiding. For the rest, it was only necessary to keep out of the way of the patrols, something made easier by the *scugnizzi* who kept vigil. "Run! The Germans are coming!" became a familiar cry in the streets of Naples. Grown men quickly adopted *scugnizzi* tactics. On hearing the cry, they would dive into the nearest alley, twist and turn to others until they had thrown off their pursuers and found an open door into which they could duck and find shelter. Thus there were plenty of men and lads in Naples on that weekend, armed and ready to fight.

Monday the twenty-seventh dawned humid and gray. A tense, armed citizenry awaited some sort of signal. The revolt had begun in Montecalvario. The first pitched battle took place that evening in the same area. The defense of the Rinascente, a department store, set the revolt ablaze.

PART THREE

The First of the
Four Great Days

CHAPTER SEVEN

Eleven-year-old Michele was a good boy. Everybody said so. He
worked in a brothel and he worked hard, especially since the telephone service had broken down. His family was extremely poor,
living from hand to mouth by a large variety of unprofitable oc-
cupations, until Michele got the job as a page boy to Madame
Carmela. Carmela was not French, but she liked to be called "Madame" because that, she had once heard, was what they called the
keepers of a team of whores in such places as Paris, London, and
New York. Carmela liked to be stylish.

Michele had begun work at the age of ten as a coffee runner—
that is to say, a boy who fetched cups of espresso coffee from the
bar to Carmela's mansion. It was all very respectable. He wore a
napkin tucked into the front of his shorts like an apron to show
his profession. But then the electricity went off and there was
practically no coffee. This was trying, but, with the coming of the
Germans, the brothel boomed. The military had limited free time,
and they had, most of them, a discriminating taste in prostitutes. In
a word, they liked to make appointments, and here the nimble legs
of Michele, now a year older, came in handy. So did the money
Carmela paid him and the food the clients brought to her from the
military canteens. Still, Michele was a *scugnizzo*. He longed to be
with the gang, and whenever he could, he slipped off his shoes and
joined them. Niello was his hero.

On the gray morning of the twenty-seventh, little Michele
crossed the Toledo, the main artery of Naples. It was quite deserted. He paused for a moment to look at the building that housed
the Rinascente. Its shutters were down, and so was the fancy

bronze portcullis that barred its entrance. It had been closed for several weeks. It was the Naples branch of huge emporia in Rome and Milan, a chain that had been the pride of the Fascist bigwigs and had catered to their tastes and those of their wives. The Naples manager—or director, as he called himself—was by no means on a level with those of the bigger cities, certainly not comparable to the head of the great store on the Corso in Rome, where both Mussolini's wife and his mistress had regularly shopped. But he had influence, all the same. His store had been protected from the looting. The German high command in Rome also shopped at the Rinascente.

Getting his breath back—for Michele always ran full tilt on any errand—he turned into the nearby alley of Montecalvario and ran up the steep slope. He found Niello's front door. He did not knock —no *scugnizzo* ever knocks. He stood in the middle of the alley and, cupping his hands round his mouth, shouted, "Hey! It's me, Michele."

He did not shout, "Hey! Niello!" That would have been unwise. If Niello did not want it to be known that he was at home, a sister or a brother or his mother would have stuck her head out of the window and made signs suitable to the occasion.

But Niello, yawning, appeared.

Michele pointed to the door. Curving his small hand, he made quick motions with it as though patting a dog. This meant "Come down immediately."

Soon the door, creaking loudly, was opened. Michele slipped inside when there was just enough room for him to do so. He pushed the door shut instantly and drew Niello to the stairs, which rose abruptly within two feet of the front door. Both boys sat on a lower step, their backs against a great balk of timber that supported the sagging floor of the first story. It had nothing to do with the bombardments; the house had been condemned as about to fall down for fifteen years.

In an excited whisper, Michele said, "You said if I heard anything . . ." He stopped without finishing his sentence, eager for encouragement.

"To tell me, yes," said Niello, and stifled a yawn.

"Well, they're going shopping."

"Who?"

"With the girls."

"*Who?*"

"It's a sort of joke."

"Who is going shopping?" said Niello sleepily.

"Isa thought of it. The joke. With that sergeant of hers."

Niello was instantly wide awake. "So the Germans are going shopping. Where?"

"With guns."

"Michele," said Niello severely, "begin at the beginning, or I shall clout you."

Michele obeyed.

Madame Carmela was a successful woman, and that meant, in her line of business, she had to be nothing if not professional. Thus her girls were provided with all the provocative equipment necessary for a well-run establishment: black lace underwear, intricate garters, thigh boots, and such. But if the truth were told, she would have liked all her employees to be dressed as ladies.

It was due to her upbringing. She had begun as a country bump-kin from Avellino, a hick town in the Apennines. She had got a job as a kitchen maid to a baron and baronessa who lived down on the plains. The baronessa had her whims: she liked hot chocolate at precisely 11:15 each morning, and she frequently com-plained that it was ill-made. One day, every man jack and jill was out in the fields because torrential November rains had put the river in flood, and all hands were at work raising the banks. Except Carmela, who was left behind to make the 11:15 chocolate. She made it, she washed her face, she brushed her dress and apron, and she served it. The baronessa fell in love with the chocolate, and Carmela with the baronessa in a perfectly chaste way. The baron-essa liked the smooth taste with not a hint of powder; Carmela loved the way that the baronessa sat at her gilt-and-leather antique desk, the way she put on her spectacles, the way she picked up her pen, the way she wrote notes on thick violet paper, and, above all, she loved her beautiful dresses.

When the money began to pour into the brothel (for Carmela had come way up from the kitchen), she bought an antique desk. It was a fake, but the best furniture fakers in the world are Neapolitan. She also bought glasses, though she did not need them. One of the tragedies of war was that she had run out of violet paper on which to write her notes, but she still sat every morning at her desk, voluminously gowned (for she had grown stout), doing her accounts.

When she had opened the brothel she had laid out a great deal of good money to dress her girls elegantly and make them ladies like herself. But professionally it did not go. Some of the girls had the figure but spoiled everything when they opened their mouths. Nothing, moreover, could stop them making an ear-splitting noise whenever they laughed, which was often. The exception was Isabella, or Isa, as she was known. Isa was quite a lady, even when she laughed.

Most of Carmela's clients during the occupation by Scholl had not been gentlemen. She was therefore delighted to welcome three young men from the Geheime Feldpolizei. Two were in their early twenties; one, of higher rank, was about thirty. They spoke adequate, if obviously studied, Italian, and were abundantly sure of themselves. They made very funny jokes about Scholl and even imitated his accent and his facial tic.

"Well," said Michele, sitting on the stairs. "It began with the chocolate."

"What chocolate?"

"What I take her. You see, I go to the bar where there's a man who knows how to make it just right with the chocolate in the boxes the Germans give Carmela and they make it and I take it and—"

"Come to the point," said Niello.

"You said begin at the beginning."

"Yes, I did but—"

"There's no but about it," said Michele stubbornly. "It began with the chocolate."

Niello sighed. "All right. Go ahead."

"Well, she wasn't there."

"Where? In the whorehouse?"

"Of *course* she was in the whorehouse. Ten o'clock onward is good for business. Men get randy in the morning," said Michele with a look of deep wisdom in his young and oval face. "I mean she wasn't at her desk. She was in the drawing room with these three Germans, and the girls. She drank her chocolate there. They had spumante. The three Germans."

Michele grew very involved at this point, but Niello was all attention, and patience. Carmela had impressed upon the girls and Michele that they should be very polite to the Geheime Feldpolizei. They looked like military police, but they weren't—that is, they were, but they worked for the Gestapo.

"I see," said Niello. "I see. Go on."

"Well, there was Isa there, and she was saying she hadn't a rag to wear nowadays because there was nothing in the shops and all that—you know how women talk. So the older man said, 'What's the best shop in town?' So she said the Rinascente, but it's bang shut up tight, she said. So one of the younger policemen said, 'We'll go shopping.' 'You can't,' said Isa. 'It's closed.' 'We'll open it,' said one of them, laughing. So they drank up and they're all coming to the shop this evening early when they get off duty. They're coming in an armored car. They're coming shopping. That's what they said. So I thought I'd tell you."

"Yes," said Niello. "You're a good boy."

Michele nodded complacently. That was what everybody always said.

Niello made a tactical decision over an exiguous lunch of black, coarse bread and an ancient salami sausage. He picked his troops for the battle of the Rinascente with great care. Ottocalli and the procession of the dead body had led to nothing, except notoriety for himself. The slum warren of Montecalvario had led to a victory. These people were his neighbors; they were the people he had been born and bred among. Every general in history has had a cohort, a phalanx, a cavalry regiment, a brigade of guards that he knew he could rely on in a crucial engagement, troops he could throw into the heat of the battle when the front was giving way, a spearhead to thrust at the enemy when the rest of his army was reluctant or dispirited. Niello decided on his Household Troops. They should be confined to the inhabitants of Montecalvario.

The slum area has a curious resemblance to the planning of an

American city such as New York. There are a number of alleys that run up the hill in a straight line, crossed, rigidly at right angles, by smaller alleys, like New York's avenues and east and west streets. So the battalions of Niello's shock troops (though each group was no larger than a few lads and boys and students) could have been named Toffa, Trere, Montecalvario I, Montecalvario II, Giardinetto, etc.

His faithful band from Santa Lucia duly arrived. They were detailed off to be messengers. Those who wished to join the battle, Niello said, must be armed and should assemble in the atrium (a sort of entrance hall) of Santa Maria della Concezione (Saint Mary of the Conception).

While he was talking to his boys (they stood in a circle watching a sham fight between two *scugnizzi*), Michele brought the vital communication. He had been the go-between for scrawled notes, which he had duly steamed open. The "shopping" expedition was to begin at 5:00 P.M. when the military police had leave. They would arrive, they said, in style. A bottle of brandy accompanied the note, "to warm the girls up."

The average age of those who joined Niello's band was low; the oldest recruits were not more than eighteen or nineteen. But faced with the deportation of their sons and relatives, this time their elders made no objection. Tempers were up.

Niello, like other commanders, was not above making a slip. He had chosen the wrong place for the rendezvous, but that was because he was still a boy, with a boy's fund of memories. He had selected Santa Maria della Concezione because he remembered it as being very spacious, and also because it was placed in a cul-de-sac, which was an exception to the rigid pattern of the alleys of Montecalvario. It was in a sort of contorted ear of irregular alleys that led nowhere and could not be found by anyone who did not know the area to perfection.

Niello had not been in the church since his First Communion, the ceremony which, among Protestants, is called Confirmation. He had learned his prayers and the rosary and some moral precepts besides. He had been dressed in a white suit with a large white silk bow tied to his arm. The suit was not his own; it had been borrowed because his parents could not afford to buy a new one, even at the cut-rate price of the tailor in Montecalvario. It had not fitted him; the trousers hurt his crotch and showed his ankles. He had mumbled his responses and taken the Sacrament from a terrifyingly high ecclesiastic who, like Niello, seemed to want to get the ceremony over as soon as possible. He had been a little boy, and the church had seemed big and vast. The rite over, and the small gathering of family friends eating sweet cakes and drinking sweet liqueurs done with, he had sworn never to set foot in the church again, and he had kept his vow.

Now, with a sinking heart, Niello saw that the atrium he remembered as enormous was actually a little over two yards in width and not very long. Boys and lads were standing outside in the alley; there were so many of them, far more than Niello had called. Niello looked up at the fantastic rococo facade of the church, with its great swags of stucco decorations. The church doors were closed, as was usual at that hour, because the priest was having his siesta.

Niello saw that this assembly was dangerous. A Fascist spy could observe it and report. A Fascist spy could lead a patrol through the winding alley. A Fascist spy could have them all arrested on the spot, and since, at Niello's specific request, they were all armed, they could be shot.

Niello went to the door of the priest's house. Watched silently by the boys and lads in the street, he rang the bell. A tousled priest, an old and irritable man, opened the door.

"You!" he said. "*You*. I guessed it would be you waking me up. What do you want, you scoundrel? Have you killed somebody? If you have, it's no good confessing. You know that, don't you? I'll have to tell the police if it's murder. Canon Law, Canon Law, my boy."

"I haven't killed anybody, but I may."

"Then don't, don't. That's all. Just don't."

"If I do, it will be a German." He gestured to the silent gang of youths.

They heard what he said. One or two raised hunting guns. Others, following suit, reached into their shirts and took out revolvers. One boy idly swung a hand grenade.

The old priest looked. He ran his fingers through his thin gray hair. He studied the faces of the boys. He knew his parishioners, even if many, like Niello, had not been in his church since their

First Communion. He knew the look in their eyes, and the meaning of the set of their mouths. He knew what was afoot.

"I can't have anything to do with it," he said. "You all know that."

Niello nodded. "But you can hold a benediction."

"At this hour?"

"Yes. Open the church. These boys have got to get inside, and quickly, or the patrols will get them."

The priest said a silent prayer for forgiveness for any sin he might be committing against Canon or any other law, but he said aloud, "Yes. All right. But you'll need women to make it look as though it's real—your mothers, sisters . . ."

Niello nodded. He passed the word. The priest disappeared and some moments later the ancient wood doors of the church creaked open and a bell began to ring.

The women, shepherded discreetly by the boys, gathered in the front pews. The lads and boys hung back and sat in the last rows, an arrangement which, in those days, would cause no suspicion, since the two sexes customarily sat apart.

Niello whispered to the priest, "Make it loud, we've got to talk." So the priest, trembling both in body and voice, began the rosary. The women responded, their voices unusually shrill, their responses very fervent. Under cover of the resulting noise, Niello muttered to his troops.

"*Hail Mary full of grace.*"

"I want ten of you to go into the store with me. Pass it on."

"*The Lord is with you.*"

"It will be dangerous. We're going to shoot it out."

"*Blessed art thou among women—*"

"I want volunteers."

"*—and blessed is the fruit of thy womb, Jesus.*"

"We can all of us be killed. Think carefully."

"*Our Father—*"

"If you want to come, put your face in your hands as though you were praying."

"*—which art in Heaven . . .*"

The boys and lads stared at the priest as he led the congregation. They felt the pistols in their shirts and trousers. They thought of the rifles that they had been told to leave outside in a convenient cubbyhole in the entrance to a neighboring courtyard.

". . . *thy will be done on earth as it is in Heaven.*"

One boy put his face in his hands.

"*Give us this day our daily bread.*"

Little as the women understood the grammar or even the proper pronunciation of the Latin words, they knew their meaning and they knew it bitterly. Their voices rose higher.

Two more boys put their faces in their hands.

"*Forgive us our trespasses as we forgive them. . . .*"

Niello tightened his lips. This was not the time to be a Christian. He coolly observed boy after boy raising his hands to his face. He would have to choose. There were too many volunteers.

". . . *lead us not into temptation . . .*"

Niello's heart missed a beat.

"*For ever and ever.*"

Or for just today?

"*Amen,*" said the priest, the women, and the boys.

The priest, in a shaking voice, intoned a hymn, and the women took it up, discordantly. Nobody was thinking of music, only of life and death.

The priest knelt in front of the ornate altar with its tabernacle. He prayed silently, then fished a small gold key from his soutane, fumbling. He inserted it into the gold-plated lock and opened the tabernacle door. Everybody but Niello bowed their heads. Some boys knelt; mentally, Niello among them, his mouth dry.

The round Host was fitted into the monstrance with its metal sunrise, tarnished and broken here and there at the tips of the sunbeams, because this was one of the poorest parishes in Naples. A boy in a worn surplice, put on so hastily that it was all awry, rang a bell. The priest raised the monstrance. He made the ritual great sign of the cross with it in benediction, but it was heavy and it swayed uncertainly.

"Bring him back, Mother of God, bring him back safe and sound," the women prayed, silently moving their lips. The boy with the bell stared at the priest, his mind full of excitement and of fear.

"The bell," said the priest irritably, and the boy rang it, too loud, to cover his confusion.

The women, the boys, and the young men filed out. Niello went first. He stood in the narrow atrium. As the boys passed, he either looked past them or gave a slight nod of his head. When the congregation was all in the alley outside the church, ten boys remained in the atrium. The mothers and sisters of these boys lingered; looked at their sons and brothers; then, fingering the beads of their rosaries, slowly went away.

One young man remained behind, although he had not been chosen.

"*Salve*," he said shyly to Niello in greeting.

"*Salve*, Osvaldo. I thought you were at the wars."

"I was."

Niello surveyed the civilian suit Osvaldo was wearing. He was a young man of some twenty years, a *guaglione*, as the Neapolitan says—a description, exclusive in all Italy to Naples, of any strapping lad. Osvaldo's suit was short in the arms and very short in the legs. Niello remembered his own borrowed Communion suit.

Osvaldo saw the look.

"I deserted. These are my old clothes. The ones they send back in a bundle when you join up."

This was the custom in those days. The recruit, the draftee, was given his uniform. His civilian clothes were taken away, wrapped up carelessly, tied with string, addressed in a clumsy hand, and sent off to his parents. It was a symbol that the *guaglione* was a soldier now and no longer belonged to his family. Fascism was full of dramatic symbols, all of which failed.

Niello smiled. "And where's your uniform? It might come in handy."

"I made a bundle of it and threw it in a street trash can."

Niello laughed loudly. "Well, good for you. But I must be going."

"Wait—I kept the rifle."

"We've got plenty of guns."

"But I know how to use it. Your boys don't."

"They'll do their best."

"The best isn't good enough when you're up against a soldier. It's you or him, and it had better be you. That's what they told us at the rifle range. I was good. I got a prize. Five days' extra leave."

"Well?"

"Can I come along?"

"Use your head. You desert the army to save your skin and now you want to risk it again. We're not playing, you know."

"I know."

"You were never one of us."

"Can I help it if my father was a butcher? They always make money."

"And you always had shoes. Those look pretty tight."

"Marching. Spreads the feet."

"Take them off."

Osvaldo's face showed the blank expression so beloved by sergeants. But he bent down. He took off his shoes and socks. Niello smiled to himself. It was a small revenge for the times Osvaldo's father had screwed the inhabitants of Montecalvario for his far-from-excellent meat.

"Listen, then make up your mind. We're going inside the store, and we're going to wait for them to break in. Then we're going to start shooting."

"Then you'd better have someone who can hit someone for sure."

"Yes. Yes, you're right." Niello surveyed him again. Could he be the spy he feared? If he was, it was too late now to do anything but kill him. A knife, perhaps. Niello thought for a moment. He decided that there was another way. "Stick close by me. Don't get out of my sight."

"Yessir!"

"Shake hands."

"*Grazie.*"

Osvaldo was not a spy. He was just the first of the many hundreds of *guaglioni*—young men—who joined the *scugnizzi* in the revolt, all risking their lives, and some to lose them.

The large building on the Toledo that housed the Rinascente was tucked into the base angle of the quadrilateral that made up Montecalvario. It made a considerable pretense at grandeur, as did all department stores. Originally a palace built in the middle of the past century, it had a great enclosed balcony high up, with columns, and below it five huge windows with rounded tops, the "noble floor" of the palace, as it is called in Italy. The chain store's

publicity men kept up some of the aristocratic tradition, in their
way. For Christmas and for sales, they would hang out strings of
flags, some with armorial bearings. The decorations echoed the
lines of laundry that perpetually hung across the alleys going up
the hill of Montecalvario behind it.

There were no flags now. The building was tightly shuttered.
Next to it is the Church of Santa Maria delle Grazie, with steps
going up to the doors. Niello told his boys to go there, inside or
outside on the steps, whichever they wished, but to look natural.
Some looked holy and went in to pray. Some looked idle, and
gathered around the old woman who was selling the first roasted
chestnuts of the season. They made lewd jokes, and spat freely.
Others leaned against the side wall. All would instantly disappear
inside the church and down into the crypt if the two sentinels,
posted in the Via Toledo, saw a patrol.

Niello detailed two of his most trusted boys to stay by him—
Aldo, the one with some education; and Eduardo, the boy who was
not very brave but had nimble legs. There would be climbing to do.
Besides, Eduardo had another asset—he knew the inside of the store,
for he had often pilfered there.

Just to be sure, Niello took Osvaldo with him as well, having
first taken him home to get his rifle from above his father's butcher
shop. That done, Osvaldo's rifle, with the shotgun or two owned by
the rest of the detail, were put in a handcart, covered with a variety of old clothing and rags, and the cart put conveniently in the
alley between the church and the store, to wait there till Niello
had found a way of getting in, and the time was ripe for action.

Niello, Aldo, and Osvaldo watched from a doorway behind the
Rinascente as Eduardo, slim, whistling a song, kicking a stone
with his bare foot, moved slowly around the building. Every so
often his bright, swift eyes took in a detail. He made the full cir-
cuit, then rejoined his companions.

"The ground floor's got steel shutters," he said. "I know because
I've seen that from inside. They're easy enough to open, just a
bar."

"Good," said Aldo.

"From the *inside*," said Eduardo. He gave the clever boy a superior smile. Aldo looked sulky and fell silent.

"Is there any way to get in?" said Niello.

"No," said Eduardo judiciously. "The windowsills are too narrow to stand on while you pry open the other shutters on the upper floors. They're just wood, but you need space."

"Could we get in through the roof?"

"You can *always* get in *anywhere* through the roof," said Eduardo.

"Good," said Aldo again.

Eduardo nodded. He looked up to the roof of the building, tilting back his head. He screwed up his eyes, pursed his lips, and grunted.

"You couldn't climb up. Those drainpipes would come clean away with your weight," Eduardo continued. "They haven't been renewed for years and they're rusting, but . . ."

"Well, go on," urged Aldo.

"*I* could do it. Another way."

"You could?" said Aldo excitedly. "How?"

Eduardo pointed to the top of the building behind the store. It was separated from the Rinascente by one of the transverse alleys. "If I could get up there," he said, "I could do it."

His eyes dancing with mirth, he watched his three companions as they craned their necks to see.

"You really *could?*" said Aldo, all admiration.

"Yes," said Eduardo. "All I'd need is a pair of black tights, a mask, a cloak, and something neat and nifty around my middle so that you, dear friends and companions, won't see the shape of my cock and balls when I *leap* through the air and—"

With a roar, Aldo aimed a kick at Eduardo, but the boy was yards away before it could land.

"All right," said Niello, with a broad grin. "Come back and let's forget Phantomas," he said, referring to one of the more popular comic strip characters of the Thirties and Forties. "You have found a way in, haven't you? Otherwise you wouldn't be so cheerful."

"Uh-huh." Eduardo, keeping a wary eye on Aldo's foot, came back. "Niello, come with me. No, just you. We'll have to go out into the Toledo and we don't want a whole crowd gawking up at the store."

The two went. They went out into the main street, cautiously making sure that the sentinels were on the alert. Eduardo pointed to a broad terrace that extended from the great arched windows on the "noble floor." It had been built when the store was a palace, for its owners to take the air in the cool of the evening.

"Look at the shutters," said Eduardo. They were of wood, and made up of slats. The paint was peeling from them. "They're much older than all the others. Too big to renew, too expensive, I suppose. I dunno. Perhaps they forgot or meant to do it, then came the war and—"

"And the second from the right is not properly locked," said Niello.

"Lock's rusted."

"Can you get up there?"

"Well," said Eduardo dubiously, "there's that sort of a railing."

It was a fancy ironwork affair, done in the once-fashionable "Liberty" style, known outside Italy as art nouveau. It was full of twirls and leaves and metal flowers.

"If I had a ladder . . ." said Eduardo.

"You'd be a sitting duck for any patrol. They'd see the ladder and you climbing it a mile off. Besides, where could we get a bloody long ladder like that? Can you climb a rope?"

"I can climb anything except those drainpipes. And by the way, that railing's rusty, too."

"Afraid?"

"I'm always afraid." There was a long pause. "If you get me some rope—and a hook . . ."

Niello put his hand on Eduardo's shoulder. "Right, Phantomas. Will do."

Eduardo grinned, but his lips were trembling.

The rope was easy. Eduardo ran off to a chandler's shop, which was just opening after the hours of the siesta. The elderly owner was stacking the shutters.

"Rope," said Eduardo. "We want some rope."

"What are you boys up to now? Rope, eh?"

"Not rope-eh, just rope. That pile there will do."

"First I want to know what you boys are going to do with it."

"Hang Scholl from a lamppost. *Hurry!*"

"Who's going to pay me?"

"Scholl."

"How, if you're going to hang him?"

"You can pick his pockets as he dangles. *Hurry*, you old fool."

"Take it yourself."

Eduardo took up the coil, slinging it over his shoulder. He gave the owner a winning smile. "Thanks."

"By San Gennaro," said the old man, mollified, "I wish you *were* going to hang him. They've taken my boy. Idiot was lounging about the station and they got him. Make it a slow death," and he laughed. As Eduardo disappeared, the chandler shook his gray head. "Those *scugnizzi*. I wonder what they're really up to. No good, I'll be bound."

The hook was more of a problem. It had to be large and solid. Eduardo, Niello, and Aldo all talked at once for a minute or two, as is the habit of *scugnizzi*. Then Osvaldo said, "If you'd let me get a word in edgewise—"

"Go ahead," said Niello.

"There are a dozen damn great hooks hanging outside my father's shop. There's been no meat on them for weeks."

Half-carcasses of sheep, whole legs and thighs of cattle, skinned rabbits, and such customarily hang outside butchers' shops in Naples, and can still be seen despite sanitary laws.

"Let's go," said Niello, and, circumspectly, he went with him.

The hook was obtained: As Osvaldo knew he would be, his father was still sleeping. For boys accustomed at Santa Lucia to lend a hand with the fishermen, it was an easy matter to fix the hook securely to the rope. The boys crouched in a small courtyard to complete the task, then they went out and stood beside the Rinascente.

"Who'll throw it?" asked Aldo. "I'm no good at that sort of thing."

"I'll do it," said Niello, and the other two *scugnizzi* nodded agreement. All the boys had joined in battles with rival gangs. They would strip to their bathing trunks and, manufacturing simple slings, would bombard one another with rotten tomatoes or peaches or oranges, to the huge delight of the stall owners who saw their wasted stock being put at least to some use.

Niello eyed the metalwork around the terrace. He swung the

rope about his head three times and then let go. The hook fell short by about a foot and Eduardo nodded approval. This was correct: Niello was judging the distance. You aim the first tomato just short of a boy; the next one should get him full in the face.

"One, two, three," said Niello as the rope swung a second time. "Got it!" The hook neatly caught a romantic design of flowers and creepers. He pulled on the rope, and it held.

"Up you go."

Eduardo thrust a piece of iron into his shirtfront. It came up against the small automatic he had hidden there, so he removed the gun and held it out to Niello.

"That's right," said Niello. "You won't need it. There's nobody inside."

"Sure?"

"I swear it."

"On your grandmother's bones?"

"On my grandmother's bones." It was as solemn an oath as any boy could want.

Eduardo began to climb. He was agile; his bare feet gripped the rope securely. He could climb the mast of a fishing boat when it was rocking in a gale.

Just short of the top, the metal flowers wilted and bent. A shower of rust fell on Eduardo's head. The boys below held their breath. Eduardo gritted his teeth. His palms sweating, he made the last few feet with astonishing speed. As he drew himself over the railing, the metal flowers and creepers crashed to the ground, and lay, the pride of some forgotten artist and craftsman, on the stones of the alley.

It was a moment's work for Eduardo to use his bar to pry open the old lock on the shutter.

"Easier than cars," he said to himself. The locks of automobiles could be opened with a thin blade, but it took delicacy of touch, it took expertise. This was journeyman's work.

The shutter swung half-open. Eduardo slipped inside the store. The half-light from the window was not sufficient for him, coming as he did from the bright outside. Slowly, the spots in front of his eyes cleared. Ten feet away from him stood a man.

CHAPTER EIGHT

Although the man stood very still, Eduardo knew perfectly well that he had been seen. A beam of light coming through the half-open shutters fell across the man's eyes and they gleamed with malice.

After a moment of terror in which he could do nothing, all his *scugnizzo* experiences rushed into his mind. He was instantly fully alert. Once, a store detective in this very same place had seen him filch a cigarette case from a bargain counter. Then he had escaped by dropping on all fours and crawling behind counters till he came to an emergency fire exit. He dropped down now and crawled.

It was harder this time, in the dim light. He bumped his head noisily against the edge of a counter, and he froze for half a minute. Cautiously raising his head till his eyes were just above the counter, he saw the man was still looking in the direction of the window through which Eduardo had come. He had his hand slightly thrust forward, holding something—something with a long projection. Jesus, it was a gun!

He crawled desperately, working his way so that he would be behind the man. Policemen always looked for a stupid second or two in the direction in which they first saw you. Then they looked left and right and left and right again as though they were crossing a busy road. Only after that did they turn right around to face about, so behind them was the place to get to.

Eduardo got there, some fifteen feet away, behind another counter. He raised himself. He cursed Niello silently but roundly, asking San Gennaro to send him the clap next time he slept with a girl. He had, after all, said that the store would be empty. He had, after all, let him climb up without a gun.

The man had not moved. He was still staring at the window through which Eduardo had come—waiting, no doubt, for another boy. Eduardo sank back to his knees. A breeze came down the Toledo, and the shutter, with a whine, swung wider. Eduardo looked to his right. There, dimly, but quite clearly enough to send his pulse bounding, he saw the legs of a man. There were *two* men in the store. A spy must have split on them.

He peeped back at the man by the window. He still had not moved. He looked back at the trousers of the second man. They were perfectly creased. He examined the shoes. They were resplendently polished. Moreover, this second man was standing on a square platform.

Eduardo coughed once softly, then more loudly. Neither trousers nor the outline of the other man moved.

Eduardo chuckled. "Take that back, San Gennaro," he whispered. "They're tailors' dummies."

He rose to his feet. From the pocket of his shorts he took a small flashlight that Niello had given him. It was very precious. The Germans had commandeered every flashlight they could lay hands on, and the long nights of the bombings had used up all but a few of the batteries. This one had come from a benevolent doctor in a hospital.

Using it, Eduardo made his way back to the window. He shone the light on the first dummy. It was dressed in a white suit; it held a panama hat in one hand and a pair of yellow gloves in the other —the perfect attire for a young gentleman paying a call in summertime. "Hope you lay her," said Eduardo.

Then he carefully closed the shutter, as Niello had told him to. He found the stairs and ran nimbly down them. He knew the layout of the store perfectly, and in no time he was at the staff entrance. The door was fastened with an iron bar that came easily away. There was an old-fashioned lock dating from the days when the building was still a palace. A minute's thrusting and probing with his metal tool and the lock yielded. Cautiously, he opened the door about six inches and whistled the opening bars of a Neapolitan song.

The door gave onto the alley at the back where the boys were waiting. Niello ran to the end of the alley and whistled another line of the tune. The boys on the steps, who were chattering with the woman selling hot chestnuts, instantly fell silent. One of them ran up the steps into the church. Once inside, he whistled softly.

An exceedingly grubby sacristan seized his elbow. "Heathen!" he hissed, his voice low in the manner of his profession. "Protestant! Don't you know better than to whistle in church? This is the house of God. Sit down, take a seat," he said with heavy irony. "Make yourself comfortable. Cross your legs." This was precisely what all children were brought up never to do in church.

But the three boys in the pews had heard the signal. They got up and slipped out the door. The boy who had whistled apologized briefly. The sacristan still held his elbow. "It's a good thing that some boys know how to behave," said the sacristan. He nodded toward another boy who was on his knees in a side chapel.

The boy rose reverently. He moved toward a stack of candles ready for the faithful to buy by putting a coin in a box. He picked up one. He glanced at the boy who had whistled. He picked up a whole armful of them and bolted for the door. The boy who had whistled shook himself free and went through the door with him. The sacristan howled in indignation.

The operation was not as neat as Niello had planned. He had forgotten the sacristan. But nothing in Naples goes exactly as predicted.

The sacristan ran out to the steps, waving his hands wildly.

"You clumsy great ox! Look what you've done!" shouted the woman who was selling chestnuts, while at the same time she kicked over her brazier so that the live coals and chestnuts rolled down the steps. "I'll make you pay for that, every centesimo. I'll tell the priest. Snatch my living out of my mouth, would you? And me a poor woman who can barely keep body and soul together!"

The tirade, at the top of her voice, deafened the sacristan, who stood making helpless little gestures of protest with his hands. Out of the corner of her eye, the woman saw with satisfaction that the boys had safely disappeared. She, too, came from Montecalvario.

Niello had foreseen that all the shutters of the store must remain closed; otherwise the Germans would suspect a trap. Hence —given the lack of flashlights—the importance of the candles.

The appointed boys were slipped into the store by the service entrance, and each was given a candle to find his way. But the candles ran out. There were far more volunteers than Niello's chosen band—two or three students, a worker, and some apprentices came in through the door unasked. The word had spread. Finally, Niello gave orders for the door to be shut.

The big chain stores of Italy were not air-conditioned. That was to come only after the war. They could not be cut up into low decks, as they are today. The palace in which the Rinascente operated had been gutted, and the store designed on American and French models. There was a great open well, rising from the ground floor to the roof, surrounded by galleries. On the four sides of each of these galleries the goods were displayed.

Niello led his troops to the second gallery. The first, as Eduardo had discovered, was for clothing and served no purpose for the coming battle. The second was better. It held suites of furniture, much of it solid and heavy in the style of the day. It would give excellent protection. He told his unit to shift the furniture to the rails of the gallery, so that it made a barricade.

In the flickering light of the holy candles, he saw his orders obeyed, but sometimes by strange faces. He tightened his belt, because he had a strange, creeping feeling in that area. He thought at first it was just nerves, but soon decided it was something more logical. When the firing started, what was to stop one of these young men whom he did not know from shooting him in the back?

"What do we do now?" said a voice from behind a candle flame.

"We wait," said Niello. "We wait till they come in. Then wait again till they've done a little shopping."

"Why?"

"Because the girls won't have guns, but the men will."

"So?" said a voice, this time from one of his own boys.

"So the men will have their arms full, so they won't be able to get at their guns, so we'll have the first round. Any more 'So's?' from anybody?"

There were none.

"When they begin to break in, put out your candles."

"Yessir," said a young voice.

A deeper voice objected. "How will we see them? It will be pitch-dark."

"So it will. So it will," said Niello, as though the thought had just occurred to him. "But they'll be in the dark as well, won't they?

And have you ever taken a woman shopping in a pitch-dark shop? No? Use your heads. Using them? Good."

"They'll open the windows," said Aldo.

"Right. Now, all of you, shut up."

He was obeyed. As he waited, Niello speculated on what it would be like to be shot in the back. Did one die quickly? Or did one thrash around like a lizard whose spine you've broken with a stick?

The girls in Carmela's brothel had to drink up quickly. Their lovers had only two hours' leave. But, spluttering, gulping, and protesting, they grew happy in a suitably short space of time. There were three of them: Isa, of course, who everyone knew was the center of the party, and two other girls for the two other young Gestapo men. All six trooped downstairs to the entrance, followed by Carmela.

"I told you," said the sergeant, "we'd do this in style," and he waved a hand at the armored car drawn up in the street. "Madame," said the sergeant to Isa, sweeping her a bow, "your limousine awaits you."

Grinning a broad peasant grin, a fourth soldier held open the door, his cap in his hand.

"Your chauffeur, Madame," said the sergeant. He was, in fact, the driver, but also an expert member of Scholl's demolition squads.

Giggling, the girls climbed aboard.

Carmela waved goodbye. She did not really like her girls being taken out; the world, even in peacetime, was such a dangerous place for girls. But she consoled herself that Isa, at least, would choose a dress worthy of a lady. As for the other two, they would certainly come back with something worthy of a streetwalker. She sighed, and closed the door.

"What's that, in that wooden box?" asked one of the girls.

"Dynamite," said the sergeant, and a wild, female shriek arose from the armored car as it drove off through the deserted streets.

Inside, the boys waited in total silence. Each crouched behind a heavy piece of furniture that, with the aid of the light of the candles, they had dragged into position against the balustrade overlooking the well of the store. The balustrade, too, was fashionably ornate, and its component parts gave ample loopholes for firing. Inexpert fingers played with triggers. Young blood pulsed in the bodies of the lads and boys.

"Gimme," said Eduardo, who was crouching beside Niello.

"What?"

"My gun."

"No. You're too young."

"I'm afraid."

"Don't be. Stick by me."

"Thanks, but I'd feel better if I had my gun back."

"All right." The gun passed from hand to hand.

"Remember," said Niello, "nobody's to fire till I give a shout."

The boys, in the silence of the shuttered store, heard the noise of a car engine outside.

"It's them," whispered a boy.

"Sh . . . sh . . ." said Niello.

There was a pause which the boys found nearly unbearable.

"You've passed it, you've passed it!" shouted the girls as the armored car trundled by the front of the store.

The Germans laughed. "Just as well we did. We don't want three charming ladies going up in little bits. Leave it to Kurt."

Kurt, the driver and demolition expert, drove past the church and some yards more down the Toledo. He stopped the armored car and, watched by a hundred eyes through the slants of shutters or between gaps in curtains, unloaded his gear. From a spool he ran out a long length of fuse. Then, carrying sticks of dynamite, he fastened them to the grill that protected the entrance to the store.

The setting of the fuse, the attachment of the dynamite, and the hundred precautions of the expert Kurt took time. The boys heard the little noises of the preparations with mounting impatience, but at last it was over. There was a flash and a roar. A great billow of acrid smoke swept through the ground floor and made its way upward. The boys began coughing violently.

Niello said, much louder than he knew because the explosion had temporarily deafened him, "For Jesus' sake, stop coughing. Pass it on," he ordered Eduardo, and the small boy, hugely delighted by the magnificent bang, crawled around on his hands and knees and gave the message.

The cloud subsided, and so did the coughing. There was another pause. Then the boys saw, from the light coming from the shattered outer grill and inner door, the three Germans and the three girls. The girls stepped gingerly over the debris. They came into the store. The leading German switched on a powerful flashlight and flashed it around.

"*Marronne,* what a stink," said one of the prostitutes. "It smells worse than—"

"Lucia, mind your tongue," said Isa.

The sergeant stood his light on a counter, rubbed his hands, and bowed deeply. "Modom," he said, imitating a floorwalker, "would Modom perhaps accept ah, ah . . ." He picked up a bottle on which the lamp was shining. "Would Modom perhaps accept a flask of Chanel Number Five with the compliments of the management and our deepest apologies to Modom for the clumsy way our doorman opened the door?"

"Thank you," said Isa, between her coughs. "Thank you for the perfume, but let's get the bleeding hell out of this."

"Ooh," said one of her fellow prostitutes. "Hark at her, swearing. And she always so ladylike," but her further comments were drowned, for a fit of coughing seized her.

Isa recovered. "First floor. That's where the dresses are," she said, fearful that her poise would desert her. "Let's hurry."

"Modom shall be served," said the sergeant. "Forward!" he said to his companions, in an effeminate voice and clapping his hands. "Ladies' wear, first floor." He bowed and, picking up his light, he flashed it around to find the stairs. He located them, then said in his usual authoritative voice, "Conrad, open a window or two. The ladies are incommoded." Both he and Conrad broke into a raucous laugh, but the soldier did as he was told.

Precisely as Eduardo had predicted, the windows were simple to open. The evening light broke into the store and for the first time the boys, hidden behind the furniture, saw the wreckage of the main entrance clearly. The Gestapo soldiers and the women made their way up the stairs. Slowly, the boys' eardrums resumed their function.

"Not a move, not a shot, till they go out," whispered Niello.

"Pass it on." Eduardo, his gun clutched in sweating fingers, once more crawled on hands and knees with his message.

It was an extraordinary situation in which to choose some dresses and hats, but Isa did not transcend the custom of her sex. She kept her male escorts waiting. First, several of the windows on the first floor had to be opened so that she could see herself properly in the mirror as she tried on hats, or held gowns up against herself. The sergeant sat on a spindly gold-painted chair and made approving or disapproving remarks, as was befitting. The boys, hearing the murmur of voices, grew increasingly restless. They watched Kurt, the demolition expert, come into the store and go upstairs.

Kurt crossed over to his superior and sketched a salute. "The streets are full of people, sir."

"It's the noise," said the sergeant tranquilly. "Too garish for you, my dear—the noise, Kurt. The Neapolitans love bangs. You should hear the noise they make with fireworks on New Year's Eve. I was brought here once as a boy by my parents. We were on holiday and—"

"I am not a traveled man," said Kurt respectfully, "but I know a gun when I see one. And these people in the street have got them."

The sergeant rose. Two or three selected dresses fell from his knees to the floor. "In which street are they?" he said in German.

"The main street, and both alleys."

The sergeant rapidly made sure that this was true.

"Girls," he said, in a voice that produced a squeak from all of them, "we've got to get out. We're—we're—" He searched for the Italian word. "We're surrounded. Out with you."

"Ow," wailed one of the prostitutes. "You said we'd go shopping in style."

"Quiet!" said Isa. She was all composure. "Do as the gentleman tells you."

The group came down the stairs and into the well of the store. The girls preceded the men. The men, as Niello had said, had their arms full of dresses. Niello waited until they were in the middle of the ground floor. Then he fired a shot in the air.

Instantly a hail of pistol and rifle shots poured out of the second floor. The boys discovered to their dismay how much more difficult it was to hit a man than the movies had led them to believe. Besides, at the very first shot the Gestapo men, dragging the screaming girls behind them, had flung themselves behind counters, just as Eduardo had done.

The center of the ground floor was taken up by a display of perfumes. The boys hit these bottles squarely. A waft of mixed scents rose from the counters.

The sergeant, peering around a corner, aimed and fired. The bullet splintered a piece of furniture, and the boy behind it gazed, open-mouthed, at the gash.

All four soldiers now began shooting, but the light from the few opened windows was not sufficient for them to have effect.

A second fusillade was the boys' answer. Then, silence. The puzzled boys took potshots from time to time to break it, but there was no move from the soldiers.

Then suddenly there was a noise of scrambling and loud female protests. The Gestapo men emerged from behind their counters. They had seized the whores and were backing toward the shattered doors, keeping the girls in front of them.

"Don't shoot!" screamed one of the girls. "Don't shoot! We're your own flesh and blood. Try and kill these fucking bastards, but don't shoot us!"

The men moved slowly backward. One or two of the boys let off their pistols, but more to intimidate than to injure. Deliberately, their shots went wild. They had no effect on the retreating men, except to make Isa scream.

"Murderers!" she yelled at the boys. "Murderers!"

The men reached the doorway, their grips on the women still firm. Osvaldo took up his rifle, slowly.

"No," said Niello sharply.

"Yes," said Osvaldo.

One of the random shots of the boys hit a display case, and there was the sound of shattered glass. The girl, who was being held by one of the soldiers, twisted violently, bending almost double to shelter her face.

Osvaldo fired.

The Gestapo man who was holding her looked up in surprise. He pushed the girl away from him, so that she stumbled drunkenly.

Regaining her balance, she bolted for the door. The soldier who had released her shook his head like a dog just fresh from the water. Then he pitched forward on his face.

"He's dead," said Osvaldo. "I got him right over his heart. Like the target they had on the rifle range."

Then there was nobody in the store but the boys, and the body on the floor.

Led by Kurt, the two remaining men of the Gestapo went through the doorway with the girls in front of them. They were in the Toledo, but it was a very different street from the one they had known. The noise of the firing had drawn the people. They stood now, lined six deep, on the sidewalk opposite the store and blocking the lane both to the left and to the right. In the front row were young men with rifles and handguns. One swung a grenade negligently. The crowd was quite silent.

The sergeant pushed Isa roughly in the small of her back. "Get in the armored car," he said. She did not move for the good reason that the sergeant had lost his Italian and spoke in German. He gave her another push and she stumbled across the sidewalk. Righting herself, she suddenly started screaming. There was nothing lady-like about her now. She shouted in the rough dialect of a country girl.

"They're going to kill us!" she screamed.

"Whore," said a male voice from the midst of the crowd.

"Whore I may be," said Isa. "But if you're going to let these dirty German pigs kill us, then if I'm a whore, so's your mother."

"Get in the car!" the German shouted, recovering his Italian.

"They're taking us away!" Isa yelled. "Look what they're doing to us! Look what they're doing to us! It's what they'll do to your sisters, your brothers. . . ."

The crowd growled. Someone fired a shot in the air.

Niello and his boys listened to this echo of their own slogan which had had so little effect. They had run down the stairs as the Germans had withdrawn. Niello had paused by the dead man. He marveled that there was no blood, just the body of someone who had fallen down, sprawling like a drunkard. He wanted to help him to his feet, but his boys were already in the Toledo, their pistols and guns at the ready. He joined them.

The girls were bundled into the car. Isa said nothing more, but the other two prostitutes set up a high-pitched wailing. The sergeant swung his open hand and hit both of them squarely in the face.

"You ready?" he said to Kurt, the driver.

"Oughtn't we to go back and get—*him?*" said Kurt. Then he added, "Sir?"

"I said are you ready to start?" roared the sergeant.

"Yessir."

"Have they tampered with the car?"

Kurt pressed switches. The engine started. Kurt tried the gears.

"All in order, sir."

"Good. When I say go, *go.*"

"Yes, sir."

The sergeant stood in the turret of the car. Very slowly he raised the machine gun. He swallowed some spittle, cleared his throat, then shouted, in careful Italian, "I am coming through. If you try to stop me . . ." He patted the machine gun.

The crowd watched him without a word. He tilted the machine gun upward and fired a burst in the air. As the echo died away, nothing could be heard except the whimpering of the slapped girls. Everybody looked at the boys with their guns standing in the doorway. The boys looked at Niello.

He made a sign with his hand. The crowd parted. The armored car rocked and roared, then slowly made its way through the lane the crowd had provided.

"Don't worry, girls," said a young man. There was no answer. He beat with his fist on the metal side. "I said don't worry. We'll come and get you. It's all up with those buggers. It's all up."

The car moved on. Niello watched it till it was well down the Toledo. It was his moment of triumph.

But he still wished he could have picked up that sprawling German in the shop, and he still wished he could have heard him say, "Thanks. I'm all right."

CHAPTER NINE

The boys were heroes. As the Germans retreated, the citizens poured out of their houses. Niello suddenly found himself seized from behind, hoisted into the air, and seated upon the broad shoulders of a workman. Upturned faces smiled at him. Hands reached out to touch him as though he were the statue of a saint. Round about him he saw the boys and lads who had won the battle of the Rinascente. They were proudly waving their pistols and rifles.

One, however, Niello noted as he swayed on the shoulders of the man who was carrying him, waved an ancient saber, and Niello was sure he had never taken part in the action. It was something he was soon to get used to. As the days went by, everybody in Montecalvario seemed to have irrefutable evidence that they had been in the store. Many conserved candles as a memento. Had they all actually been there, the Rinascente would have been as packed as it used to be for a winter sale.

He looked around him to find one of his own *scugnizzi*. He saw Eduardo. The boy was swinging his pistol idly and looking up with sad eyes at Niello's triumph.

"Listen!" shouted Niello at the top of his voice. The cheering died away. "There's the boy who got us inside. Nearly killed himself." He pointed to Eduardo.

There was a great shout from the crowd, and instantly the small boy was hoisted onto willing shoulders. Up in the air, beside Niello, he still looked sad.

"Smile," said Niello to him over the heads of the crowd.

Eduardo managed an unenthusiastic smirk.

"What's wrong, Eduardo?" Niello asked.

"I'm hungry," said Eduardo, then much louder, "I'm *ever* so hungry."

"He's hungry!" shouted Niello.

There was a cry from the crowd and a bustle. Somebody started a lewd song about the Germans that had been composed to an old tune in the air-raid shelters. Before it had got to its third verse, a motherly woman was elbowing her way through the crowd.

"Stand aside," she said. "The poor boy's hungry!" In her hands she held two lengths of sausage. The crowd parted as though she were a princess. She handed one to Eduardo and another to Niello. Eduardo fell to eating his without delay, only pausing to wave it in the air as he chewed on the lump he had bitten out of it.

Niello, grinning sheepishly, took a clasp knife from his pocket and cut himself a slice. He ate it slowly, envying Eduardo's appetite. He was worried. Everything in Naples ended in songs and a *festa*, much too soon. The Germans, he knew, would come back.

"To Piazza Plebiscito!" somebody shouted, and the cry was taken up till it echoed from the buildings that line the Toledo. By now, many others of the *scugnizzi* had been hoisted on shoulders. A rough procession was formed. The *scugnizzi*, grinning broadly, waved weapons in one hand and candles in the other. Thus the candle became a medal of merit.

The Piazza Plebiscito is a vast square, the biggest in Naples. It is a hundred paces from the end of the Toledo. On one side is the huge bulk of the Royal Palace. On the other is a great colonnade, semicircular in shape, with the domed Church of San Francesco di Paola in its middle. On the side where the Toledo ends is the Palace of the Prefect, the major civil authority of the city. It was from this building that some of Scholl's orders had, ostensibly, issued. The functionaries, all loyal Fascists, looked at the teeming crowd from the windows, some of them very pale in the face. One of the watchers was the prefect.

On the balcony of this palace a hero had once waved to the crowd—Giuseppe Garibaldi, something of a *scugnizzo* himself in spirit, a man who with a tiny army had helped to free Italy from another conqueror. The Neapolitans had cheered him so incessantly that an aide had appeared on the same balcony. He had quieted the crowd with a single famous phrase: "Hush! *He* is sleeping."

"We have clearly forbidden any assembly of more than three persons in Plebiscito," a small nervous man in a black shirt said to the prefect. "We can't allow this. Who knows where it will end? Who knows what Scholl will say?"

"Yes," said the prefect. "We must disperse the crowd. How?"

"Yes. Well—eh—um—" said the little man. "We could—eh—call the carabinieri."

"And if they join them?"

"Then—um—the fire brigade perhaps."

"No," said the prefect, with a slow, cynical smile, "*you* go out and tell them *I* want to sleep."

The little man said, "Yes, you're right. There's nothing we can do, nothing really. Just wait and see."

"Look," said the prefect, "they're hoisting the *scugnizzi* on the horses."

The piazza includes two bronze statues of heroic size. They show two past kings of Naples (both foreigners) mounted on horseback. One is Ferdinand I, the other is Charles Bourbon III. Only a handful of Neapolitans can tell you anything about these monarchs, but everybody in the city likes the horses. These colossal animals are regarded with affection and respect. In normal times, any *scugnizzo* daring to clamber onto them would be chased off with blows and cuffs. Now the boys were being hauled up hand over hand, till as many as six sat on them, some in front of the kings, others on the horses' immense hindquarters.

Niello refused to join them, though he laughed heartily when the boys kicked the metal flanks of the beasts and waved to him. He shook his arm free from an enthusiastic middle-aged man with the air of a schoolteacher, who wanted Niello to join his companions.

"No," Niello said. "I've something to say."

"Say it up there."

"No. Down here will do."

The middle-aged man clapped his hands above his head to attract attention. The crowd near him stopped cheering the boys on the horses and listened.

"Our new Masaniello has something to say."

Immediately a group was formed around Niello. The people stood in a circle, with some yards of space between him and them. It was the traditional act of respect paid to some citizens that the Neapolitans admire. Such a person need only stand still in a piazza with the air of one who wishes to speak, and a crowd will always take up formation. Previously this gesture was reserved only for gray-haired gentlemen, immaculately dressed like the dummy in the store, who would then give advice to the hoi polloi, the mob who were always held to be in need of guidance from their social betters. Now it was one of the mob itself, a boy in a dirty shirt and trousers, his hair uncombed, a pistol in his hand.

"Listen," he said. "They'll come back."

"We're ready for them."

"That's just what we aren't. You saw that machine gun. He fired in the air. Just a flick of his wrist and he could have brought it level and fired it straight at you."

"God have mercy on us," a young woman wailed.

"He will if you aren't fools."

Eduardo was riding in front of Ferdinand I, who towered feet above him, staring over the boy's head. Niello was speaking within yards of the base of the statue. He looked up. "Eduardo," he said, "tell them how we didn't get shot in the store."

Eduardo stuck out his chest. He made a wide, oratorical gesture and all but fell off the horse. Clutching King Ferdinand, he recovered his balance and dignity.

"Niello said, 'Go to the second floor.' Niello said, 'Move the furniture to make a barricade.' So we did. And when those bastards started shooting, they hit the furniture, not us. One bullet was as close as *this* to me"—he held a finger two inches away from his head—"but it just went into a sideboard or something. Was it a sideboard, Niello? I forget."

The crowd raised a cheer for Eduardo's bravery. Eduardo, who had not lost hold of his sausage even when climbing onto the horse, grinned, waved it, and cut himself a huge slice.

"So that's it," said Niello to the crowd around him. "When they come back, they've got to find us all behind barricades. Block off Montecalvario. Block off the Toledo. While they're trying to shift you from behind, shoot at them from the windows up there." He pointed to the top floors of the buildings that lined the end of the Toledo.

"What with?" asked a woman. "I mean, what do we make these —these—" The word was new, the word was long. She was lost.

"Barricades. Walls." Niello supplied the word. "And you make them with any old junk, as long as it's thick and heavy."

"Junk?" said a man with silvery hair. "I've got more junk than anybody in Naples." He pointed toward San Carlo Opera House. The crowd laughed, for behind those walls the relics of hundreds of operas lay moldering in the basement. And as everybody knew, this was the man in charge.

"Hey," he said to the boys on the horses. "You *guaglioni*. Come down here and help me bring it out."

Joyfully the boys clambered down, but Niello stopped them.

"Wait till it's dark, when you'll not be seen," he said. "I want it to be a nice surprise for the Nazis in the morning."

September 28 dawned in a sulky sky that threatened rain. Outside Scholl's headquarters a yawning German soldier checked over his Fiat automobile. It was a good, sound car, and he had commandeered it himself from its Neapolitan owner, at the point of a gun. But you could never be sure. There was always sabotage—and the possibility that when he turned the ignition key and pulled that knob *there* to start the engine, he would be blown up by a bomb. Not that he really thought such a thing could happen; it was just that the checkup was part of his instructions and he followed them meticulously. As for himself, he had seen plenty of occupied towns in Europe, but never one as tranquil as this. "Supine" was the word he heard in the mess each day to describe the Neapolitans. Of course, he had heard of spots of trouble here and there, but it always died down so quickly. And he had expected them to be all full of fire. If, when the war was over, anybody told him that the southern Italian was hot-blooded, he would put him straight. Supine. He must remember that word to use when he got home at last to the wife and kids. What tales he would have to tell!

There was no bomb, as far as he could see. He looked at his wristwatch. He smiled as he remembered how hastily the man had handed it over to him: even with a smile, and the sketch of a Hitler salute. Supine. He would have time for a coffee before the usual run: All broad streets—those were the orders since that trouble with the ragamuffins in Ottocalli—Via Vittorio Emanuele, Via Salvator Rosa, down into Piazza Dante, along the road they call the Toledo—though clear as day there were signs saying it was Via Roma—to the Prefect's Palace, and then the envelope to hand over and the receipt book to get signed.

He looked at the sky. It was a pity it was so misty. In fine weather the view over the bay, with Capri and Ischia, was stupendous. That was something else he would tell the wife and kids about. Many of the men planned holidays here when the war was over. There were plenty of Germans on Capri, rich men who knew what they were doing, like Krupp. Goethe had raved about the bay, so he had been told at school. He had never read him, but that was another thing he meant to do when the war was over.

He entered the canteen. "Heil Hitler," he said to some men who were there, but he only muttered it. The regulars didn't like it. But it was in Army Rules, and, after all, there was that skinny eagle clutching a swastika, a badge they all wore.

"Good morning," said a corporal he knew. "There's been trouble on your route. Have you heard?"

The messenger sipped his coffee. "No. What happened?"

"There was a shoot-out in a store on the Toledo. You pass that, don't you?"

"Yes, I do. Was it serious?"

"No," said another soldier. "Just some urchins robbing the place. Some of our men caught them at it."

"I haven't tasted coffee like this for years," said the messenger. "Makes up for having to deal with these lying scoundrels. I'm surprised to hear there was shooting. They're so . . ." "Supine" was the word he wanted, but just at that moment it slipped his memory. He drank his coffee noisily.

"Just kids playing cops and robbers," said another corporal.

"Yes. Well, I must be off." He left the canteen.

The usual thick envelope was handed to him, with the receipt book. He exchanged salutes and drove off.

The bay was hidden in mist. The broad streets were empty. He turned into Piazza Dante with its pink palaces and fancy archways. He gave the brooding statue of the Poet of Heaven and Hell a wave as he always did, for luck. Goethe. He must read Goethe when all this was over.

He drove on down the Toledo toward the Prefect's Palace. On his right he saw the hill of Montecalvario. His mouth opened wide in surprise. He slowed the car.

Each of the narrow alleys that ran into the Toledo had been blocked off by barricades. Boys sat on them, swinging their bare legs, watching his slow progress with steady, hostile eyes. Young men peered over the tops, with here and there a rifle lying across the pile of furniture, boxes, and scrap iron.

A boy shouted to him. What he said was "Where are you going?" but the messenger did not understand it. From the next barricade, another boy asked him, "Where did you steal that car?" The messenger did not understand that either, but the hostile laughter from behind the barricades conveyed menace.

The messenger looked right down the Toledo to the final piazza. There stood the Palace of the Prefect, red-bricked, massive, and reassuring. The messenger was very frightened, but the sight of the palace told him what to do. His duty.

It had been the most exciting dawn Montecalvario had ever known. As soon as Niello and his boys had mentioned the word "barricades," everybody, with that immense Neapolitan enthusiasm which is the other side of the medal of their lethargy, wanted to get to work immediately.

It needed only a few words from the hero of the shoot-out at the Rinascente to point out the folly of this. Night was coming on fast. There was no street lighting. Flashlights were scarce and, in any case, would draw the attention of a night patrol. These had become infrequent because so little took place after dark, but the occasional round was still to be heard and seen. With the new order for recruiting forced labor, such night rounds might increase in number; picking up sleeping young men and carting them off to forced labor would be very typical of Scholl's mentality. It would be far better to wait for the first light of dawn, and then, working at top speed, block off the streets.

Everybody agreed. Everybody went home to bed. But that night, very few slept.

With the first glimmer of dawn from behind Vesuvius, the boys were up and about, knocking at doors, calling people softly by name. Their spirits were high. This was like the time when, in the early morning, they had dived into the cold waters at Santa Lucia for the first arms of the rebellion. After that, it had seemed that the revolt would never come—that it was just an adolescent dream of adventure. But now it was here.

There were difficulties. The woman who had asked what they would make the barricades with turned out to have her reason: Such pieces of furniture that the people had were treasured. Grandfather's sideboard and grandmother's table were all they had left to their descendants. Shopkeepers were shopkeepers—they loved their counters, their shelves (even if they were empty), and the packing cases in which were hidden away all the stock they had left. People, shivering in the damp September dawn, stood about and argued in subdued voices.

Niello gathered his boys and lads. Strange young faces—of deserters from the army, of students, and of some who were past their youth but eager for action—looked at him as he stood in an alley.

"Loot the Rinascente!" he said. A shout went up. "Quietly, you donkeys!" he said. "*Quietly*," and held a finger to his lips.

The admonition was completely ignored. An air of *festa* swept everybody. Men, women, and boys poured in through the broken doorway and soon were lugging out the very furniture behind which the boys had hidden. Nor did the heroes of that encounter fail to point out the bullet holes. They stepped around the body of the German soldier, which still lay where it had fallen. The Geheime Feldpolizei clearly had not been anxious to report to Scholl their expedition with a party of whores. The Gestapo had its dignity to maintain in front of nonprofessionals. The body of their comrade would be found by one of the patrols.

The priest from the church next door settled this problem. Carrying a revolver in one hand and holding his little book in the other, he gave the dead man a hasty absolution and had him carried away to the basement. He then joined in the building of the barricades.

The *festa* continued, and it was found that among the revelers

(San Gennaro be thanked) were two or three night watchmen of the banks and official buildings that lined the Toledo. They had keys; keys opened doors; women came and went carrying pompous chairs, while men and boys dragged out large tables which civil servants and bank employees had spent a dreary lifetime for the privilege of sitting behind.

By the time the sun was up and shining fitfully between swiftly drifting clouds, the barricades had been built.

The messenger had come to the end of the Toledo. A barricade stretched across the road. Men and boys with guns peered over the top of it; guns poked through interstices. Beyond lay the Palace of the Prefect.

The messenger stopped his car a few yards from the barricade. He adjusted his uniform neatly, he set his cap correctly. He rose. In his left hand he held the envelope it was his duty to deliver. His right hand rested on the butt of his revolver, the holster duly unbuttoned.

He held up the envelope.

"I have a message from Colonel Scholl to your prefect," he said, in correct and clipped German.

A noise like that of barking and growling dogs rose from the barricade. This was the Neapolitan burlesque of German; it represented the way the German language sounded to ears accustomed to the mellifluous accents of Italian.

The messenger smiled. He had heard the sound from *scugnizzi* before, but they had always run away the moment he had raised an open palm as if to strike them. The barking and growling increased, mixed with some laughter. This time, the *scugnizzi* were not running away.

The messenger waved the envelope, smiling desperately. "Message," he said in Italian. "Prefect." "Must." "Urgent." "Very urgent." Then, mustering all the grammar he knew, "Me pass? Yes? Me pass, please? Please."

He heard voices as though in discussion. Then a slim young man of about eighteen appeared on the top of the barricade. He had glasses and the air of a university student, a somewhat nervous one, for it was clear from the way he constantly looked back and downward, apparently arguing, it was a job he was reluctant to do. Finally he shrugged his shoulders. He took out a white handkerchief and waved it.

"Good," said the messenger in German. "They're seeing sense."

"They're doing nothing of the sort," said the student in serviceable but plainly learned German. "They want me to tell you to go back."

"I shall not," said the messenger. "I have this envelope to deliver to your prefect, your lawfully constituted authority."

He felt proud of the last words, but they were lost on the student.

"The prefect's gone. Run away. Last night," said the student. "That building's empty." He pointed to the palace.

"You're lying," said the messenger. "All you Italians are liars."

"It's empty, I tell you. We raided it for arms last night at midnight and there was nobody there."

"You're lying."

The student said something in dialect. It was, in fact, a harmless request for the people behind the barricades to let off a few guns to show that he was telling the truth. The Germans had deposited a great quantity of arms in the Prefect's Palace, meticulously rendering up to the civil authority the arms they had seized from the citizenry.

A rattle of shots rang out from guns and pistols pointed in the air. The messenger, seized with a sudden panic, pulled out his revolver and, aiming at the first target visible, shot the student. The bullet hit the lad squarely on the forehead. The force of it carried him off his feet. He dived backward and hit the pavement behind the barricade with the full length of his body. The back of his skull split open.

There was a moment of horrified silence from the Neapolitans. Then Gi-gin, the thirteen-year-old member of the band who had an uncle in the Customs Guard, climbed in his slow, sleepy way to the top of the barricade. He held a grenade in his hand. He drew the fuse and, seemingly losing interest, waited the prescribed seconds, then he flung back his arm in a smooth gesture. The grenade flew from his hand.

It landed on the messenger's car. There was a flash and not very much noise. The messenger's face disappeared in a welter of spurting blood and torn flesh. Then he fell over the windshield of the open car, quite dead. It was the first of the hundreds of hand grenades that were to be used in the next four days of the revolt. A moment later, the car was blazing.

Niello's fear that he might be shot in the back by those who, to all appearances, were fighting on his side was a scarlet thread that ran through the whole revolt. It was not really a question of "traitors." It was not a question of fifth columns and quislings, bought by money to betray. There was no cloak-and-dagger. The men who were on the German side, the convinced Fascists, had every argument to support them. For twenty-one years, Italy had been under its own regime, its own invention, its own way of life, much admired by the Germans, and even by some of the notoriously democratic British. Now here was a gang of dirty, swearing, thieving street boys urging the populace to rise against Italy's trusted allies, the Germans. It was not as though the fascist regime had been swept out of existence. Mussolini was still alive and kicking; there were even reports that he had set up a new government in the North. You could not believe everything that you heard on the radio from Rome. Still, you could *believe*. These boys believed in nothing, not even the Catholic Church.

It was true that the Prefect's Palace was empty. It was true that the prefect had fled—who would *not* flee from a howling mob? So reasoned a true-blue Fascist who watched the death of the messenger, peeping through drawn curtains from a handsome top-floor apartment on the Toledo. He went down the stairs, crept out of a back entrance, and climbed the long hill to the German headquarters in the Parco Hotel.

Scholl hollered, Scholl stamped his foot, Scholl's provincial accents grew more than his interpreter could cope with. The Fascist informer (or patriotic messenger, according to one's standpoint) was so alarmed at the acrobatics of Scholl's cheek muscle that nobody at headquarters had a clear idea of what actually was taking place at the end of the Toledo. There was a mob. There was a boy. There was a murder. Napoleon had said that he could have put down the French Revolution with a whiff of grapeshot. Scholl had no grapeshot. But he had a tank. One stood daily on guard at the entrance to HQ, more for show than for anything else. Scholl gave orders that this tank should immediately drive down the Toledo. At the first sign of resistance, the tank should fire, at random.

The tank moved slowly down the Toledo from Piazza Dante. There was no resistance. People were watching from windows, but the road was empty.

The tank drew level with the alleys of Montecalvario. For the first time the Germans saw the barricades. The officer commanding the tank stood in his observation post, half exposed. The gunner within pressed the lever that worked the motor, which in turn swung his cannon slightly to the left and to the right, to see that all was ready for action.

The commanding officer gave his orders. "We shall fire if there is resistance."

The tank ground on, leaving tracks on the asphalt of the road, which had grown soft during the hot summer months and had not been repaired.

Suddenly a shot rang out. It hit the plating of the tank and ricocheted.

"Fire! Fire at the first stories."

It was a technique that had been used frequently in other parts of Europe. It was frightening, but avoided a massacre.

The first shots hit empty buildings, sending glass and woodwork flying from windows. Then there was a wild shrieking. Flames burst from the first floor of an apartment house. A young girl ran out onto a balcony, her clothes blazing.

"Mamma!" she shouted. "They've killed mother!" She attempted to climb over the railing, lost her balance, and fell onto the side-walk. Boys and men leaped over the barricades of the alleys, and to cover them, a hail of fire was directed at the tank. A student took his jacket—his only jacket and a symbol of his social rank—and beat at the flames coming from the burning girl. They sub-sided, but the girl was dead. The boys and lads dragged her small body into the shelter of a great portal built in the days of coaches and horses. Flat on the paving of the entrance, they watched the battle.

The tank moved forward toward a new barricade, the one that stretched right across the Toledo.

Niello squatted beside a machine gun. It poked out between a table that lay on its side and some beds with their mattresses. A deserter from the army, a boy of nineteen, manned the gun. Niello held the belt of ammunition. The nineteen-year-old, his eyes red with rage, was about to fire a burst when Niello stopped him.

"Wait."

The tank came nearer. The commander said to his gunner, "Use the machine gun, straight ahead, at the barricade. Traverse it for forty feet."

The gunner adjusted his weapon with care, checking that its parts were in good working order. He took his time. He foresaw that very shortly the tank would crash through the barricade and the rebels behind it would be running for their lives as he sprayed them with bullets. What fools these Italians were!

At that moment a *scugnizzo* jumped over the barricade. He was dressed in a torn shirt and shorts made from stolen camouflage cloth. He was making signals with his hands. There was no more shooting. The gunner held his fire. Perhaps these Italians had at last seen sense.

The boy, smiling, held out what looked like a Thermos flask. It seemed a very peaceful gesture. But the commander gave no order. The tank continued to approach the barricade at full tilt in order to destroy it.

The boy bent down. He rolled the seeming Thermos flask toward the tank, and then, with the agility of a chamois, remounted the barricade.

"Stop!" the commander yelled at his driver. But the tank moved forward. The Thermos flask rolled under its tracks. There was a bright flash and the tank rocked. The driver was flung up against his panel of instruments. He leaned back, blinded by blood from his forehead. The hand that was to have pulled the lever to slow the tank fell useless. The tank, one of its tracks put out of commission, slewed violently, mounted the sidewalk, and rammed into the huge stones that made up the street-level wall of an ancient palace.

A rain of bottles with flaming rags and gasoline inside them fell on the tank.

"Fire!" said the commander.

The gunner, shaking his head to clear it from the shock of the collision, tried the mechanism which would have brought the cannon around to point at the barricade.

"No go. It's jammed," he said.

"The machine gun," said the commander. But the tank now had its rear pointing toward the barricade. The machine gun fired, but its shots covered only a small portion of its target.

More incendiary bottles fell on the tank, and gas was flaming in several places. The heat inside rose.

"Radio for help," said the commander to the operator who sat in the back. "That stupid swine Scholl should have had us covered with an armored car."

The operator fiddled and swore. The firing from the barricade continued. Then an enormous bottle of gas was flung at the tank. The gasoline had been stolen from an army dump, and the jar was one of those used for storing wine (a demijohn), which became a favorite weapon in the revolt. Two stalwart lads were needed to hurl it, but they were invisible to the Germans.

A sheet of flame enveloped the whole machine.

"Radio's bust. A valve's gone," said the operator.

"Both of you," said the commander to the two remaining able men, "open the escape hatch. We've got to get out of this or be roasted alive. When you're in the open, put your hands up."

"Yessir," said the gunner. "What about the driver?"

The driver heard. He wiped the blood from his eyes. "I'm all right," he muttered, and edged himself up from his seat.

The escape hatch, low down, had four bolts. None of them jammed, and soon the men were outside. They crouched behind the tank until the driver had fully recovered his senses, then they put up their hands and cautiously came out into the street.

"Hold your fire!" Niello yelled, but he was too late. A burst from the machine gun hit the radio operator and he pitched forward on his face.

A great cheer rose from all the barricades. The boys and lads poured over them. Some pointed guns at the prisoners. Others stood around the tank in a circle, as though it were a bonfire. The radio operator still lay on the ground, but he was moaning. The machine-gun fire had caught his arm and shoulder, and his uniform was soaked with his blood.

A woman of Montecalvario approached him. She gently turned him over. She lifted his head. He looked at her in fear, then suddenly his staring eyes softened. "Please, please," he said.

The woman called to the boys. "Help me get him indoors."

The boys stood silent.

"Do as I tell you!" she said.

"But he's a German," said a lad.

"Yes, but we're not," said the woman. "He's just a boy like you. What's come over you all? Would you like to lie bleeding in the street with no one to help you?" She tried to lift the wounded man herself, but he was too heavy.

"Come," said Niello to the boys standing around him. "She's right, you know."

So the *scugnizzi* and the woman carried the German to safety.

Thus ended the first battle and the first victory of the first four great days of the rebellion. Elsewhere in the city, for the whole of that day, the revolt flared.

CHAPTER TEN

"Ask Lenin," the sarcastic student had said to the youngster who quoted the sage too much, to shut him up when everybody in the refuge had wanted to go to sleep.

Antonino Tarsia in Curia asked Lenin ten times a day, more often than an old woman consulting San Gennaro. True, it was a long time since Lenin had died, and a long time since Antonino Tarsia in Curia had read a line of him. But that was not the fault of Antonino Tarsia in Curia. Tarsia in Curia was a Communist, and years ago la signora Tarsia in Curia had made him hide all his books by Lenin and Marx under the floorboards because of the Fascist spies. And there the rats had got at them, for the dwelling of the Tarsias in Curia was a very modest one, in spite of the rolling thunder of their name. Nobody quite knew what the name meant, but it was generally believed to be some sort of title awarded centuries ago by the emperor of Byzantium.

Perhaps. At any rate, signor Tarsia in Curia was a slim, slight man, so his mother had always called him Antonino—Little Tony. Little Tony was a humble gymnastics instructor, but in his dreams he led Italy to a glorious communist revolution. Then everybody might well call him Little Tony with the respect that the unregenerated Russians called the late and deservedly assassinated czar Little Father.

Antonino, then, was a dreamer. Often he would go for solitary walks by the sea and look out at the island of Capri. Lenin had been an exile there. The ignorant inhabitants could not pronounce his name, so they had called him signor Trin-Trin. Lenin had laughed good-naturedly. The ignorant Neapolitans insisted on calling Antonino Tarsia in Curia Little Tony. Good-naturedly, he laughed. Sometimes, gazing at Capri, he wondered if he should grow a beard. But signora Tarsia in Curia had put her foot down.

Sometimes, like Trin-Trin, Little Tony wrote pamphlets about the coming revolution, with bits of the works of Lenin that he could remember or what the rats had left. Signora Tarsia in Curia burned them. She need not have. The Fascists knew Little Tony for what he was—harmless, a talker, a dreamer.

Then, suddenly, it seemed that his dreams were coming true.

The institute where Little Tony taught gymnastics had been bombed to rubble, so there was nothing for him to do but to sit on a chair outside his house. He had, for a while, continued to go to his local coffee bar where, with great caution, he would expound his ideas of the coming revolution. When the armistice had been declared, he had gathered quite a little following. Then the coffee had run out and the owner of the bar had put up his shutters. Thus, it was on his chair outside his house that Antonino Tarsia in Curia heard the great news, brought by one of his respectful listeners at the coffee bar, a young man who had once been his pupil.

"*Professore!*" (Antonino was not a professor, but he had the grave and knowledgeable air of one, even when he was demonstrating how to climb a rope, so the title was awarded him by common consent of the coffee bar.) "*Professore!*" The young man was jubilant. "It's come! Just as you said it would."

"What?" said Little Tony dreamily.

"The *revolution!*" shouted the young man.

"Sh-sh-sh," said Little Tony. "Not so loud. You'll be heard."

"What's it matter?" said the young man, only slightly lowering his voice. "The Fascists are finished. It's just as you always predicted. The dictatorship of the pro—"

"I don't mean the Fascists," said Little Tony hastily. "I mean my wife. She doesn't like politics, you know, and she's kept me out of trouble all these years and—"

Seeing the look of disappointment on his ex-pupil's face, Little Tony pulled himself together. He gave his informant an extraordinarily piercing look; if he could not copy Lenin's beard, he could produce Lenin's look at will. "Come," he said decisively. "Let us walk by the old school."

They had, in fact, to walk over parts of it and around other parts, as the bricks and beams lay in piles on the ground. Still, the space was the same. Little Tony looked into it, and listened gravely.

His pupil, stumbling a little in the rubble from his excitement, told him of the barricades, of the fighting, and of the victory over the tank.

Little Tony returned home. He found his wife at her ironing board, pressing his trousers, for Antonino Tarsia in Curia was a dandy. Nobody had ever seen him untidily dressed. Nobody had ever seen him without a waistcoat draped with a watch chain, nor without a jacket with its lapels pressed flat and a flower in the buttonhole, nor trousers with a knife-sharp crease, and shoes polished daily by the shoeshine man on the corner. Revolutionary he might be, but he was also a Neapolitan. Besides, as he often said, had anybody ever seen a picture of Lenin in dungarees, or even in shirtsleeves, suitable as they might have been to his political theories?

Little Tony hung up his panama hat on the stand that took up most of the hallway. He walked with an assured step into the room where his wife was at her ironing.

"My dear," said Little Tony solemnly, "it's come. The moment I have waited all my life for."

Giuseppina tested the heat of her iron an inch from her cheek, then offered her cheek to be kissed. "What moment?" she asked placidly as she leaned on the ironing board.

"The revolution," said Antonino with noble simplicity.

"Then you'll soon be shouting for your best trousers. I thought these would do," she said, pointing to the pair on the board, "seeing as how there's nothing much going on these days. But if it's the revolution, you'll be needing your white with the gray stripes. I'll go and get it."

When the moment had come for signor Trin-Trin, the Germans had sent him in a specially sealed train across Germany to Russia. For a moment, while Giuseppina made domestic thumps with the wardrobe doors, Antonino had a vision of a plane with a red star on its wings making a secret landing to whisk him away to—

"Here it is," said Giuseppina triumphantly, holding up the suit. "Thanks be, the moths haven't got at it during the summer."

—But whisk him to *where?* Not Russia, like Lenin. They had already had their revolution. The fact was, said Antonino to himself, nodding his head, he was one up on signor Trin-Trin. The revolution was here, in his own Naples. He was the center of things. They would be coming to him soon, for advice, for leadership.

He went into the bedroom and began to change his clothes. He was very thoughtful. His wife returned to her ironing.

With one leg in his beautifully creased trousers, he paused. Speaking through the open door, he said, "My dear, you *do* know what I am talking about, don't you?" Sometimes she did, and sometimes she didn't, but she never minded being asked.

"I should," she answered. She lifted up the top of the iron and blew into its container of glowing charcoal. "You've been talking about it for twenty years, and for twenty years I've been keeping you out of trouble because of it."

Antonino inserted his other leg and buttoned his fly with a certain sense of satisfaction. "You've done your bit for the cause," he said generously. "Now you'll get your reward."

Giuseppina laid aside the trousers and took up some of the brightly colored handkerchiefs her husband wore in his breast pocket to match his tie and socks. "I've always thought you had a right to your own opinions," she said, thumping the iron decisively.

Antonino was now in his waistcoat and was threading his watch chain through the loops. "That's well said, my dearest, well said indeed."

"What worried me," she went on, "was the way you kept on babbling them about everywhere when you knew the Blackshirts didn't like it. Still," she said, blowing once more on the embers, "your . . . mother . . . *huh* . . . warned me you were always a chatter . . . *huh* . . . box."

She clamped down the iron. She leaned on the board. She gave her husband a long, steady look. "It's not a revolution," she said. "It's just a bunch of no-good kids who've got hold of guns. I know. I heard about it in the breadline."

"There *are* some young people involved," said Little Tony, coming in from the bedroom. He picked up a correctly colored handkerchief from the pile and tucked it into his pocket. He gave the edge an experimental flick so that it flared out, just so much and not more. Giuseppina ran her eyes over her husband. It was her greatest, perhaps her only, pleasure. He took a flower from a vase and put it in his lapel. "And being young, they will need leadership. I have spent my life leading the young."

"I do turn you out nicely," said his wife. "Everyone says so. Well, Tonino, my dear one, from all I hear, these boys aren't like the ones you keep on the hop round your gym. They're *scugnizzi*. You'd better leave your money with me." She held out her hand. Obediently, he felt in his pocket and handed over his very slim wallet.

"I don't expect you to understand just yet," he said, with that detachment which comes to men whose eyes are fixed on far horizons, "but you will see that soon it will be all different. So very different. Well, I must be going."

"Where?" asked Giuseppina. "Oh, I see. To the revolution. Well, don't get too close."

"No," he promised, with a little smile. After all, leaders are never "close," out there in front, alone. He left his home. He picked up the chair on the doorstep on which he had been forced to sit far too long, and, tidily, put it back in the hall.

The neat figure in its white-and-gray-striped suit walked toward the corner on which he was to meet the young man who had brought him the good, the historic, news. The young man seemed tongue-tied.

"Well," said Antonino Tarsia in Curia, "to the barricades."

"It will be rather a long walk," said the young man apologetically, "and I couldn't find any means of transport. Still, there's some action in Piazza Mazzini, I've heard, and that's only about five minutes away and—"

"Then," said Antonino, "to the barricade that is only five minutes away," and he smiled an ironic little smile. He hoped the young man would notice it. These moments had a way of getting nailed down in history. For instance, Piazza Mazzini was approached by a steep slope that was actually named Tarsia, after one of his ancestors. That would be symbolic, very symbolic. But the young man led him by a much more devious path.

"That white suit," said the young man breathlessly as they climbed the hill. "Sharpshooters."

"But I can see no barricades," said Antonino a little peevishly as he surveyed the Piazza Mazzini. In truth, there was nothing to be seen at all, except the statue of a hero and a great number of pigeons which were cowering on every available ledge.

It was, in fact, difficult for Antonino to get a steady view of anything. The young man had led him through an abandoned shop to a small courtyard. From the entrance Antonino could peer out at the square; but every time he did so, his guide seized him by the slack of his jacket and pulled him back.

"But where are our people?" demanded Antonino. "*Our* people?"

At that moment a shot rang out. The pigeons whirled into the air and gyrated wildly in the sky. Another shot followed, and there was the crash of splintering glass.

"I think *our* people must have taken to the upper floors," said the young man prosaically. "At least from the sound of the last shot. You see, the boys did mean to erect a barricade, but no sooner had they got here than—"

There was the sound of another shot, and then several more. The pigeons, who were just about to settle once more on their ledges, rose again in demented circles.

"—than," the young man went on, pulling Antonino back to the shelter, "the sharpshooters began. We'd forgotten something."

"What?"

"You can't build a barricade with half a dozen Fascist crack shots tucked away in the top stories. That building there is one of their meeting places. No one could think of what to do, so I said I was going to meet you, so they said, 'Ask him,' and so, well, so here you are, and what shall . . ." A rattle of fire from an automatic weapon drowned his words for a moment. Then from a floor above the courtyard came the high-pitched scream of a boy. It stopped suddenly, then gave way to a strange gurgling. "What shall we do?" the young man finished, but his voice was a whisper and his eyes wide with fear.

Antonino Tarsia in Curia opened his mouth, but no sound came from it. The side door of the shop burst open. Swaying on the doorstep was a lad. He had torn open his shirt and held it in his two hands. There was a great red hole in his chest from which blood was pulsing.

Antonino found his voice. "Gianpaolo! Gianpaolo!" he shouted. Then, to his guide, "He's one of my boys from the gym. Help him! Call a doctor!" Then he relapsed into mere babbling.

Gianpaolo twisted his mouth into a little smile. He tried to say something, but only a red froth came from his mouth. Then he pitched forward. As he fell, he slid against Antonino's white-and-gray-striped trousers. He lay quite still on the flagstones of the courtyard.

Three of his companions came running from the shop into the courtyard. They were adolescents of his age, and all carried guns. One of them said to Antonino, "Are you a doctor?" but Antonino did not answer.

"I said, 'Are you a doctor?'" the lad shouted hysterically. "You look like one."

Antonino shook his head.

"Christ," said the lad, "then get out of the blasted way. Come on, the lot of you. We've got to get Gianpaolo to the hospital."

One of his companions, who had turned Gianpaolo's head so that his face showed, said: "I think it's too late. The bastards have done for him."

"Never mind," said the first boy. "Lift him up. Carry him out the back way."

The boy was lifted, but his lolling head showed that it was as his companion had said. Gianpaolo was dead. Antonino watched as his body was carried away, leaving a trail of blood on the flagstones.

The young man who had been his guide said, "Look at your trousers."

They were red with blood.

"You can't go through the streets in those," said the young man. "The Germans will shoot you on sight. Wait here. I'll go back and ask your wife for another pair."

"Yes," said Antonino. "She was just ironing—she was just ironing—" Then he burst into uncontrollable tears.

The man who had shot Gianpaolo wore boots. Had he not worn boots, he would never have shot down an adolescent born and bred in the man's own city. But to a Neapolitan, footwear is very important. Even today they have a saying: "All you want is your health and a pair of new shoes and everything looks rosy." That is why Antonino had his shoes polished every day, so, although they were not new, they looked it.

Boots were as important, but more serious. Boots came into fashion with the Fascists. Mussolini preferred them. If Julius Caesar liked men around him who were fat, this new Caesar liked men about him in boots. It gave a military air to what was, regrettably, turning out to be a most unmilitary nation. It was his boots, then, that gave the man who shot Gianpaolo the courage to do his duty by the Duce. Boots, again, were the cause of the next action of the boys against the Germans. Not only the boys; this time there was a girl, one who made for herself a niche in history. Her name was Maddelena Cerasuolo.

Maddelena worked in a boot- and shoemaking shop in the periphery of Naples. She had begun to make boots when she was eleven—that is to say, in the 1930s, the noonday of fascism. There was, of course, plenty of work for bootmakers.

But one day, when she was twelve years old, Maddelena took the day off, like the rest of her workmates, put on her prettiest dress, and went to the *festa* of Piedigrotta. She went alone, because both her mother and her father worked in the same small factory, and were glad of the *festa* to put their feet up for the day. Besides, everybody knew that Maddelena was a very responsible little girl and would not get into mischief. The piggy bank was broken by one of her older brothers (as was the custom on Piedigrotta) and her savings were put in her purse. She wore a white dress with flounces; a white bonnet with artificial flowers; white stockings; and black shoes. She looked for all the world as though she were going to her First Communion.

For the festival of Piedigrotta, the whole seafront of Naples was lit with fairy lights. In the piazzas, popular singers with orchestras sang Neapolitan songs. But the real attraction was the long line of hundreds of temporary stalls that stretched around the whole curve of the bay. They sold candles and gewgaws, but pretty gewgaws, such as you would never find in more solemn shops. There were cheap toys, and balloons, painted china, and jewel boxes of clever inlay; and there were jewels to put in them—not real jewels, but paste rubies and emeralds and diamonds and coral worked into brooches, rings, and necklaces. Maddelena wanted a necklace.

She walked past a dozen stalls dripping with necklaces that had crucifixes on them, or holy medals. But she ignored them. She wanted a real necklace, a *heathen* necklace, if you will, which would make her feel a woman and not show that she just said her prayers.

She had gotten halfway along the bay before she saw it. It was draped around a small velvet bust. The velvet was moth-eaten and dirty, but the necklace was perfect. It was the pride of the stall. It outshone the crucifixes and the holy medals, glittering in the myriad beams of the fairy lamps. There were three diamonds, then a great red ruby, three diamonds again, then another ruby, and so on all the way around to a pendant of emeralds that ended in a teardrop pearl. For a moment Maddelena thought it must all be genuine, but then she knew of course that it was not. She asked the price. So far beyond the money in her purse was the sum the stall owner quoted her that for Maddelena it might just as well have been genuine.

She began to bargain. She fumbled with her purse to tempt the stallkeeper to a quick sale, but he would not budge in his price. She bit her lip. Tears pricked behind her eyes, and she dropped the purse. Instantly, a raggedly dressed *scugnizzo* snaked between the people, stooped, and picked it up. The stallkeeper, an old man, shouted a warning and aimed a feeble slap at the boy. He dodged it without effort. Maddelena was just about to raise the cry "*Al ladro*"—"Stop thief"—when to her astonishment she saw that the *scugnizzo* was standing a few feet away, holding out the purse and smiling at her. It was such a beautiful smile that Maddelena's heart bounced under her white dress—and well it might, for in all her life, Maddelena never forgot it.

The *scugnizzo* was dark, almost as dark as an Arab, and perhaps Saracen blood ran in his veins—for, centuries ago, they had held the country around Naples. He had full lips, and a straight nose between large eyes shaded with long lashes. Black curls tumbled over his forehead. He, like Maddelena, was about twelve, and he had dirty feet because he had no shoes. Maddelena instantly wanted to make him the most elegant shoes that had ever been made, because she had fallen in love.

So had Corrado. It was not that Maddelena was particularly

good-looking; she had too much forehead and too little a nose. But he had fallen in love with the look of sadness in her eyes when she found she could not have the necklace, and he had fallen in love a little with himself. That sad, almost brokenhearted look on Maddelena's face had caused a wave of manly feeling to sweep over him, a masculine sense of being able to put everything right for the girl. After all, for a *scugnizzo*, it would be very easy.

It was done in a moment—the correct moment, of course. A parade of decorated cars and carts always formed part of Piedigrotta, and people gathered on the sidewalks to watch and throw confetti. It passed now.

Maddelena had dawdled a little, looking back at the boy. Then both she and the old man who owned the stall joined the crowd to watch the cars. The back of the stall was sheltered by a tarpaulin. The tarpaulin was split in the middle. The cars passed, the old man clapped. A young arm stretched through the split, and young fingers lifted the necklace from its worn velvet stand.

Corrado kept the necklace in the pocket of his trousers until the last day of Piedigrotta. Then everybody crowded to hear the leading singer of the day, and he knew he would find Maddelena among them. He did. The singer finished, the crowd dispersed. Corrado followed Maddelena, and Maddelena knew she was being followed. She went into the park that lay behind the seafront. There, behind the plinth of a classical statue, she lingered. Corrado lingered, too. Then he brought out the necklace.

It was the beginning of a long romance, but it had to be clandestine, because a *scugnizzo* was by no means the sort of boy that a family of shoemakers with steady jobs would welcome. As the years rolled by, Corrado grew more beautiful in Maddelena's eyes, and Maddelena became more and more of a fascinating puzzle to Corrado.

They would meet in places where they would not be observed, and they would kiss and hold hands and hug and then talk. This last exercise always seemed to Corrado something of a pity, but it was unavoidable. Maddelena wanted him to go straight. The conversations varied very little.

"But how can I marry a *scugnizzo?* My mother would never

hear of it. And I can just *hear* what my brother would say. Why don't you let me get you a job? A steady job?"

"I get by."

The words he used were, "I arrange myself." It is a phrase that covers brilliant guesses which might make a fortune, petty crimes which might produce a meal—all in all, a skill, inborn, which helps the Neapolitan to deal with a perennially hostile world.

"How I hate that '*mi arrangio*,'" Maddelena would burst out. "At home we never use it. Don't you see that's why everybody looks down on us, us Neapolitans—the Romans, the Milanese, the Germans? We arrange ourselves. Ugh! At home we work. Making boots and shoes and—"

"Boots and shoes and boots and shoes and boots and shoes. . . ." Corrado would intone mockingly.

"And why not? It would be an honest living for you. For—for *us*."

Corrado would shift his feet, lower his long eyelashes. "I don't like the smell of leather," he had said once, but once only.

"So you think *I* smell of leather!" Maddelena had almost shouted, and stormed off, not to be seen for days.

When they would meet again after one of these arguments, Corrado would be contrite. Once he suggested that at the next Piedigrotta they should give the necklace back to the old man. "A sort of beginning of my new life," he had said humbly.

"Then what will I have to remember you by?" Maddelena had said.

"Well . . . something else. . . ."

"And how would you get that? Don't answer. I know. By *stealing*."

"Ah, well, maybe."

"There you are, you see. What good would giving back the necklace be?"

"We could give it to San Gennaro. People do, you know. To be forgiven and all that rubbish."

"Give *my* necklace to San Gennaro, to be forgiven?"

" 'Sright."

"But *I* didn't steal it. *You* did."

" 'Sright again," Corrado had said in a resigned voice, and he gave up trying to follow all this reasoning. It was, he supposed, because she had that high forehead that she was so brainy. It was the same when, one hot summer when he was sixteen, he tried, at last, to seduce her. She would not allow it—she bit him—until he promised to get a steady job. Once again, he could not quite follow her reasoning. As he said to some of the other *scugnizzi* later, he was not proposing to poke her with a pay packet.

So they quarreled, and did not see each other again until Corrado was one of the *scugnizzi* who fought the Germans.

CHAPTER ELEVEN

Maddelena lived next to her workshop, and if the name of the road was any indication, it was the most desirable residence in Naples. The boot-and-shoe factory was on the Road of the Throne; the next road was the Road of the Salvation of Paradise, and, in case those names smacked too much of religion, the two roads were joined by one that was named after Petronius Arbiter, the author of the *Satyricon*, that catalogue of classical vice and luxury. The man who named this particular Neapolitan slum must have been a scholar and a wag.

But still, it was a respectable slum, as Maddelena incessantly told Corrado, when she was speaking to him. When Corrado had obstinately remained a *scugnizzo* who knew how to arrange himself, she dropped him and took up with another boy friend, this time from the splendidly named streets, and from the respectable family of the Januzzis, and named, as was entirely proper, after San Gennaro.

But she still wore the necklace. She was seventeen now, and when Piedigrotta came around, it was not proper that she should wander alone. She was taken out by Gennaro or other admirers. They all agreed that, spend money as you might, she never seemed to enjoy the *festa* as she should have. She looked about her a lot, tossed her head when she was asked if she was looking for someone, and even refused to eat the traditional stick of nougat, called *torrone*, on the excuse that it made her teeth ache.

For years the factory did well. Its boots were on all the right feet, and orders were plentiful. While Maddelena cut and stitched and rubbed, she was content. It was when she went out into the bright sunshine that she began to wonder if Corrado had not been right after all. At one Piedigrotta (the last before war turned out all the fairy lights) she had caught a glimpse of him. He was taller, he walked with a charming swagger, and his skin was glowing. It made Maddelena look at her hands, and she was particularly snappish that *festa* with her young cavaliers.

You cannot make a good pair of boots out of our human skin, but it is not so very different from that of animals more useful to bootmakers. It softens with the chemicals you must use, but unfortunately it wrinkles as well. You cannot go round to the shoeshine man at the corner and have your hands and face polished. Each morning that Maddelena put on her necklace and looked into the tarnished mirror on her chest of drawers, she saw that her hands and that tall forehead of hers were showing the signs of her profession. She was growing prematurely old. Corrado, with all his reprehensible ways, was not.

Still, a steady wage was a steady wage, a good job was not to be sniffed at. One day she would marry a sensible boy and leave the workshop to raise a family. She spent happy hours walking down the Toledo with its smart shops and looking at all the expensive beauty lotions that would one day take away her wrinkles, if only she could find a husband who could afford them. Things were not so bad.

Then came Scholl, and disaster.

On September 27, the day before the first battle of the barricades, a Fascist official who lived on the Road to Paradise presented himself at the workshop. With a good deal of beating about the bush, he told the proprietor that he had received orders from Scholl to arrange that the factory should be brought into line with, as he put it, the overriding necessities of the war.

The proprietor got out a bottle of wine and said he would be delighted to make boots for the Germans, or anybody else. The Fascist official refused the drink in an embarrassed manner. The proprietor inquired if the boots he had made for him were comfortable, and the official grew even more embarrassed because he had not paid for them. So he blurted out the truth. The next day the Germans were to come with a truck and take away everything in the workshop, including the stock of leather, to send to Germany. The workshop was then to be blown up. The truck would come precisely at 3:00 P.M. and the official was entrusted with the job of seeing that the owner, his staff, and the neighbors did not make trouble. If they did, there would be shooting.

He left. The news spread. The poetically named streets filled with white-faced people. Without the factory, how were the employees going to eat? Where would they go? And how could the Germans blow up the workshop in such a crowded slum without destroying the whole block?

That night, nobody slept. September 28 dawned gray and chilly, with a slight drizzle. Men and women went to the workshop from force of habit, but stood about or sat on the tables, talking till the proprietor turned up.

At first he was full of vigor. He had a plan. Everybody was to help. All the stock and all the unworked leather was to be moved to a secret destination. He clapped his hands, bustled about, gave orders, until the Fascist neighbor knocked at the door. His belt unbuttoned, his hair tousled, and his chin unshaved, he said, with numerous apologies, that he had forgotten to say that removing anything from the premises would be considered an act of treason against the Reich and would be punished, he was very, very sorry to say, by being put against the wall of the workshop and shot. It was all very regrettable, but after all it was the fault of the Americans and the British. Were they not even now invading the sacred soil of Italy?

With that he left, but remained at the window of his apartment, ostensibly reading the morning's issue of *Roma*. This announced further victories of the German and Italian forces everywhere except Salerno, where it recorded planned withdrawals to prepared positions.

The proprietor, little to the surprise of his employees, underwent one of those sudden reversals of mood so familiar to the Neapolitan. He despaired; he threw up his hands; he flung boots about at random and then burst into tears. An employee gave him a swig of jealously preserved Italian cognac. His courage returned. He announced defiance. All would leave, and he personally would lock—*lock*, he repeated—the door and throw away the key.

This was done. Maddelena watched, disgusted.

It was while they were all standing outside in the street that the news arrived that the *scugnizzi* down in the center had fought and had captured a tank. The small knot of her workmates buzzed in excited conversation. The Fascist at the window looked worried, folded his newspaper, and disappeared. The proprietor, annoyed at attention being drawn away from his act of defiance (he had not yet actually got to the point of casting away the key), said that the doings of a band of worthless guttersnipes were of no interest to serious people in serious times like these, but Maddelena was not listening. She knew what she had to do.

It was a long walk, but fortunately all downhill. Maddelena reached the Toledo. The shops that sold the beauty preparations she would one day buy were all shuttered. One building had a great hole torn in it where the tank had fired at random. Maddelena walked even quicker. Sunless as the day was, it was warm, and she was sweating. But the sight of the hole made her shiver. She said a little prayer to the Madonna that Corrado should be safe, and that she would find him.

Soon she came to Montecalvario, and, wide-eyed, saw the barricades. A youth shouted at her, waving a pistol. He told her to keep off the Toledo; any minute now the Germans might come back. Thoroughly alarmed, Maddelena noticed for the first time that she was alone in the street, except for the young men and the boys on the barricades.

She turned abruptly and took a narrower road that ran parallel to the Toledo. She had not gone far when she came across a group of *scugnizzi*. They were holding, gingerly, several flat metal objects. A young man, a soldier from the evidence of his disheveled uniform, was giving them orders. The boys, obeying, carried the metal pieces into the middle of the street.

Maddelena stopped. "Have you seen Corrado?" she asked them, but they were too intent upon their work to reply. The soldier waved a hand at her to go away, but he did not take his eyes away from the boys.

Since nobody seemed to know Corrado, she changed her tactics. Niello's name was being bandied about the whole city, so she said, "Niello. I must find Niello. I've got news about the Germans."

The soldier looked up briefly. "He's at San Francesco's," he said. She nodded her thanks and began to run.

The soldier roared at her. "For Christ's sake, keep off the road! Stay on the footpath."

She stopped and did not move.

"The road's mined, you silly little bitch," one of the boys shouted, adding a good round *scugnizzo* epithet. "That's what these things are."

The thought of her narrow escape left her breathless for a while, and it was a minute before she had enough courage to go on her way. Then, hugging the walls of the buildings, she made for the Piazza Plebiscito.

Nearing the piazza, she was stopped. The side road that led to it was blocked by a pile of stones and rubble from a nearby bombed building. Balks of timber completed the barricade, but it was not like those others she had seen. A boy stood behind it, and the barricade reached only to his waist.

He pointed a rifle at her head. "Hey, you, where d'you think you're going?"

"Corrado. I want to find Corr—or Niello—I want—"

"Bugger off," said the boy, jerking up his rifle. "Niello's busy. And mind how you go, or you'll get your pretty backside sent sky-high."

Maddelena eyed the muzzle of the gun.

"It goes 'bang' and we all fall down," said the boy sarcastically. "Get moving."

"I won't," said Maddelena. "I've got to see Niello. Where is he?"

"Over there under the portico. You his girlfriend?"

"Yes," said Maddelena desperately.

"And a lying little cunt you are at that. He doesn't have a girl friend. What's your game? Nobody gets past this barrier without the password, and you don't know that or you'd have said it." The *scugnizzo*'s eyes suddenly went very cold. He cocked his rifle. "Back off," he said.

Then, across the rubble, she saw Corrado. He was leaning against one of the bollards that marked off the piazza. He, too, held a rifle. Across his shoulders was a bandolier, and on his head a soldier's helmet. Maddelena thought she had never seen a human being look so beautiful.

"Corrado!" she shouted at the top of her voice. "It's me. Maddelena. I've got to see you. It's urgent. Life and death."

Corrado stirred. He looked across the square at her. Slowly, maddeningly slowly, he strolled across to the barrier. When he reached it, the young sentinel said, "Who is she?"

"She's all right. I know her."

It was, thought Maddelena, said much too coolly.

"Niello said to watch out for informers," said the sentinel importantly, "and in particular, young skirts. They're the ones the Nazis use. He said." The sentinel finished lamely, because Corrado, slightly smiling, had climbed the barrier and gone over to the girl.

"*Buon giorno*, Maddelena," he said with old-fashioned courtesy. "I hear you're looking for that no-good lazy thief, Corrado. At your service."

Maddelena, her nerves at the breaking point, flung herself upon him. He took her in his arms. The bandolier hurt her cheek a good deal, but she did not mind at all.

"So *he's* your boy friend, too, is he?" said the sentinel. "How many have you got? One on every corner? Oh, all right. Come on over. Whatever Corrado says goes with the boss. Come *on*. Look lively.

"Girls—huh!" he added as, helped by Corrado, she scrambled over the barrier.

San Francesco di Paola is a perfectly round church built in the neoclassical style—that is to say, it is very like the Pantheon at Rome. It was put up because the various kings of Naples wanted something to look at from the windows of their vast palace other than the Mediterranean Sea on one side and a lot of tumbledown houses on the other. Since the round church did not fill in the panorama, it was given two sweeping porticoes, like two arms. Between the arms in the vast piazza were two statues, one of which Eduardo had ridden in his moment of triumph. One portico arm reached the Prefect's Palace, now deserted. In the other, Niello had established his headquarters. It was very convenient. The roof gave him shelter from the irritating showers that constantly, on this September 28, swept in from the sea. The spaces between the columns gave him a good view of what went on in the piazza. Somebody had produced a table from a nearby café, and Niello sat on an upturned box.

All this Maddelena saw as she crossed the piazza and came up to the portico. She held Corrado's hand very tightly because everywhere there were young men and boys with guns, strolling about or standing with their legs apart, scrutinizing everybody who passed in front of them. Maddelena had never seen Piazza Plebiscito with so few people and so businesslike.

A small group stood around Niello's table. One or two were in uniform and were clearly deserters from the Italian Army. Others were in civilian clothes and looked like apprentices, shop assistants, and such. The rest were *scugnizzi*, and these clearly ruled the roost. They all bore arms. Some had steel helmets. Leaning against the columns near the table where Niello was sitting were several very serious-looking boys with submachine guns. As Maddelena approached, they took their shoulders off the columns and slightly raised the barrels of their weapons. Maddelena tightened her grip upon Corrado's hand. It was not at all the reception she had expected. *Scugnizzi*, everyone knew, were noisy, active, laughing, swearing, and very much boys. These *scugnizzi* seemed as though they had grown up overnight in everything but their stature.

Near the portico, Corrado said a word and he and Maddelena were waved forward, not without some very close looks. Inside the portico, Corrado made her wait. Niello was indeed busy. He was eating sunflower seeds from a twist of paper. The seeds are a Neapolitan delicacy, but he was putting them to a new use. As, one by one, his henchmen reported news, he placed a seed on a map.

Corrado bent toward Maddelena and whispered in her ear. "There's fighting all over," he said.

Niello looked up from his map. "I thought I said no girls or women this side of the barriers. Who's this, Corrado? Ah, the girl who jilted you. Right?"

Corrado dropped his heroic stance. He shuffled his feet. "Right," he mumbled.

The boys standing around the table grinned. Corrado had made much of his attempts to seduce the girl they were now looking at. His anecdotes had been entertaining at first, then tiresome, then banned by unanimous consent as a topic of conversation.

Niello nodded toward their intertwined fingers. "Made it up?"

Corrado said nothing.

"Yes," said Maddelena.

"She's brought news," said Corrado hastily. He was blushing so deeply that it showed even under his dark complexion. "The Germans are going to blow up her workshop this afternoon and . . ." He poured out the story. Niello listened.

"Where exactly is the factory?"

Corrado pointed to the map. Niello took a sunflower seed from his lips and put it on the Road of the Throne. He gazed at the seed for a while. The boys stood silent. "We could do with trouble there," he said. "The more places the better. If we bunch up too much, we're done for."

He looked up at Maddelena. "Can you cook?" he said suddenly.

"Yes. When mother's ill I always—"

Niello did not let her finish. "There's a kitchen over there," he said, and pointed. To Maddelena's astonishment, he was pointing at the Prefect's Palace. "If it's locked, the boys will break in. See if you can rustle up some coffee, camomile tea, anything, and get the stove to work. Now, off with you."

Corrado let go of Maddelena's hand and touched her shoulder. This meant, in the elaborate gesture language of Naples, that she should go without question. Had he touched her forearm it would have meant that she should stay. So she went.

Niello detailed off a boy to accompany her. It was little Michele, the boy from the brothel. He was, as ever, a mine of fractured information, and as he trotted beside her across the wide piazza to the gray and red palazzo of the prefect, he prattled happily.

"It'll be a second time if we do," he said.

"Do what?" Maddelena was torn between her desire to bring Corrado something hot and tasty and wholly unexpected, which he would eat or drink and then look at her and say, "Yum! Delicious," and a much deeper resentment at being dismissed to the kitchen by a street boy like Niello, who, after all, would probably only be a seven-day wonder, something with which Naples was only too familiar. Besides, she wanted to be with this new Corrado, Corrado the warrior.

"Do what?" she repeated absently as they approached the palace.

"I've told you," said Michele.

"Tell me again."

"If you're going deaf, you should wash your ears out," said Michele, in the politest of tones. It was one of the witticisms he had picked up in the brothel. He notched up his treble voice to its highest. "As I've said once and say again, it won't be the first time we've broken down a door." Then, dropping his conversational pose, he said, "Look yourself," and he pointed.

The two great doors of the Palace of the Prefect gaped on their hinges. Great slashes made yellow wounds in the ancient wood. Beside the broken portals a sentinel lounged, a rifle cradled in his arms. He presented the gun.

"Halt!"

"It's me," said Michele.

"I know it's you," said the boy sentinel patiently. "Who could mistake that ugly face? But you've got to have the password."

"*Butta.*"

"*Butta* what?"

"*Soldi.*"

"Pass, friend. Your girl friend can stay behind if she wants to."

The two passed in. "What did all that mean?" Maddelena asked. They both stood under the vast entrance to the palace, big enough to take two coaches side-by-side and shelter them under the gloomy roof from the rain.

"It's Niello's idea. It's what we used to say in Santa Lucia. 'Throw money, throw money.'" His young voice echoed eerily in the vault.

Michele's hand crept into hers. "You ever been here before?" he asked in a small voice.

"No, thank the Madonna," she said, and squeezed his hand.

"Neither had I till we broke in. Not this part, at any rate. It was fun. Hatchets," he went on. "Hatchets. Of course they could have, but they didn't."

"Didn't what?"

"Girls do ask a lot of questions, don't they?" said Michele. He withdrew his hand from hers. "They could have shot the lot of us as we came in."

"Was Corrado with you?" asked Maddelena.

"Questions, questions," said Michele in a bored voice. "'Course he was. First in. No, second. Next to Niello. They could have got them both. Tat-tat-at-atatatatat." Then he took a step forward, clutched his breast, staggered, and fell on the floor, but slowly, so as not to hurt himself. He gave a realistic imitation of death throes.

"Stop it, stop it, *stop it*, you clown," said Maddelena, and covered her eyes.

Michele, a little piqued at this reception of his acting, got up. "What's the fuss? They didn't. I told you they didn't. Because."

With her hands still over her eyes, Maddelena said, "Because what?"

"Because nobody was there. They'd all run away."

Maddelena recovered. "Well, stop chattering like a parrot and show me the kitchen. If you know where it is."

" 'Course I do. I delivered bread there once when my brother was ill with fever. Come on."

She followed him through a corridor and then down some steps to a basement. Some more corridors, and then Michele stopped before a door.

"The kitchen," he said with a grand gesture.

Maddelena tried the door, but a large iron lock, plainly very old, held it fast.

Michele knitted his brows dramatically. "What do we do now?" he said. "They have foiled us."

"You've been reading too many comics," said Maddelena. She shook the door violently. But foiled, it seemed, they were.

"There is just one chance," said Michele. "Put your fingers in your ears." When Maddelena was slow at doing this, he said sharply, "Do as I tell you, you silly cow."

As she obeyed, he slowly unbuttoned his shirt; then, to Maddelena's dismay, the top of the fly of his shorts. Then she saw that he had a belt around his bare body, and a holster. He took a small automatic from it. He blew down the muzzle, then sighted it along its short barrel.

Her fingers in her ears, Maddelena said, "Don't point that thing at me."

Lifting a cynical eyebrow and smiling a little crooked smile, he aimed the automatic at the lock.

He fired. The shot made a tremendous noise in the corridors of the basement, reverberating back and forth. When the echoes had died down, little Michele had quite lost his composed air.

"Phew! What a hell of a row! Still, it's done its job. At least," he said as he pushed the door, "it should have."

But it had not. The huge and rusty lock had a decided dent in it, but it still held.

Maddelena took her fingers out of ears. "Now what?" she asked.

"Questions, always questions," said Michele. He replaced the gun and buttoned his shorts and shirt with deliberation. " 'Now what?' you ask," he continued when the gun was safely away. "Now I climb through the back window of the pantry. It's always open to let the air in."

"Did you know that before you made all that horrible din?"

"Of course. My brother showed me. I used to slip in and steal the meat when we ran short. Did it only last week. Good meat. Can't think where they get it from. Of course, the military have got pull, and as for the Germans—"

Maddelena cut him short. "Then why did you fire that gun?"

Michele regarded her sagely. "I see why Corrado dumped you. Fancy marrying a girl like you! Questions—morning, noon, and night," he said, his voice fading as he made off down a long corridor.

The larder was as Michele had described. It was a storage place before the days of refrigerators, thick-walled, with a window easily opened to the cool night breezes, and hung, even now, with hunks of meat and bacon. Along the walls were shelves with brown ceramic jars, arrays of bottles, and strings of red peppers, tomatoes, and onions. Boy and girl stood surveying it, their mouths watering.

"It's a good thing the boys didn't first," said Michele. "Otherwise they would have been here forever."

Maddelena was opening jars and pulling out drawers. She was about to say "What?" but having been rebuked (and maybe Corrado *had* tired of her questions), she said, "I think I know what you mean."

"Do you?" said Michele. He had found a box of biscuits and spoke through a mouthful. "A lot of people don't. I've a funny way of speaking, but my mother says I'll grow out of it."

Maddelena tested a carving knife with her thumb. She began to carve a slice off a hanging side of bacon. "Yes," she said. "You meant that if the boys had discovered this kitchen they'd—"

"They'd never have found the armory. That's where my pistol came from. There were rifles and shotguns and pistols and bombs and hundreds and millions and thousands of bullets and—"

"And you can't eat bullets," said Maddelena briskly. "So to work, my boy. To work."

"You can *bite* them," said Michele. "You used to have to bite

them when they cut off your legs before they had anes—athis—"
The word "anesthetics" was too difficult for him, and he was glad
to cover his confusion by running to and fro, fetching and carrying, chopping up wood and piling the huge old fireplace with coals
he found in a bin, all to Maddelena's stream of orders. He was,
after all, a good boy, and everybody always said so.

Very soon slices of meat were sizzling on the iron grill over
the fire while Maddelena turned them with a long fork and Michele
cut open loaves of a whiteness he had not seen for months. It was
not a fancy meal that Maddelena prepared; a loaf, pointed at both
ends and cut lengthwise, with the meat laid hot between the halves,
would be, she knew, a *scugnizzo*'s banquet. It was tasty, it was
nourishing, and, above all, it could be eaten while you walked
about. You could satisfy your stomach while your eyes missed
nothing of what went on in the streets.

Three large basketloads had been carried out to the colonnade
and emptied by hungry boys. Rifles had been stacked against columns, strong white teeth had bitten into the bread that seemed
like manna, and a couple of bottles of wine (all that Niello would
allow) had been passed from mouth to mouth. Maddelena, brush-
ing hair out of her eyes, sat on the plinth of one of the columns
and bitterly reflected that not one of the boys and lads had offered
her a word of thanks. In Naples, one does not thank women for
doing the household chores. These boys might be fighting that man
Hitler (she told herself), but they agreed with him on one thing:
a woman's place was in the kitchen. She studied Corrado. He was
picking his teeth with the blade of a pocketknife while deep in
conversation with Niello. She wondered for a moment if she really
did want to marry him. But he looked so handsome with his
bandolier, she decided that she did. She smiled and waved at him,
and he nodded and said, "Yes." She felt a flush of pleasure, but it
subsided rapidly when she realized he had looked right through her
and was answering something that Niello had said.

"This is no place for a woman," she said aloud. And at that very
moment she decided that she would *make* it a place for at least one
woman—herself, Maddelena, provided Corrado was there to see
her do it.

Niello was rapping with his knuckles on the table with the map. The boys gathered round. The routine of Santa Lucia still held them: food had been supplied; they had eaten; and now for orders.

"Pasquale."

"Yes, Niello."

"Have you seen Annunziata?"

"Not since the Americans got over the mountains. It's become too risky for her to move about, I think. They're shooting spies."

"Does anybody know just how far they've got?" said Niello.

"I do." It was a newcomer, a tall, thin lad of some seventeen years.

"Where're you from?"

"Pompeii. Family's there."

"Doing what?"

"Selling rosaries, pictures—you know, that junk."

"That's right," said Gi-gin, in his sleepy way. "His cousin married my eldest sister and he brought us some food. Walked all the way."

"And my brother," said the lad from Pompeii, "is the sacristan."

Niello was all attention. "At the Sanctuary?"

"Where else?"

The Sanctuary is a church with a miraculous picture of the Madonna. But from Niello's viewpoint, it was its tall bell tower, rising eighty meters into the air and built with the offerings of the faithful.

"Could you see the fighting?"

"If I could, I wouldn't be here. The Germans shoot anybody going up the tower. They've got observers there with binoculars, damned great things on tripods, and a radio. Still . . ."

"Still, what?"

"They can't stop the sacristan going up his own tower, can they? Particularly since he spun them the yarn that he's shortsighted. He takes them booze when he rings the bells."

Niello leaned forward with two hands on the table. "How far have the Americans got?"

"My brother says they've taken Castellammare." This was the shipbuilding town at the foot of the mountain barrier on the Naples side.

"Good."

"Not so good. They've got stuck at Nocera."

This was about halfway between the foot of the mountains and the sacristan's observation post.

"Trouble is," the lad from Pompeii went on, "the Yankees can't even go out into a field to take a crap without the Nazis seeing them. Then the Germans open up with all they've got. And that's plenty. The piazza's all torn up with the tracks of mobile guns."

Aldo, the boy who could read *Roma*, spoke up. "The paper says 'prepared positions.' I thought it was the usual lies—"

"It seems it isn't," said Niello.

Another boy said, "The Yankees must be bloody fools. Why don't they blow that tower to bits?"

"And have half the countryside at them with pitchforks?" said the lad from Pompeii, and there was a murmur of agreement.

Tens of thousands of city dwellers and peasants had taken their marriage vows in the Sanctuary. A bomb on the church would be, for them, as bad as a bomb on the pope's Vatican.

"How long do you think it will take them," Niello asked, "to reach here?"

The lad shrugged. "Weeks, perhaps. Look at the time they took to get over the hills."

Niello nodded. Eighteen days had passed since the landing at Salerno. He looked out between the columns to where the slopes of Vesuvius stretched out almost to the bay. The Yankees would have to come along that way, and the skirts of the volcano were a first-class place for gun emplacements.

The lad from Pompeii seemed to read his thoughts. "The Nazis have machine-gun posts all along the road," he said.

"Did they stop you?"

"Once. I told them I was carrying food in my bag, and they weren't interested. They were looking for wristwatches, but I'd sold mine a month ago. So they waved me on."

"Nice of them," said a listening boy.

"Yes," said the lad. "They still let us walk about our own country."

"If you don't carry a wristwatch."

Niello took his eyes away from the volcano on the horizon and brought his gaze back to his band of boys. "It's going to be a long time before it *is* our own country," he said. "Meantime, we've got a fight on our hands."

"Well," said little Maurizio, "we won the first battle," and he looked at his hero with admiration.

"We did," said Niello. "In the wrong way."

Then, under the portico, Niello laid down the lines of the tactics that the boys were to follow. He had first told them to fight and run. But that served only to inflict pinpricks on the enemy. He next had told them to build barricades. At the time, that had seemed to be the right thing to do. Now, a more experienced strategist, he told the boys what was wrong. As was his custom, he did so by question and answer. Boys do not listen to long speeches, especially on a full stomach.

He pointed across the piazza to the barrier over which Maddelena had stepped. "How high do you think we should make that barricade when it's finished?"

"Three meters." "Twice my height." "Big enough to hide behind when they start shooting." The voices came eagerly.

"How high must it be to stop a tank like the one we've captured?"

Nobody had a ready answer. Some boys scratched their heads, others frowned. One very small *scugnizzo* stood with his legs apart, his hands clasped behind him, and his chin sunk on his chest.

"What," said Niello, pointing to him, "does Napoleon Bonaparte say?"

"Very funny," said the boy. He abandoned his pose. "I was only just thinking. That's allowed, isn't it, Duce?"

"It is. And what do you think?"

"Well, a barricade, never mind how high, can't stop a tank. It can go right through it just when it wants to, and a nice sticky mess it would make of all of us behind it. So I was just thinking that it's bloody silly building them. But you said build, so we did."

"But we won, we won," said a dozen voices.

"Once," said Niello. "We took the Germans by surprise. Now they know what we're doing, well, little Napoleon here is right—"

"My name's Carmine and I'll thank you to use it," said the boy, but he gazed around at his companions with a proud look. It wasn't often that Niello paid a compliment, however left-handed.

Niello went on. "It's true I asked you to build barricades, but I've done some thinking, too. Barricades are all very well in the history books, but that was when they fought on horses. Horses shy at anything high that they can't leap over. Tanks don't. There's nothing the Germans would like better than for us to build barricades all over the place, and then to send in their tanks to knock them down."

"So what are we to do?" said a new recruit, still in the uniform trousers he wore when he had deserted from his barracks.

"Build barricades all over the place," said Niello.

"Yessir," said the young soldier automatically; but then, "Yes, but, what the hell? You just said—"

"The men in the tanks are like the horses," said Niello. "They don't like things they can't see over. They won't be happy till they've smashed through them and found out what is on the other side."

"And there won't be anything," said Aldo brightly. "Because we'll have run away. That's pretty clever."

"*We* won't be there," said Niello. "Quite right, Aldo. But something else will." He nodded to a serious-looking young man with thick spectacles. Maddelena recognized him as the youth who had warned her off the street.

"There'll be mines," said the young man, but without enthusiasm.

"Boom, boom, BOOM!" shouted some of the *scugnizzi*. "Up they go!" and they clapped their hands with delight.

"In the movies, yes," said the young man, wearily taking off his spectacles and polishing them. "The ones they showed us from Abyssinia when we were training. But in fact, the damned mines are as temperamental as those horses you were just talking about, Niello. Sometimes they go off when they should, sometimes they don't. Sometimes the tanks miss them, God alone knows how. Then, if all you boys are not going to be there, what's to stop them sending a team out with mine detectors?"

"But just a minute, just a minute," said a boy. "You gave me that mine to roll at them, and it did the trick."

"It was nice work," said the young engineer, putting his glasses on again. "I'll give you that. Nice work. But I've seen those mines blow up just where you want them and the tank goes blithely on. Tanks," he said, and shook his head.

Everybody's spirits were dampened.

"But then," said Gi-gin, who, in his lazy way, had been following the conversation with his eyes half-closed, "why," he asked, opening them, "do we have to build the damned things? It's a sweat."

Niello answered him, marking his points with an upraised finger. "We'll build them everywhere to give the Germans something to think about. To worry them. To keep them busy knocking them down. As for us, *we* fight them from the rooftops, from windows, from everywhere we can hide. We'll build the barricades all over the city, so as soon as they get rid of one of them, those radios of theirs will start bleating about another. *We've got to make this whole thing look much bigger than it is. It's our only chance.*"

The boys regarded him curiously. It was unusual for Niello to be emphatic.

"And just one more thing. I don't want any heroics. That's not going to get you anywhere except get you killed. And I don't want that to happen. I like you all too much. And I cannot," he said, lowering his finger and giving the boys a broad, inclusive smile, "think why." With that he turned to the map and, calling one or two boys to him, began, in a low tone, to give orders.

Then he looked up and spoke to Maddelena. She gave a slight start on hearing her name. When the talk of barricades had begun, she had been caught up in a daydream. She had seen those pictures in a history book, the one that told of the revolution of the people of Milan against the Austrians. Barely hearing what Niello was saying, she saw herself on the barricades beside Corrado, a flag in one hand, a pistol in the other. Corrado fell, wounded (only slightly, a scratch), and she dragged him to safety.

"Are you listening?" asked Niello.

"Yes."

"I was saying you'd better get back. I'll send some boys with you. Your area is a good place to make trouble. But you keep out of it. Corrado, see that she keeps out of it, will you?"

"Sure."

"Good. This is too serious to have girls mucking about in it. Come with me. I've got transport for you—of a sort."

Maddelena sighed, and rose. Things were not going at all as she planned. But at least Corrado was going back with her.

She fingered the necklace he had stolen for her and said a little prayer to the Madonna of Pompeii to keep him safe. Then she followed Niello obediently.

CHAPTER TWELVE

The Germans arrived with Teutonic promptness exactly on the hour that the Fascist had announced. In all, there were thirteen men; some in a motorcar, others in a truck. The way that they jumped simultaneously out of all four doors of the car, or leaped down from the truck, made a pretty picture of efficiency and determination. They were quite unaware that the muddled Neapolitans, notorious for never keeping an appointment, had arranged a welcoming committee, because it was, as Niello had advised, invisible.

Niello had taken Corrado (followed a few steps behind by Maddelena) to see the transport he had promised. They passed a series of automobiles parked in the courtyard of the deserted Prefect's Palace. Corrado eyed them with joy, but Niello said, "Lovely sight, isn't it? If only we could fly around in those. But there are those license plates. We'd be stopped by every patrol."

"No problem," said Corrado cheerfully. "I know a gang that can fix you up with any plate you choose. They steal cars and—"

"And there's the color. Official blue," said Niello.

"Spray job," said Corrado succinctly. "Now that truck there. Give my boys time and they'll turn that into an ambulance—siren and everything. One job they did was so good that when they ran into a real accident on the Via Foria they had to take the injured to hospital. Spoiled everything."

"Why an ambulance?"

"Robbing a post office."

"Ah," said Niello, full of comprehension. "That must be the Gambastorta lads."

"Right first time."

Maddelena, listening to this, had a twinge of conscience. Perhaps her family was right. What would life be like married to a man who knew car thieves? For a moment she thought of quietly walking away and going home to safety and respectability. But *walking?* This time it would be uphill, and Niello had promised transport. Corrado kept bad company, and bad company corrupts good manners, so her mother had said. But—and she stole a glance—it did not corrupt good looks. She stayed.

"I'll think about it," said Niello. "But just now you haven't time for a spray job."

"God, no," said Corrado, collecting himself. "Those buggers are due at three."

"So you'll have to make do with what I've got for you. Over there." He waved a hand toward a wall, where, in neat wooden supports, there was a row of bicycles. "When they cleared out, they left these. Don't argue. I'll explain. It isn't only the Gambastorta gang that can think up tricks. Oh!" he said with a change of voice. He turned to Maddelena. "I suppose you can't ride a bike."

"Suppose again. I can," said Maddelena determinedly. She was telling the truth, in a way. She had tried and gallantly fallen off. She could try again.

"Good," said Niello. Then, "Jesus, no, it isn't."

"Why?" said Corrado. "I've seen her. She's not very good, but she can wobble along if I'm there to steady her."

Maddelena felt a little flush of pleasure that he had remembered their little trip into the countryside one splendid spring day. It had been marred only by the fact that she was sure the bike was not Corrado's, nor, as he maintained, his sister's.

"Skirts," Niello said. He ran his eye over the parked bicycles. "It doesn't seem that the prefect's staff included a midwife. No girl's bikes. You'll have to walk."

Some forty minutes later, two German officers were indulging in their favorite topic of conversation, the extraordinary behavior of the Neapolitans. The first officer called his dog to heel, and was duly obeyed. The second fixed an eyeglass.

"But just look, just look at those boys." The other officer looked. The dog sat, and looked. "Here they are in the middle of a war which that jackanapes of a Duce has lost for them. Their city is in ruins and most of them are starving. And here, bless my soul, they're practicing for a bicycle race."

"It's a popular sport," said the other officer, patting his dog. "The winners are national heroes."

"But now, *now*," protested his friend. "And they look as though they haven't a care in the world—to say nothing of the fact that the slim boy with the sort of turban round his head doesn't seem to be able to ride properly."

"Hans, *sit*," said the other to his dog, who showed signs of wanting to chase the procession of athletes. "On old iron like those, you can't expect an Olympic performance. But I suppose they're thinking of the time when we've settled this little job for them and the piping times of peace come again. Why the führer saddled us with these as allies, I shall never know."

"He must have had his reasons."

"No, Hans! Hans, come *here*." But the dog had slipped his leash and was in full cry after the squad of boys.

They were dressed in the sweat shirts emblazoned with commercial advertisements that is the uniform of competitive cycle races. Their own trousers and shirts were in the small haversacks strapped to the carriers behind them, together with some pistols and a hand grenade or two. The owner of the sports store who had kindly lent them their clothes had been delighted to do so. He agreed with Niello: it was the sure way of getting past the patrols.

As for Maddelena, with her hair painfully tied up under her turban, the barking dog was a sore trial. She would have fallen if it had not been for the strong arm of Corrado holding her on her correct course. But at least, she said to herself, she would not have to turn up to face her family in the little shorts with writing on them that the other boys of the squad were wearing. They had found her a pair of trousers. The owner of the sports shop, a man with respectable views like herself, had insisted upon it.

"Hans, come here, you disobedient animal," said a voice in German behind them; and to the relief of everybody in the frantically pedaling squad, Hans obeyed.

When the boys and Maddelena arrived at the Road of the Throne, the inhabitants were as puzzled as the German officers. But not for long.

"No questions," Corrado said in a masterful manner. "We're from Niello. Get us inside as quickly as you can."

Doors were readily opened, and the boys, sweating profusely, were given water to drink and a place to get into their proper clothes.

"Were you stopped?" somebody asked, but Corrado, toweling himself, said, "No. We just sailed past everybody. Some soldiers even clapped. But there were a couple of bastards who set a dog on us. That was a bad moment. I thought Maddelena would fall off her bike, and if that turban of hers had come undone, God help us all. But she was game. She's wonderful—Oh!" he said, and covered his bare torso with the towel. "I didn't know you were here."

"It's my house," said Maddelena, standing in the doorway. "Welcome. It's the first time you've been in here, isn't it?"

"Yes."

Her father had been helping the boy. "You're not Corrado, are you?"

"Yes."

"The—er—"

"The bad lot. Yes."

The older man took his hand. "As my daughter says, welcome."

"Aren't you going to change out of those trousers?" Corrado said to Maddelena. "It doesn't look proper. Not for a girl."

"Doesn't it?" she said. "Pity. No, I'm not going to change. I like them."

The Neapolitans are natural-born journalists. When there is any news of a sensational nature, it is automatically exaggerated and blown up to twice its size. The word spread in the whole area that Niello had arrived with scores of his now-famous *scugnizzi*, and that he had sworn on the bones of his grandmother that he was going to give the Germans a fight.

There was a small stretch of grass and shrubs that divided the place, and it was here that young men and boys flocked, ready and willing to join the hero. There was considerable disappointment when it was found that the *scugnizzi* numbered no more than eight, and that Corrado, not Niello, was their leader. There was even more disappointment when it was known that the *scugnizzi* had not come loaded with submachine guns, flamethrowers, and high-velocity rifles. The pistols they produced from their knapsacks seemed very tame.

Time pressed. The Germans were due very shortly. Corrado mounted a stone bench and addressed the crowd of boys and youths.

"How many of you have a gun or a pistol?"

A few hands were raised—among them, to Corrado's surprise, that of a young priest.

Corrado continued. "Niello taught us to go straight for where the arms are. In their barracks. Where is the nearest one?"

"Piazza Gesù and Maria," said the priest, "next to my church. And there's nobody there." With that, he opened a few buttons of his soutane and extracted a pistol from the recesses of some mysterious garment. He handed the gun to a young man standing next to him. "I can't use it because of my *gonnella*. But you can."

There was a laugh and a cheer. A *gonnella* is a skirt and it is impolite slang for an Italian priest's dress.

Maddelena heard all this from a window. The talk of skirts reminded her she was in trousers. Prudently she decided to remain indoors till the lads had something to distract their attention to other things.

"To the barracks," said Corrado; and Maddelena, watching from her house, admired the authority with which he spoke, and the way that the others trooped after him.

The barracks were as the priest had promised—deserted. A door was forced and the crowd poured in. As in the other barracks, there were rifles to be found, and ammunition. A deserting soldier had no wish to carry armaments; nor did their officers, when they, too, deserted, wish to draw attention to themselves by making a great fuss about giving up the guns—and, in any case, to whom? To what civil or military authority that would not promptly arrest them? Like the employees at the Prefect's Palace, they had simply walked out. All over the Italian peninsula, the Italian Army was on the move, sagely going home to mother.

There were a number of standard rifles, some heavy officers' pistols, and, in a rack, a few old-fashioned rifles with long, broad bayonets. They had probably belonged to some ceremonial guard of honor, but they greatly took the boys' fancy. Among those boys was Gennaro Januzzi.

Armed, the boys and young men of the quarter gathered once more in the green space to hear Corrado's instructions. Maddelena chose this tense moment to appear among them, and she went straight to Corrado's side. As she had guessed, the excitement was now such that her male dress drew only passing comment, and that favorable. Even the young priest only sighed and shrugged his shoulders. But she caught Gennaro's eye as she stood at Corrado's flank, a pistol in her hand. She saw that Gennaro was jealous.

In any other place, one boy being jealous of another boy over a girl is amusing, especially to the girl. But in Naples, jealousy does not smolder, it flares. Gennaro was armed with one of the guns with a bayonet, and Maddelena did not like the way he looked from her to Corrado and from Corrado to the gun. She wished the Germans would hurry up.

The proprietor of the workshop had completed his act of defiance. The door was securely locked, the key not, as planned, thrown away, but hidden, in case things should turn out better than expected, in the ample bosom of his wife.

The Germans arrived. They kicked the door down. Orders in crisp voices sent some men inside and others to fetch explosives from the truck. And at last the boys, hidden in their houses, saw a flamethrower.

Corrado, Maddelena, and her father watched from behind the shutters of Maddelena's house. Gennaro was beside them; for, as a good sound local boy who admired a girl, it was his right to come in and out of her house as he chose.

Maddelena's father said, "Corrado, we must do something. I fought in Africa. I've seen our own troops use those things. I've seen them blow up buildings. I've—I've done it myself. They'll set the whole quarter ablaze. Those cans they're carrying in now hold gasoline. Once the fire gets going, there's no stopping it. We shall be homeless."

"Or dead," said Gennaro bitterly. "Well, Corrado, when do we start taking action? You seem to be the military genius around the place."

Corrado bit his lip. "Niello said to hold our fire until they'd loaded up and were outside. You can't hit them while they're still in the workshop."

"And what if the place is blazing away and the explosives go off?" said Maddelena's father. "Did he reckon with that?"

"I don't think he did," said Corrado, hesitantly.

"So we wait here till our heads are blown off or we're burned to a cinder," said Gennaro, a sharp edge to his voice. "As for me, I'm going to start shooting, and you can court-martial me for mutiny afterwards, General."

With that, he pushed open the shutters, leveled his rifle, and, sighting it along the bayonet, fired into the open door.

Instantly a rattle of fire broke out from a dozen houses. There was a pause, then the Germans replied, crouching down at the windows of the workshop. Again there was silence. From out of a doorway, a boy threw a hand grenade. He misjudged his distance, and the hand bomb exploded fifteen feet away from its target, on the roadway.

"Mother of God," shouted Maddelena's father, "don't do that, you silly little fool! There's explosives in there. Can't you use your eyes?" He had leaned out of the window to deliver his warning. Shots flew from the workshop, and Corrado hauled him back to safety. A bullet came accurately through the opening and shattered a mirror on the opposite wall.

The boys and young men held their fire, bewildered. A sergeant appeared in the doorway of the workshop and signaled with his hand. A pistol cracked and he dodged back inside.

"I think they want to talk," said Maddelena.

"I think I want to fight," said Gennaro. Shielding himself as well as he could, pressed up against the wall, he once more pointed his rifle out of the window.

Maddelena's father said, "Talking's the only thing that's going to get us out of this mess. What do we gain by shooting? We can't kill the lot, and it needs only one man to bunk out of the back door after he's lit a fuse. And that'll finish the lot of us."

"And," said Corrado, "if one of those fool boys lobs a grenade into a window, that's the end of the party."

"Couldn't you just nip out and run down to your precious Niello and ask him what the hell we should do?" said Gennaro with heavy sarcasm. "It'll only take you about an hour, there and back on your bike. And you can wear those pretty little shorts of yours."

"Where's Maddelena?" Corrado said. The three looked about them, but she was no longer in the room.

"I'll go and see," said her father. "I hope to God she's not going to do anything silly. When she gets an idea into her head . . ."

He found her in the main bedroom. She had a walking stick and she was tying a white pillowcase to it by its corners.

"Tell Corrado to cover me in case they start firing," she said calmly. "Though with this it shouldn't be necessary. Mother's best pillowcase," she said, smiling. "It's a good thing she's away with auntie in Caserta."

"Stop doing what you're doing," her father roared at her. "Whatever crazy thing you mean to do, stop it at once."

Maddelena calmly tested the knots in her improvised flag of truce. "If it's crazy, then you're the mad one, not me," she said. The knots held. She waved the flag on its stick experimentally. "You put it quite clearly to those silly boys: the Germans can't blow up the workshop without finishing us all, and they can't get out without our mowing them down. Well, when things are like that, what do sensible people do? They make a truce. I'm going to them and I'm going to say, 'Leave our workshop alone, and we'll leave *you* alone.' You're quite right, father. Quite right. You always are."

"Me?" said her father in a bewildered voice. "*I'm* right? And you're going to tell them all that? *You? A girl?*"

"Yes, me, a girl. You know what will happen if you go, or the boys go? They'll expect a trick. We're Neapolitans. They always expect a trick from the likes of us. So they'll shoot first and talk afterward. They won't shoot a girl in cold blood. Have they ever done so yet?"

"If that's your game," said her father, "then you'd better let them know you're a girl. Let down your hair."

"Holy Mary, I'd forgotten," she said, and stretched her arms behind her head and let her hair fall loose from the clasp that held it. "Right again, father. Now, is that all right?"

"Nothing's all right. Everything is crazy."

"No. It's just a draw, like football. They can't do anything without getting killed. Neither can we. And all for a load of stinking leather. Now that *would* be crazy, if you like. Well, father? Do you agree? Those boys don't know their heads from their backsides. They've never fought a war. But you have. You got wounded, and that's why you're not fighting this one. But you know what war's like."

"Yes. It's not football."

"But you do have truces. I remember your telling us. How you had flags like this and went out to bury your dead. Both sides. The blacks and ours. I remember your telling us that when I was just a kid, no higher than your knee."

"We had truces," said her father reluctantly. "But—but—" He sought desperately for an argument to confute her. "But we talked. We had interpreters to talk their horrible lingo. You don't know German. They don't know Italian."

"I've noticed that. One of them does, though. He came to check over the stock before they served the order. I listened to him. He talks Italian bad, like they all do, but he understands it when you talk back to him."

"And he's there? Are you sure?"

"Quite sure."

"I don't know what to say."

"Yes you do. I'm your daughter."

For a long moment they faced each other, he quite still, she combing out her hair with her fingers to make herself securely feminine.

"God go with you," said her father at last.

Corrado and Gennaro were both outraged when she, in a few words, told them what she meant to do. They talked volubly, and together, shouting each other down.

Her father stopped them with a gesture. "It's no good arguing with her. She's my daughter and I know. Besides, she's right. If anybody's going to talk to these swine, a girl will be best."

"I'll go," said Corrado.

"Hell you will," said Gennaro. "If anyone goes, it'll be me," and he made to seize the makeshift flag of truce.

"What you boys can do if you want to show yourselves men,"

said Maddelena's father, "is to go with her as far as this side of the road and cover her with your guns. That's what we always did to make sure the blacks didn't do us dirty. Don't go further than our front door. That's the rules of war. She has to walk out quite alone. But the first sign of trouble, like them aiming a gun, shoot. And for the love of the Madonna, shoot straight. I'll be at the window covering her too, in case you boys miss. And, Maddelena—"

"Yes, father?"

"If they shoot or you hear us shooting, chuck away that flag and go flat on the ground. Then crawl back."

"Crawl, father?"

"Yes. It's not pretty. But war isn't. All right." And he nodded to all three. As they went, he closed the shutters of the window. They were of wooden slats and much eroded by the sun and the rain. With the butt of his rifle, he broke three of the slats and made a loophole. Through this, slowly, he thrust the last two inches of the muzzle of his gun.

The Germans looked through the splintered windows of the workshop.

"There's a boy with a flag of truce," said one of them.

"It's about time," said another. "Chucking those bombs about like maniacs—they'll blow us all to blazes."

"Watch out for monkey business," said the sergeant. "There's a couple of those guttersnipes with guns covering him."

"No shooting," said the officer. "Not till I say so."

"Yessir."

There was a pause. Maddelena slowly made her way across the road, the flag held high. Gennaro's hand on his rifle shook with tension, but he gritted his teeth and finally steadied it. No good relying on the dirty *scugnizzo* next to him if trouble blew up. He'd run, the coward.

One of the German soldiers spoke up. "Sir?"

"What is it?"

"It's not a boy, it's a girl."

"In trousers?"

"Yes, sir. Look at her hair."

"And her boobs," said another soldier, daringly. "She's got a pretty pair."

"Silence."

"Yessir."

"Sergeant," said the officer, "what do you think? If it's a boy, damn the flag. It'll only be a trick. We'll get him. If it's a girl . . . well . . ."

"You can't tell in this stink-hole of a town," said the sergeant, full of worldly wisdom, as is the way of experienced sergeants dealing with officers younger than themselves. "I've seen it in Rome. Boys dressed as girls, flaunting themselves up and down the road like whores. It makes you sick."

"We had it in Berlin, till it was all cleaned up," said the officer.

"Yessir. All cleaned up as you say."

"But they didn't have their hair down below their shoulders—"

"Or boobs," muttered the soldier.

"Quiet," said the sergeant.

"Yessir."

Another pause. Maddelena was now a few feet from the workshop door, walking with a steady step, though the flag of truce wavered in the air.

"It *is* a girl, sir," said the sergeant.

"No shooting," said the officer. "They mean to give in, otherwise they wouldn't have sent a girl. Women are women in Italy. I daresay they've bullied their men."

"Right you are, sir. And the men aren't men."

"*La mamma,*" said the officer in a derisive tone. "I daresay she's taken a hand."

"Yessir," said the sergeant.

"Leave it to me. I speak their language."

Maddelena went into the darkness of the doorway and was lost to sight of the two boys.

"Now what do we do?" said Gennaro urgently. "They could rape her and we'd be none the wiser."

"Stay here, like her father said," replied Corrado.

"And like *I* say, you're a stinking coward," whispered Gennaro, his low voice adding venom to his comment.

"It's no good calling each other names," muttered Corrado. "Niello said, 'When you make a plan, stick to it. The Germans do. That's why they walk all over us.'"

"I agree with your precious Niello," said Gennaro. "I've made a plan and I'm going to stick to it. I'll be back in a moment."

"Where are you going?"

"Mind your own bloody business," he answered, and he was gone.

When Maddelena's eyes grew accustomed to the gloom in the workshop, she saw the thirteen men in their field-gray uniforms scattered about the room she knew so well. One of them, tabs on his shoulders, detached himself and came toward her. She lowered the flag.

"*Ja?*"

She could not quite make out who he was. "You speak Italian?" she said. "I have message. Message."

"*Nicht* speak Italian," said the man, in a monstrous accent. "Heinrich! Forward."

Another soldier whose rank Maddelena could not distinguish came toward her. He seemed very menacing. She raised her flag again.

"*Kaputt,*" she said hastily. "*Kaputt!*" The word meant surrender. Unfortunately, it was one of the very few words of German she knew.

Heinrich came quite close to her. He peered into her face. "White flag not mean to *kaputt,*" he said. "White flag mean to talk. To talk then. *Presto.*" Like all foreigners with little knowledge of the language, he used only the infinitive form of verbs, because it was much easier.

Maddelena let out a little sigh of relief. She knew the code very well, as did every Italian who had to do with foreigners. Usually, it was a matter of bargaining or begging. Now it was a matter of life and death. Her mouth suddenly went dry.

"You not to blow up this place," she said. A little spittle providentially came on her tongue. "You to blow up, then you to die. We all to die. We not want to die. You want going back"—the code slipped her for the moment—"home. Mamma. Wife. Kids." She recovered and was more fluent. "We to say you, 'You to go free. We to do nothing.'"

The man showed no sign on his face. She waved the flag. "We to make peace. You to make peace. We to go back to mamma, wife, kids. You to go back to mamma, wife, kids. Otherwise, all to die. You. Us. To die. *Gute?*" Another word in the language of bargaining had come to her. "*Ist gute?*" she said.

There was talking among the soldiers in German. Maddelena shut her eyes in order not to see the pistols that were pointed at her head. While the German chatter went on, she saw herself back at her table. She drew in the smell of leather, the smell Corrado had not liked. Behind closed eyelids she saw the shaping knives, the iron lasts, the needles, the thread, and the beautiful, fine, soft boots. It saved her from fainting.

The German chatter that Maddelena could not understand was precise and to the point. The officer who had first spoken said to Heinrich, "Are they surrendering?"

"Not quite. They are making an offer."

"*They* are? Who the devil do they think they are? Tell them we're here to blow up the place and we'll do it. So they can cut the gabble."

"Trouble is, sir, *they* can blow it up any time they want to. With us inside."

"Tell her there will be ten of them dead for every one of us. Put up against a wall and shot. Shot."

"We're dealing with *scugnizzi,* not sensible men."

"Talk German."

"We're dealing with boys. They might do anything. They might do it any moment."

"Sir?" said the sergeant.

"Yes, sergeant?"

"She's got a flag of truce."

"What the hell does that matter? She's just a girl, not an emissary in uniform. If she *is* a girl."

"She's a girl, all right," said Heinrich.

"May I speak, sir?" said the sergeant.

"You may."

"We do want to get out of this. We didn't expect opposition."

"Are you suggesting we run away from a gang of boys and—and a *girl?*" said the other man, spluttering a little.

"Not run away," said the sergeant. "There's a big building just two houses away. School or orphanage or something.* I noted it when we drove up. It's empty. We could hold that for hours if we could get inside. One of my men could slip out of the back door and get help from headquarters."

"And how are we going to get out of here? Are you suggesting we walk out of that door with our hands up?"

"Certainly not, sir. I'll create a diversion. With the girl."

"Take care of yourself, Sergeant. Very well, carry on."

He turned to the soldiers and, in a low voice, gave them their instructions.

The sergeant approached Maddelena. He was a big man and he towered over her.

Suddenly he broke into a roar of German. "You insolent little whore! Go back to the brothel you came from! Do you hear me? And don't wave that rag in the faces of German soldiers!" he shouted.

Maddelena, who had not understood a word of this, felt the walking stick twisted violently from her grasp. A piercing pain in her shoulder made her cry out. The sergeant took the stick and broke it across his knee. Then he seized her by her twisted shoulder and arm. She cried out in agony again, but he held her firmly. Once, when she tried to free herself, he struck her heavily in the stomach so that she was breathless. He dragged her toward the door, and then pushed her through it. As he followed her into the open, he said to the officer, "Now, sir. *Now!*"

Corrado, his heart beating wildly as he heard Maddelena's screams of pain, saw her thrust with force into the road. She fell on her knees, and Corrado raised his rifle. But she scrambled up again and he could not fire. At the same moment, out of the corner of his eye, he saw men running toward the deserted building. At his window, Maddelena's father, peering through the broken slats of the shutters, could barely make out what was going on.

But Maddelena remembered his advice. At the next push of the sergeant, she flattened herself deliberately on the ground. She rolled a little, and then, on all fours, she scrambled away.

At that moment, Corrado fired. His aim was poor, for he trem-

---

* Known locally as the *cento camerelle*, or "one hundred small rooms." This description follows closely the report in Aldo de Jaco.

bled with shock. The sergeant grasped his shoulder, then ran with the other men to the empty building. It had been uninhabited for a long time and its large door swung on rusted hinges. The sergeant, without closing it, disappeared inside, his hand still clutching his shoulder. Blood was staining his uniform.

Maddelena crawled to Corrado's feet. He helped her up. She was weeping with the pain of the manhandling and could barely stand.

"Inside," said Corrado. "Inside the house."

She obeyed, stumbling.

Corrado looked at the building into which the soldiers had disappeared. As he did so, the shutters were flung open and a hail of fire swept the roadway. Bullets spattered against the stucco of the wall behind him. He fired back wildly, but soon was driven to take shelter.

He chose a narrow alley that was a cul-de-sac, and backed into it, keeping the palazzo with the Germans in view. They were now firing sporadically, replying whenever there was a shot from their opponents. During a pause in the conflict, Corrado suddenly heard a voice behind him.

"Running away, eh? Just as I said."

He turned to see Gennaro. The lad had come out from a doorway. Behind him was a group of boys. Gennaro had his gun with the bayonet, and so had two or three of his followers.

Gennaro struck a martial pose, his feet apart, the butt of his rifle grounded. " 'Fight and run,' " he said. "That's your great Niello's advice, isn't it? Or was it just 'run'? Where's Maddelena?"

"Safe at home, I think," Corrado replied.

"You *think*. Well, *I* think you haven't guts enough to stand by a woman when she's in trouble."

"You went first," said Corrado indignantly, but he felt that his manner was that of a little boy replying to a taunt.

"And do you know why?" answered Gennaro. "I went to gather some boys with an ounce of pluck. These," he said, and with his free hand gestured behind him.

A burst of fire from the Germans made talking impossible for a while.

"Bravo," said Corrado, when he could be heard again. "Bravo to the lot of you. But what are you going to do?"

i tedeschi barba
rocifiss
ssolini
Badoglio
allea
avitù ci
ati
urelio
Ruggier

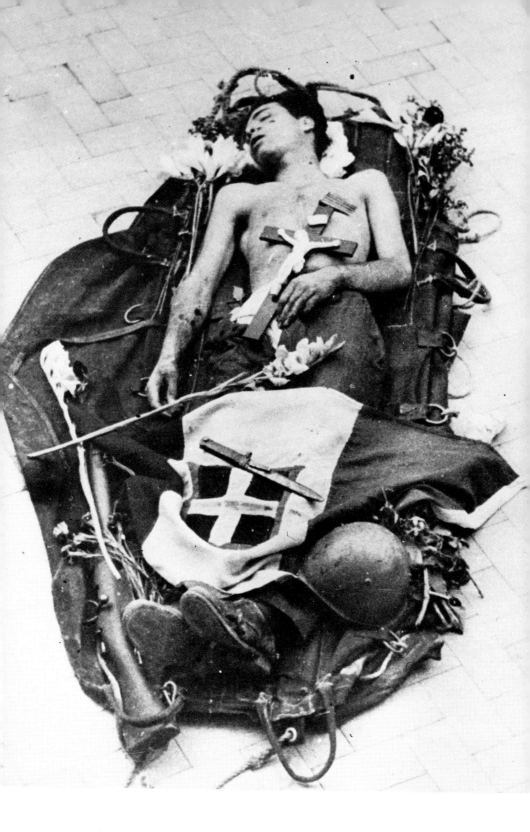

ROBERT CAPA-MAGNUM

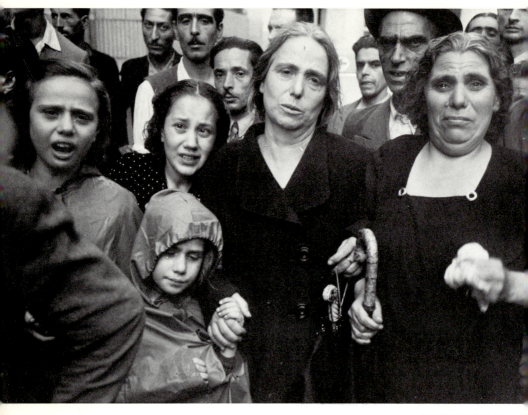

"Go out there, if you'll be so good as to get out of our way."

"They've got every inch covered."

"Dear me, dear-oh-dear-me," said Gennaro. He turned to his followers. "News from the battlefront. Our friend informs us that it's *dangerous*. And I always thought that war was *safe*." His blood grew hot. The excitement of the shooting, the feel of his rifle, and jealousy made his head throb. "And this is war!" he shouted hoarsely at Corrado. "Not bag-snatching and picking pockets. Get out of our way. What are we going to *do*? We're going to charge right into those swine and drive them out at the point of this, *this*," he said, and pointed to the bayonet on his rifle. "Like my father and my uncles and my grandfather did when they went to war. Where were yours? Faking illness? Cleaning out the officers' latrines? Come on, boys."

He held up his hand high above his head. He made a sweeping gesture, one he had seen a dozen times in films and on the covers of magazines telling the stories of Italy's wars.

"Forward!" he shouted, and, pushing Corrado roughly aside, he and his followers made for the space in front of the German refuge at a run. He held his rifle in the classic position, both hands clasping it, the bayonet pointing at the enemy.

It was a magnificent act of sheer, raw courage. All who saw it were astonished. It astonished the Germans. They held their fire in a moment of amazement. Then they shot him dead through the heart.

He lay on the roadway, face down. The moment he had fallen, his followers took to their heels, running back into the cul-de-sac, or to wherever refuge first presented itself.

For long minutes, neither side fired a shot. The sight of the slim boy lying sprawled on the road, the sudden end of a young life, stilled everybody. From the windows, women prayed that he would get up, walk away, be alive again. Even the Germans wished it.

But he did not. Then a gray-haired man very slowly opened a door. Cautiously he stepped out into the open. He stood for a moment, quite still, as though waiting to be shot. Then he felt in his breast pocket and took out a white handkerchief. His hand shaking, he held it high above his head.

"What you want?" said a voice from the palazzo in rough Italian.

"My son," said the man. "My son."

"To raise your other hand," said the voice.

The man obeyed.

"Forward." This time the command was in German, but the man understood, the words resembling each other in the two tongues.

"*Grazie.*" His hands raised, the handkerchief now crumpled into a ball, Gennaro's father came forward. He knelt beside the boy. Very gently, he raised the boy's head.

"Gennaro," he said. "Gennaro. It's your father. Are you all right? Say you're all right. I'll carry you back. It's your father. Talk to me."

Gennaro's eyes were open, far too wide open. His father lowered his head again, but, so that the boy's features should not touch the hard stone, he first laid the handkerchief under his son's head. Then the man looked up at the windows and at the palazzo. Slowly he shook his head. To the watchers it sent a message of a hope lost forever.

He rose. He picked up his son. He swayed a little under the weight, then walked with him to the door of the house from which he had come.

He climbed the steep stairs to the first floor. Three women stood on the landing. One of them was Gennaro's mother. As the boy's body came into view, she said firmly, "It's not Gennaro. I know it's not Gennaro." Gennaro's face could not be seen and she continued to say, her voice rising in hysteria, "It's not Gennaro. It's one of those other boys. Bring the poor boy in here. Who's to tell his mother? Who's to tell his mother? Bring him in here. Poor boy."

The father wordlessly carried the body to a bedroom. He laid it on the bed. The mother went in, the two other women following her closely, holding her elbows. Gennaro's head lay on one cheek on the pillow. His mother looked into his open eyes.

"Gennaro!" she cried, and the two women caught her as she pitched forward.

CHAPTER THIRTEEN

Maddelena did not faint. Nor did she go to comfort the mother. She knew that this would be done. The two women who, as soon as they knew that Gennaro was dead, had stood at his mother's side would stay there until he was buried, and for as long after as the first bitterness of grief exacted. If she wept, they would dry her tears; if she did not weep, they would gently tell her stories about her dead son until the pent-up tears flowed. This was Naples. Heartbreak had its ritual, it was so common.

Instead, Maddelena was seized with an anger as deep as that which Gennaro had felt. But it was cold, the lasting, brooding anger of the Neapolitan, very rare, but which, once it came, might endure for a lifetime. She was angry with Gennaro for being so foolhardy. She was angry with the Germans who had killed him. She was angry with her father, who, for all his expert making holes in shutters for his gun, had not fired it. She was angry with the war and its waste.

But she was angry above all with herself. She had failed in her mission of truce. She had been frightened of the soldier's rough, hurting hands. She had been frightened, she knew, of the pistols pointed at her. She could not bring Gennaro back; she could not stop the war; but never, she swore to herself by the Madonna and all the saints that she could remember, never again would she be frightened of guns.

She sought Corrado. She had been impatient of his cool ways, of his *scugnizzo* air of being knowledgeable. But it was that which she now wanted.

She found him behind a house, surrounded by the *scugnizzi* he had brought with him, but also by dozens of local boys, and with them young deserters from the armed forces and a student or two. They were listening intently.

"We don't fight from the street," he was saying. "Street fighting is all very exciting, but when you've got your enemy two or three stories above your head, looking down on everything you do, it's bloody silly. No. We fight from the terraces. We fight from the roofs, if they'll take your weight and give you cover. But the terraces are best."

Terrazzo, in the poorer quarters of Naples, has not the grand meaning that it has elsewhere. A terrace is not a wide promenade, giving onto some view. It is a narrow balcony, some five feet long, far too narrow to accommodate a deck chair. It has an iron railing, and behind it are French windows, always shielded by wooden shutters; some solid; some, like that of Maddelena's father's, with slats. The terraces are not meant for enjoyment. They are meant for hanging a line to take in the family washing. There is no other place. The roofs of the houses, built (and often jerry-built) decades ago in another century, are sloping and unsafe; hence Corrado's warning—it was easy to go through them. It was this that played the decisive part in the battle of the Road of the Throne.

One of the *scugnizzi* said, "But what d'you mean? You want us to stand out on a terrace and stay there like pigeons till they pick us off?"

"No. Which of you fought at the Rinascente?"

Two boys put their hands up.

"Good. You remember how Niello told us to pull up the furniture and make a barricade?"

The two boys nodded.

"Now, the best furniture to stop a bullet turned out to be a bedstead with a mattress, didn't it?"

"Yes," said one of the boys. "I was behind one. But Mario here was behind a bookcase, and he nearly got his packet. A bullet went right through the back."

"Cheap wood," said Mario. "Never trust those big stores."

"But there's nothing cheap about a matrimonial bed and a double mattress, is there?" said Corrado.

"Made to stand up to wear and tear," said another *scugnizzo* with a chuckle.

"All right," said Corrado. "We know you've got a dirty mind, but don't corrupt these little angels here."

He turned to the little angels. "Now, I want you to go back and tell your parents to pull their beds over to the window, mattress and all, and stand them on their sides. Then open the shutters wide, but mind you don't get *your* packet while you're doing it. Do you all understand?"

They did, and the battle of the terraces had begun.

For a while, all was so quiet that the Germans thought they had won.

"Pity about that boy, sir," said the sergeant, "but it seems to have done the trick. It's tamed the lot of them. I suppose they thought it was going to be all fun of the fair at the shooting range."

"Yes," his superior agreed. "We'll just wait for Wolfgang to get back with help, and then walk out. It almost looks as though we needn't even wait."

But the mattresses and the beds had been moved behind closed shutters. Now, at the sound of a blast on a whistle that Corrado had borrowed from a town policeman who had taken off his uniform to join the fighting, the shutters were flung open. Heads popped up over the beds, fired, and ducked to safety. Bullet after bullet tore through the windows of the palazzo; and the Germans, taken by surprise, could think of no better defense than lying flat on the floor.

But that did not last. Training had taught them how to fight in such town battles; they had fought them in Europe street by street. They found nooks of safety, then flattened themselves against walls and ducked out to fire. They went to the top floor of the palazzo, one by one, and there mustered for action.

The top floor, underneath the attic, had been the servants' quarters. Its windows were merely narrow ovals, meant for decoration more than use, which is the manner of baroque architecture. They made admirable embrasures for automatic weapons. Soon the combatants of the Road of the Throne were receiving as much as they sent and more. The noise was tremendous. There were wounds on both sides. One soldier, a grenadier, was incautious, and was killed, but only those in the house in which he was fighting knew, so the fury of shooting from the other houses was in no way diminished.

"Sir," said the German sergeant, "we'd better cool off the shooting. We're running short of ammunition."

"Those buggers aren't," said the officer. "Where in God's name are they getting it from?"

It was after Corrado had sent the boys and youths and some of the older men to erect the window barricades that Maddelena said, "Well, I'll be off to do my bit. Are you coming with me?"

"No. I'm going to join your father and we'll manage the bed between us. *You're* not coming with *me*."

The indignant glare that Maddelena gave him made him smile.

"If you think because I'm a girl I can't handle a gun—" she began, but Corrado cut her short.

"Just because you're a girl, I think you can handle not a gun but dozens, and bombs and grenades, too. Those boys are going to have a fine time pulling the trigger, but they've got to have something that comes out at the other end. Back there in the gardens, hidden in the bushes, there's a whole arsenal that we looted from the barracks. I want someone to carry it to the fighters. I want someone who isn't afraid of a stray bullet hitting them with an armful of other bullets or even bombs. I want someone who knows every back door and every stairway of this quarter. I want someone who can keep the boys supplied. That someone's you. At least, I hope so. That is, of course, if you don't think I'm being bossy. You said I was once. Remember?"

"Did I? That must have been when you were still a boy. You're a man now."

"Getting on for one, I suppose."

"Fast. I'll do as you say."

"Thanks. Go to that bit of green and trees behind those houses. You'll find one of us there. Bring bullets first, then hand bombs. There's a machine gun, but I don't think we've got anyone who knows how to work it. But it's the bullets we'll be wanting. Take care of yourself."

She turned to go, then turned back. "Now I know—" She hesitated. "Now I know what Niello meant when he said, 'No heroics.' "

There was a silence between them.

"Did you like Gennaro?" said Corrado, with a thin thread of voice, as though he feared the answer.

"He liked *me*," said Maddelena. Then, to turn the drift of their talk, she asked, "What do you think they'll do? The Germans, I mean."

"I don't know. But I bet they don't know either. They sent off a messenger, but we took care of him. Off you go."

The messenger had left by the back door of the palazzo with a scribbled note asking for urgent help. He opened the door carelessly and took four steps into the road. Then he let out a roar of pain, for a bullet had smashed his thigh. The noise brought his companions, who, sheltering as best they might, dragged him by his arms back into the house. His bellows of pain echoed through the empty palazzo and reached the top floor.

"What goes on?" said the officer.

"I'll go and see, sir."

There was a little desultory firing for a while, and then the sergeant came back. His shoulder was in a roughly made sling, stained with blood.

"Casualty, sir. Hit in the leg. He's safe. But he needs a shot to kill the pain."

"When they sent us to clean up a pack of cobblers, they didn't think to send a medical unit," said the officer, with sarcasm. "Send someone else."

"With respect, sir—"

"What is it?"

"It's no use. We're surrounded."

"God in heaven."

"Yessir."

"Try and get that man to be quieter. In this damned place, it's eerie."

"Very good, sir. I'll try."

Maddelena went to the patch of grass and trees. She passed through an iron gate in some railings and looked about her.

"Psst! If you're looking for me, I'm here," said a high voice.

A small boy came cautiously out from behind the bole of a tree. It was Eduardo.

"Password," he said; and then added, "Of course I know who you are. You're the girl in trousers. But that isn't the password. Besides, they said they'd send somebody for the ammunition, but I didn't expect a girl. So you've got to say the password."

"Er—" said Maddelena.

"Well, of course, if you don't remember it, I'll have to tell it to you, because of course I know who you are and you know who I am so it'd be silly to stand chewing the rag, especially since things sound as if they're getting pretty hot."

"*Butta*," said Maddelena, remembering.

"That saves a *lot* of trouble. Follow me and I'll lead you to the arms dump."

It was roughly concealed with dried branches of a palm tree and some plaited matting. Eduardo lifted a branch, and Maddelena saw boxes and a pile of grenades.

"Jesus," said Eduardo, "I wouldn't like your job. Carrying all that stuff. I'm on guard because Corrado said, 'You're not very brave, Eduardo, I know, but this is a safe place.' But I mean, suppose an airplane flew over and saw me and dropped a bomb. On this. And me."

Maddelena moved away some more of the covering. "I don't think an airplane really could see you. After all, you're not very big."

"I suppose so," said Eduardo reluctantly. "But it could *swoop*. Then what would I do?"

"Run like hell."

Eduardo brightened. "Oh, yes, I'm very good at that. Well, to work. What are you going to take first?"

"Corrado said bullets."

"Bullets coming up," said Eduardo briskly, and loaded her with three boxes.

She carried them to the houses, kicking open back doors, which she knew were never locked, climbing the stairs, and coming into the front rooms where men and boys were crouched behind their makeshift barricades. One student said to her, "Keep up the good work. We're firing five to their one. They can't hold out much longer."

But the enemy were trained and disciplined soldiers. The boys and the citizens of the Road of the Throne were amateurs, wasting their ammunition. The soldiers conserved theirs, firing sparingly, but with effect. An hour passed, and then another. Still the battle went on. Maddelena's loads seemed to grow heavier and heavier, the stairs to grow steeper.

She found Corrado with her father. Both were at their barricaded window.

"Good girl," said her father, and turned to fire. Corrado aimed, but then laid down his gun.

"Taking potshots like this isn't going to shift them," Corrado said. "It looks as though we'll have to starve them out. Or—" He stopped and frowned in thought. Then he repeated, "Yes. Or—"

Maddelena wiped the sweat from her face. A light drizzle had begun and then stopped. There were patches of blue in the sky, but the air was close and clammy.

"Or what?"

"I can't stop to explain. But the next time you come, bring hand grenades."

She went, her legs now very weary, back to the stretch of greenery and the dump. "Corrado said 'hand-something,' " she told Eduardo in a tired voice. "Hand—hand—oh, I've forgotten."

"Leave it to me," said Eduardo importantly. "I know just what he means." He gave her a hand grenade, and then another. "You ought to have a belt or something, to sling them to," he said fussily, "but since you're a girl, you'd better carry one in each hand. Don't be frightened," he added, swinging a third grenade carelessly. "They're quite safe until you pull the pin. Then you count one, two, three, and"—he made as if to throw the bomb—"boooom!"

"Don't," said Maddelena. "You frighten me." Then, remembering her vow, said, "Throw it, eh? I must have a try." She, too, swung a hand grenade.

"Careful," Eduardo shouted, and fled behind a tree.

Back in her home, Corrado took the bombs. In return he gave her two glass bottles with rags stuck in their tops.

"Where is there a roof that's about fifteen feet, not more, from that palazzo?"

"Round the back. What are these?" she said, looking at the bottles.

"You'll see. Now, I'll need two things. One is a water tank or something like that to hide behind, because on the roof I'll be a sitting duck."

"Number fifteen," said Maddelena. "That's got a storage tank."

"And the other thing is I'll need an assistant."

"Me."

"It'll be dangerous."

"One sitting duck ready and willing," she said, and, tired as both of them were, they smiled at the echo of their way of talking in happier days.

The roof was easily gained, for the family who lived on the top floor had joined in the fighting. Their terrace faced the back of the palazzo, across a narrow lane. A middle-aged man with a large belly opened the apartment door to them. Corrado explained what he wanted.

"It's risky," said the man. He held a double-barreled shotgun in his hand and under his armpit. From the way he kept patting it, Corrado could see he was a hunter. Game in the countryside around Naples is small and scarce; hunting is a cult, rather than a sport. Every hunter is inordinately proud of his skill as a marksman, true or imaginary.

"Since we shot that messenger, they've put four men at the back windows over there."

Corrado cautiously peered out. The back of the palazzo had no architectural pretensions. There were no windows at the level of the servants' quarters, but above them was an attic with narrow openings to let in the light. A rifle barrel projected from one of these.

The huntsman rattled on. "One's got an automatic gun, but it kicks up as he fires and he hasn't done us any harm as yet. But if he sees you on the roof, he'll spray the place. You can go if you like—it's your skin, not mine—but if you do, I'll tell you what. I'll keep them down under cover. All I need is to see one inch of one of their ears, and I crop it for them!" He patted and stroked his gun.

"Thanks. I'll be grateful," said Corrado. "Now kindly show us the way to the roof."

"Us?" said the huntsman. "You don't mean to take Maddelena with you?"

"He's not *taking* me. I'm going with him," Maddelena corrected primly.

"I don't hold with females getting anywhere near firearms," the man began on what was obviously a favorite household theme, but Corrado was already loping through the apartment in search of the exit to the roof.

"There's a ladder in the corridor," the man called, and then to Maddelena: "You're certainly a brave girl. But don't worry. Rely on me." He patted his gun once more. "I'll see that no harm comes to you. And don't let that boy get you into doing anything foolish or dangerous. Just hand him up what he wants and come back here."

"Right," said Maddelena, and followed Corrado.

She found Corrado up a ladder and half out of a trapdoor. She tugged at his trouser leg.

He looked down at her. "There are two water tanks side-by-side which look just right for us," he said. "Follow me, but keep flat against the tiles till you get to the tanks."

He disappeared. Then he stretched a hand back and relieved her of one of the bottles, so that she could climb properly. She envied his military belt, from which hung the two hand grenades. Soon she was on the roof, flat, as ordered. The tiles were still slippery from the shower.

Shots rang out, and she held her breath. But none were directed at the roof. Then she heard the sound of a shotgun.

"That's our host," Maddelena whispered. "I hope he's as good a shot as he says he is."

"Our gallant huntsmen are dangerous, but not to anything they're actually aiming at," said Corrado; and Maddelena, in spite of a fast-beating heart, managed to giggle. Soon she was lying beside Corrado in the shelter of the two rainwater tanks.

Corrado peered around them. "Nicely judged," he said. "You chose the right house. I can reach it. I'll have to stand up though, and that's a pity."

To emphasize his words, a shot was fired from the palazzo. This time there was no doubt that it was aimed at Corrado, for it hit the roof and broke some tiles. Two barrels went off in quick succession below them, and, to confirm Corrado's opinion of Neapolitan huntsmen, a rattle of shots hit the roof: whoever had seen Corrado's head was obviously still firing.

"Just as safe as the birds and the rabbits," said Corrado with a grin. "Oh, well, here goes."

"No!" said Maddelena. "No, don't."

He looked back at her. "Eh?" he said. "Did you say something?"

She bit her lip. "No. Nothing." And in a moment he had leaped to his feet. He drew the pin of his hand grenade and then hurled it with a sweeping movement of his arm that almost caused him to lose his balance. The explosion of the bomb and the patter of bullets all around them came together.

"Did you get them?" asked Maddelena breathlessly.

"I'm not after *them*," said Corrado. "I'm after that skylight in the roof. And I missed it. I've made a fine mess of the tiles, but it's a hole I want. I'll have to try again."

This time Maddelena was so sure he would be hit that she closed her eyes. "Hail Mary, full of grace—" she muttered. Again the roar of the bomb, again the bullets, and—she was crying with relief —again Corrado was by her side.

"I've done it," he said triumphantly. "Now it's your turn with the bottles."

"You mean get up there and throw them?" said Maddelena in a very small voice.

"Didn't you know girls can't throw things?" said Corrado, grinning widely, and Maddelena did not mind at all this reflection upon her sex. "No, I'll do that," he went on. "What we've got to do is to set the rags alight. They've pretty well soaked up the gas and—" He took out a cigarette lighter. "Stolen," he said, "from a little old lady who smoked cigars."

An evening breeze was blowing across the tiles, and the lighting up was not simple.

"You should just have seen her," said Corrado, carrying on his joke as he strove to light the rag. "Damn. It's gone out again. Get closer to me. Closer. Make a windbreak. Twenty a day, great long things like they draw Churchill with in cartoons. I was doing her health a good turn. Snuggle up. Put your arm around me. That's it. Good. At last."

The hand grenade had crashed through the glass of the skylight and exploded a foot from the floor of the attic. Two of the four soldiers, the two who were nearest, fell to the floor groaning, and one with his hand clutched to his stomach.

"Get them away from the skylight," said one of the uninjured soldiers. "The swines will throw another."

The two were dragged to safety.

The attic was furnished with iron shelves filled with old documents, tied up with faded tape and clearly forgotten as being of no further use. "Behind those stacks," said a soldier.

When all four were there, one of them bent over his wounded companion.

"How are you?"

"Bad," said the man, holding his stomach. "Sorry."

"And you?"

But the other was in a dead faint.

"We've got to get them down below. Maybe the others can do something."

They were lifting the first of their wounded down the stairs when the gas bomb came down through the hole. It exploded. By the time they got the soldier to the landing below, the documents were blazing. Another bomb followed, falling into the midst of the fire. Long flames leaped up and set fire to the dry wood of the struts of the roof. When the second soldier was down from the attic, all of them were choking and coughing. The servants' quarters began to fill with thick black smoke.

The smoke made it impossible for anybody to stay in the servants' quarters. The Germans moved, carrying their casualties, to the main floor of the palazzo.

"We'll have to get out and put them in the truck. That one's in a bad way," said the officer.

"Yessir," said the sergeant. "We can try shooting our way out."

"With that cross fire from the windows? Then who's to carry *us* when they get us, as they will? No. We must ask for terms."

"You mean surrender, sir? I think that's wise, sir—"

"I do *not mean surrender!*" his superior roared at him. The noise he made was so great that it could be heard through the shattered windows in the piazza. A spatter of rifle fire greeted it. The officer and sergeant promptly squatted to be safe, and that did nothing to assuage the officer's anger.

The sergeant put his hand to his shoulder. The wound was beginning to bleed again, and it hurt. "No surrender, sir. Of course, sir," and he winced.

"I have two badly wounded men on my hands," said the officer. The sergeant screwed up his eyes and let out a barely stifled groan. "And one walking wounded," said the officer graciously. "That makes three casualties. By the international rules of war as subscribed to by the Red Cross, I have the right, as the officer in charge, to ask for safe-conduct from the enemy to seek a place where I can find medical help."

"Provided," said the sergeant, "you do not ask to cross enemy lines—*aaaaaow!* Sorry, sir. My shoulder's acting up."

"There are no enemy lines," said the officer.

"No, sir. Only a pack of cobblers—in your words, sir. From which of the cobblers shall we ask safe-conduct, sir? Begging your pardon—*ahhhhh*—for my ignorance."

"There was that girl. She spoke German."

"Yessir. There was that girl. She did not speak German, but Heinrich spoke a little Italian—"

"Then the thing is settled. Your arm is giving you trouble, Sergeant. I can see that."

"Thank you, sir."

"But I'll soon get you to the medics. Heinrich!"

"Sir."

"Listen carefully."

"Yessir."

Maddelena and Corrado had rejoined Maddelena's father. Heinrich appeared at the big central window of the palazzo. He cupped his hands. He yelled.

"He's got guts," said Corrado. "We could pick him off as he stands."

"He'll bust them," said Maddelena's father, "if he goes on at that rate. What's he saying?"

" 'Girl,' " replied Maddelena. " 'The girl.' "

A voice from one of the houses outbid him in sheer noise. "What girl?"

"The girl in—*lange Hosen*."

There was a moment of silence.

"He means trousers," said a rather high voice coming from a ground-floor shop.

"That's the tailor," said Maddelena's father. "He should know. He's been doing a roaring business in them for the Germans."

"In what?" said Maddelena.

"Trousers."

"Ah, so I'm the girl. Well, I'd better go and see what they want."

"No you don't," said Corrado, commandingly. "Not till we've made quite sure it's not a trick. I'll go with you. We'll both go to the front door. Then I'll go out first. If they take a potshot at me, don't come out yourself. Right?"

Maddelena nodded, and they went. Corrado opened the door slowly; slowly he walked out onto the road, his hands by his sides; slowly he turned his head toward the big window with its messenger.

"You want lady?" he said. Maddelena, hidden in the hallway, saw him through the frame of the open door. For her it was a frame for a picture of a hero.

"*Ja!* Lady. Girl. To talk."

With the same nonchalance, Corrado strolled back to Maddelena. He took her hand. He led her out onto the roadway. He had all the grace of a young man leading his partner to a waltz. But Corrado, the *scugnizzo*, had never been asked to a dance in his life.

As she came out onto the road, she looked at the place where Gennaro had lain. There was not much blood. But she saw not Gennaro but Corrado lying there. The vision was so clear and so convincing, she clutched Corrado's hand until it hurt him.

"It's all right. I'm here," Corrado whispered. "I won't leave you."

She took her eyes away from the roadway and focused them, with difficulty, on the soldier at the big window. The negotiations began.

There was much exchange of Italian in the easy grammarless infinitive. Corrado released Maddelena's hand and stepped back behind her, like an aide to an ambassadress—which, in a way, he was.

"They want to take out their wounded," she said to him at last. "Not to shoot. I mean, no shooting. Something about rules of war."

"Rules of war, my ass," said Corrado. "Tell them to come out with their hands over their heads."

The message was conveyed. Heinrich turned and spoke to his commanding officer, who very briefly appeared in the window.

"*Nicht!* No hands over head. To leave guns, to leave pistols all here in house. To leave behind. *Ja? Gut?*"

"Stiff-necked pack of sods, aren't they?" said Corrado coolly. He gave a long look at the top story. It was burning well. Clouds of smoke were pouring from the servants' quarters.

"We'd better get rid of them," he said at last. "If that fire gets too much of a hold, God knows if the firemen can put it out before it catches your houses. All right. Tell them to come out with their hands like *this*." He held them away from him, as he had seen in the movies.

"*Ja, ja, ja,*" came a barrage of acceptance from the big window, and the messenger disappeared inside.

And that was the way the victory of the Road of the Throne ended. The Germans came out, carrying their wounded. They loaded them onto the truck, then got on themselves. They had no weapons. They kept their hands away from their sides. Then they drove away.

Maddelena flung her arms around Corrado's neck. He kissed her briefly, then said, "I owe you an apology."

"What for, what for?" she said. "We won, we won, we *won!*"

People were pouring out of their houses, and they took up her cry: "We won! We won!"

"Yes," said Corrado, and he had to put his lips close to her ear because the rejoicing was making such a din, "but I swore. And I know how much you don't like me to use rude words. You've always told me so, and—"

But he did not finish, because she had given him a light, but significant, kick on the shin.

The owner of the workshop that had caused the battle ran through the broken-down door into the factory. "They haven't taken a thing," he was saying over and over again. "Not a thing. The key. Where the hell did I put the key to the storeroom? The key! The key!"

His wife was just behind him. "Maruccio," she was saying. "Maruccio. Here. You put it here. It's on the ring with the door key." She put her hand into her bosom and took it out.

Maruccio snatched it. "Why didn't you say so before?" he said.

"Keeping me waiting. Always keeping me waiting. Ah, women, women!"

Then the storeroom door, with all its precious piles of leather behind it, was opened.

PART FOUR

The Second Day

CHAPTER FOURTEEN

The Neapolitan in talking about Eremete Bonomi twisted an English proverb: it is a bad boy who does not bring somebody some good. And bad boys brought Bonomi all the good in the world.

He was the governor of the boys' prison of Saint Efremo, and although there is no record that he ever converted a bad boy to a good boy, the boys certainly converted him in an outstanding way.

Bonomi's well-paid job as the governor was not really very exacting. In far-off 1943, there was little idea that prison should reform the prisoner and turn him out a law-abiding member of society, especially in Naples. After all, in that city there was no law-abiding society into which he could be turned out.

But laws there were, and magistrates to enforce them when not to do so would be embarrassing. For instance, men who murdered their wives out of jealousy, or women who poisoned their husbands to free themselves to go with a lover (and, there being no divorce, there was no other way to get free quickly), had to be imprisoned. Financial crookedness on a large scale also had to be punished, unless the criminal had had the common sense to get himself enrolled into the Fascist party and had risen sufficiently high in the ranks. Bonomi was in no way crooked, but he was a good Fascist, although, as we shall see, very open-minded about the whole thing.

As for the boys, the majority of those in his temporary care were *scugnizzi*. It was not part of Bonomi's duty to put his *scugnizzi* on the straight and narrow path; after all, he knew as well as they did that a straight and narrow path was an excellent place for picking pockets. But there were boys who had got into fights with knives, or who had butted dignified policemen in the belly with their heads, or who had simply sprained an ankle when running away, and had thus been, awkwardly enough for everybody, caught. Such had to be punished, and they were sent to the boys' prison, for varying terms, none of them long.

The punishment was in other ways, also, far from severe. In the first place, some of the boys had regular meals for the first time in their lives. In the second, they were separated from bad company, such as their parents, who might well be burglars, pimps, confidence tricksters, car thieves, and such. Very few rebelled against the confinement. When one did, the warders marched him off to an empty room, told him to take off all his clothes, and then set about him with a leather belt.

Equally, very few attempted to escape; although, from the old building in which the prison was housed, escape would be easy. It had, however, to be reported to the police. The carabinieri would, as we have seen, keep the usual watch on the boy's home, and back he would go to prison. Here his friends and companions would welcome him, and tell him not to be such a fool next time; there were worse places to be in Naples than Bonomi's jail.

Bonomi's life, then, was a contented one. His one severe jolt was when the government in Rome announced figures to show that fascism had notably reduced the rate of juvenile crime in Italy. The cult of youth, much encouraged by Mussolini, had, it was said, brought a new moral fiber into the nation, and so on and so forth. Bonomi saw his job threatened, until a high Fascist assured him that the whole thing was made up in order to annoy the British foreign secretary, who had just imposed sanctions upon Italy.

Bonomi had been in the army, though not in a fighting capacity. He had the rank of lieutenant colonel and habitually wore military uniform, but he was in no way a martinet; he got along with everybody, including the *scugnizzi*. It was his outstanding characteristic. In the course of the Four Days, it took people's breath away.

During the hours when the rules said the boys should be given exercise, they gathered at the ground-floor windows of the prison. These were barred. They provided space for only three or four boys at a time, and there was much competition for a few minutes of converse with the passersby. The sentry at the gate would ask these passersby to kindly pass on, should the conversation threaten to be prolonged. This was not only because prison rules strictly forbade any such thing, but also to give the other boys behind the bars their fair chance. Bonomi never interfered with this practice. To separate the *scugnizzi* from their beloved streets would have been inhuman cruelty, and Bonomi was not a cruel man.

To keep some sort of order behind the mob at the window, boys would make appointments with their visitors. Thus, one boy's brother would be asked to come at four, another's sister only during the morning break, and others only on Sundays.

Maurizio had a cousin inside, Andrea, a lad of sixteen, jailed for being in a waterfront brawl and having a knife longer than the law permitted. A man had died in the fight, but nobody thought Andrea had been responsible. He had been jailed as a lesson to *scugnizzi* to keep their fighting to themselves.

Maurizio's relationship with Andrea was socially complicated. Andrea, a handsome, rough boy, had been a previous favorite of Maurizio's commendatore. When Maurizio arrived on the scene, Andrea had seen at once that he was no match for Maurizio's charming ways. With a tact which the commendatore found surprising in so muscular a boy, he withdrew. When he was jailed, he sent an urgent message to Maurizio that he was in need of money, since gambling at cards was one of the principal pastimes of the prisoners. Maurizio instantly recognized his obligation and spoke to the commendatore, who recognized his. An allowance was provided to meet gambling debts and other needs, such as cigarettes, and Maurizio was deputed to pass by during the break before supper every Tuesday and hand it over.

This he did, even on Tuesday, September 28. He was late, because of all the excitement, but faithful. By the time he arrived, storm clouds had gathered. Heavy drops of rain were beginning to fall as Maurizio, close up against the bars, passed over the money and then said:

"I'm sorry for you, I really am. You don't know what fun you're missing." He narrated the battles of the day. "And it's all over Naples. They're fighting everywhere. Niello says the more places the better. And it's real fighting. I've seen dead bodies. And blood."

In Maurizio's narrative, the gutters ran with it. Boys crowded to the window so that Andrea was pressed painfully against the bars. The sentinel left his post and listened eagerly.

Then a voice came from an upper window. "Guard! Send that boy away. At once!"

It was Bonomi. He waited until Maurizio, obeying the sentinel, had disappeared down the street, then he put his head out of his office door and, stopping a passing warder, said, "I want all the boys in the chapel immediately."

The boys assembled with looks of apprehension. The chapel was a place of punishment; not, of course, of beating, but discipline that the boys feared more. Mass was said each morning, and had to be heard kneeling for most of the time. The chaplain, a kind man, could manage to get through the ceremony in twenty minutes if he chose. On the other hand, he could draw it out interminably, taking longer than the pope himself. If the boys had been a nuisance the day before, Bonomi would ask the chaplain to be at his slowest. Worse, there could be an evening benediction, with hymns, the rosary, and even a homily. It looked as though the boys were in for the latter punishment, and they were not happy.

The chapel was dark and cold. There had been no electricity for days. To make matters worse, the storm that had been threatening broke with violence. Rain drummed on the roof, and the gloom was made even more depressing by the flashes of lightning that lit up the boys for a split second, then plunged them back into darkness.

"Vittorio," said Andrea, "for God's sake, hurry up with the candles."

Vittorio's small voice fought with a clap of thunder. "Is there going to be a benediction? I'm not allowed to light the candles unless there's going to be—"

"There'll be a murder if we don't get some light soon," said Andrea. "Get moving."

Vittorio was the boy selected for that week to do duty as the principal altar boy. In better days it had been his task to light the twenty or thirty candles surrounding the tabernacle that held the Sacrament. Boys were supposed to watch the process and repose their minds in something called "holy recollection." The candles made a cheerful blaze, and the boys recollected their sins, usually with pleasure. Now there were only two candles, the warders having taken most of the stock, one by one, to their homes.

The thunder rolled. The rain increased, and the two candles flickered. Then Bonomi was seen coming in from the door used by the priest. He had a powerful flashlight, which he shone on the boys.

"All present?"

"Yessir."

"This is not going to be a benediction," said Bonomi, and there was a noise of subdued cheering. Bonomi smiled. "You have done nothing wrong," he said, showing how much he was in tune with the way boys thought, and there was some laughter. "But you *might*." He moved to the small pulpit, adjusted the flashlight so that it shone on his face, and began:

"All of you boys have heard rumors of what is going on in the city. Now, many of you have had reason to know that I am a well-informed man. Not much happens that I don't know about."

There was a murmur of agreement.

"Then let me tell you that all the stories of fighting and revolt are nothing but tales put about by the agents of the Americans and the British. This is something that always happens in war. Secret agents," said Bonomi, with emphasis. "You boys have seen films about secret agents. Yes?"

There was another murmur of assent.

"That's what's happening. There has been some looting, and our brave allies the Germans have had to do a little shooting to put it down. Don't forget it might well be your own homes that these scoundrels are looting. It might be your own sister that they are holding up at a gunpoint. It might be your own mother whose wedding ring they are tearing off her fingers. That's all that's happening. I want no trouble here, and I don't expect it. You've been better fed than most of your own families. Am I right?"

Again there was agreement.

"Now one of the secret agents has been captured and he has confessed. The Americans and the British mean to try and starve this city into surrender because they know they can't capture it by fighting. That means there are hard times ahead. Well, I've taken precautions. Stay here and behave yourselves and there'll be enough food to fill your bellies until the huge forces that are coming now— and I mean *now*, at this moment—down the road from Rome fling the enemy back into the sea. Trust me. I'm a well-informed man. Now, dismiss. You can go straight to supper."

There was a quick scramble and the chapel was empty. The rain increased in fury, but Bonomi was content. His formula always worked.

His formula was that in dealing with boys you had to be just one jump ahead of them. You had to know just what they were cooking up in their silly minds before it came to the boil. You had, in his favorite phrase, to be well informed.

In the days when Guglielmo Marconi (now Senator Marconi) had been conducting his remarkable experiments, Bonomi had believed while all scoffed. When radio and the microphone came into existence, Bonomi had installed a hidden microphone in the boys' dormitory, a revolutionary idea. Little, it was true, came through clearly enough to be a basis for action, except the lurid swearing and the obscenities. Bonomi, on the advice of a colonel in the carabinieri who was a great friend of his, in the end fell back on the well-tried system of the informer.

Now, while the storm rattled the windows of the prison, one such informer brought him his supper on a tray.

Massimo, the informer, was a boy of sixteen, with neat hair, a well-washed face, and shrewd eyes. He was a member of a family of smugglers that was proud of an ancient lineage—all smugglers. He could boast of one forebear who was hanged as far back as the Spanish Occupation. He was not a *scugnizzo*; in fact, he looked down upon them as wastrels. He considered that he was in trade. If he could not, without stretching the language, say that he earned an honest living, at least it was earned. His family did not steal, and neither did he. As he saw it, they merely cut prices, and that was something every merchant did when he could.

He was, at the moment, in prison, but he bore no resentment toward the authorities for that. It was understood that from time to time a smuggler had to be arrested for the sake of appearances, to prove that the authorities were not taking bribes, which they were. It was one of those things that just happened—like, in other countries, doing jury duty.

"And so," said Bonomi, as he began to eat his supper, "what have you to tell me? Did my little talk impress the boys?"

"Yes, sir."

"They believed me, eh?" said Bonomi, chuckling with his mouth full.

"No, sir. They think that bit about secret agents is a lot of cock. That's their word, sir, not mine."

Bonomi swallowed his mouthful and forked another.

"Well, well, maybe I was not at my best. The thunderstorm may have put me off a little. But at least we needn't expect trouble, need we?"

"Yes, sir, we need. Tomorrow morning, after Mass, they are going to lock you in your bedroom and then set the place on fire. After which they are going to join the fighting."

Bonomi remained with the forkful half-raised to his now open mouth. Before he could say anything, there was a loud ringing of the bell at the main door of the prison.

"I'll go and answer it, sir," said Massimo.

"The porter will do that."

"No, sir. He's gone home."

"Home?"

"Yessir. Home. And he's not coming back. So have the warders. They slipped out after supper. You see, sir, there *is* fighting, and the boys *will* set the place on fire, and the porter and the warders *don't* want to be here when that happens."

The ringing of the bell was now accompanied by thunderous knocks at the door.

"I think I'd better open it, sir, with permission. I think I know who they are there outside."

"Who?"

"Well, sir, looters. Not my word, sir, yours."

Bonomi laid down his knife and fork and waited. The ringing and the knocking were repeated, furiously. Bonomi's appetite left him completely. Plainly, Massimo was right. The porter was no longer there, and this was thoroughly upsetting. Bonomi, a good Fascist, had always run his prison with what had been known in the Party as "English precision" (that is, until that abominable foreign secretary had imposed sanctions). One was prompt in answering doorbells, telephones, and letters. One also walked with a good brisk pace, like the Duce. That was the whole fun of fascism. The rest, admittedly, could be messy. But that was not Bonomi's concern; he was only a humble lieutenant colonel in a soft job, working toward his pension.

He opened a drawer, took out a pistol, and slipped it into its holster. "Let's go," he said.

Massimo led the way with Bonomi's big flashlight. The doors

creaked apart. For a brief moment, Bonomi wondered how Massimo had become so familiar with the way to find the keys, and the way to manipulate the several locks. But what met him when the doors swung open drove such thoughts from his mind.

A group of men—mostly, at a quick judgment, in the prime of life—stood outside in the rain. They all had weapons, and these were all pointed at the lieutenant colonel. Bonomi laid his hand on his pistol holster. Then he thought better of it.

"What is your business?" he asked sharply, in the authoritative voice that had become the fashion for all members of the Party.

"We are the Committee for Liberation," said the man in front.

"I have never heard of it," said Bonomi.

A voice from the back of the group said, "We have only just set it up," but the man who had first spoken said, "Be quiet."

Then he went on: "We are not here to bandy words. The whole city has risen. We are fighting the oppressor."

"For a Better World. For Equality. For Justice," said the same voice at the back.

"Be quiet," said the man in front.

At the moment, these men were making no great impression, and they were aware of it. But history would do them justice. They would later be known as "partisans," those intrepid fighters against tyranny, who, later, in the north of Italy, were to perform feats of great courage and daring. They have become familiar in films and books: men almost invariably in raincoats with belts, and holding guns or automatic weapons.

That was in the prosperous North. These men were Neapolitans. They had guns, but no raincoats. Those who had possessed them had pawned or sold them long ago for food. They did, however, have umbrellas, mostly a sober black, but one or two brightly colored, which they had borrowed from their wives.

The storm at that moment produced one of the quick, drenching showers, over soon, but very wetting, that are characteristic of a storm in the Naples area.

"I don't understand," said Bonomi. He spread his legs apart and put his hands on his hips.

"Your days are numbered," said a very short man in a menacing voice. "Your sort, I mean," he added.

"Are you going to keep us standing outside in this dreadful weather," said the first man, "or can we have a civilized colloquy?"

It was a lovely word. Rhetoric was one of Bonomi's weaknesses.

"I'll give you exactly five minutes by my wristwatch for a colloquy. You may come inside."

They came inside quickly, dripping water from the brims of their hats. They gathered in the arched and covered space beside the porter's lodge.

"To begin," said the first man. "We know you have arms. Every prison has, in case of revolt. We need arms and ammunition to distribute."

"To the proletariat," said one of the band.

"And others," said another argumentatively.

"To all Freedom Fighters," said the spokesman, wrapping up the matter neatly. "You will give them to us."

"I will do nothing of the sort," said Bonomi. "I am an officer and a Party member. I have taken an oath of allegiance to His Majesty the king. I intend to abide by that oath."

"Ah, but where *is* the king?" said one of the men.

"On the lam," said another.

Bonomi rose magnificently to the occasion. "I do not know what you mean by your vulgar expressions. But if His Majesty is in difficulties, that is all the more reason why I should be loyal to my oath. What else," he said resonantly, "is an oath for?"

Nobody spoke. There were subtle answers to the question and they were being found all over Italy. But, wet as they were, the armed band could not think of one.

The leader knew that in such a crisis there was only one answer for a revolutionary. He raised his rifle. "I could shoot you dead and just walk in and take what we want," he said. "That would absolve you from your oath."

Obviously the man was educated. Obviously he did not want to shoot. Obviously, said Bonomi to himself, I am being a damned fool; they might pull the trigger any moment. Bonomi's scalp crawled.

"We don't *want* to kill you," said another man.

"My wife wouldn't like it if we did," said another in a most reasonable voice. "You were good to our boy when he got into trouble."

"Mine, too," said another.

Bonomi licked his dry lips. "I suggest an honorable compromise," he said. "I will hand over to you my pistol. That is mine. I bought it myself with my own money because," he added, a little carried away, "the government issue was no good at all. I have a perfect right to do that. I also have the right to do my duty and not let you get at the guns. You are reasonable men. You are idealists. I can see that."

"We are," said two of the band together, while the man who had spoken before repeated, "We are fighting for Equality and Justice. And," he went on as this time nobody told him to be quiet, "for an end to Repression, from whatever quarter it may come."

"I shall consult my colleagues," said the leader.

They turned their backs on Bonomi to make a huddle. Bonomi noticed, with a flash of his military training, that they were now pointing their weapons at one another.

"We agree," said the leader, turning back to him. "I do not, myself, agree at all. I would not have started this mission if I'd thought it was going to end with one miserable pistol. But you have won good opinions from the people, and from now on—mark my words and mark them carefully, Colonel Bonomi—it is the will of the people that will prevail."

Bonomi handed over his pistol, adding the belt and holster for good measure. The leader immediately strapped it around his own waist.

"We bid you goodnight," he said.

"Goodnight," said several of the others; and one said, as he got outside, "Look, it's stopped raining."

Bonomi felt unsteady on his legs. Then he took one or two deep breaths and felt better.

"Massimo," he said. "Massimo. *Massimo!*"

But Massimo, like the porter and the warders, had gone home.

———

The storm had abated, but it seemed to have transferred itself to Bonomi's mind. His staff had deserted him; Massimo had vanished into thin air while he was dealing with strange men talking treason. He returned to his meal, which had congealed on its plate. He could not eat it. He was not any longer a well-informed man—and without that, what was he? A soldier on the shelf, earning his living out of naughty boys, who had threatened— No! The thought was too much for him. He would go to his best friend.

He put on his greatcoat. He went out by the back door, to

which, thank heaven, only he had the key. The streets were quite deserted and dark. He switched on his flashlight and made his way to the one man who, he was sure, could make him well informed again.

He found the apartment house. It was dark except for a window or two where some form of extemporary lighting lit up the rooms of his friend. He rang. There was no answer. Again he rang. No answer once more. It seemed that another porter had left his post. But why?

A window opened above him.

"Yes?" It was his friend.

"It's me."

"Shine your light on your face."

"Surely you know my voice. Oh, well—" He did as he was told. "Ugly as ever," he joked feebly.

"I'll throw down the keys. Lock the door after you."

It was with this chilling welcome that he met his long-time counselor and guide. He, too, was a colonel, but a real one, in the carabinieri, and attached (though few knew it) to army and Party intelligence.

He led Bonomi straight to his bedroom. An open suitcase was on the bed, and various items of clothing, civilian as well as military, were scattered around it.

"There's a little Campari left in the bottle in the dining room. It's all I can offer you."

"No, thanks. You're—you're going somewhere?"

"Tonight. My wife's gone already."

"Where?"

"Capri. My cousin has a villa there. He says that on Capri they don't even know there's a war on unless they listen to the radio. Seems the Allies have left it to itself. Not a bomb, not a shell. No doubt the British and the Yanks want a nice rest in a nice place when they take over."

"Will they?"

"Without doubt. The Germans aren't going to defend Naples. They're making a stand at Cassino. The monastery's ideal. High up over the only road fit for tanks. It'll be a long business."

He put some shirts and jackets into his suitcase. He went to a chest of drawers, and while he was rummaging he said, "Worried, old friend?"

"Believe it or not, that Massimo you told me to use as an informer—he's slipped off, by the way—"

"He always was a boy with his head on his shoulders. Ah, there the damned things are. My best cuff links. The British are dressy."

"Massimo told me that the boys . . ." and he repeated his news that they meant to lock him up and burn down the prison. "Can that be *true?*" he asked, with pathos.

The intelligence man pressed down the lid of his suitcase, which sprang up again because the case was very full. He paused in his packing.

"I don't think they mean to burn you to a crisp. That's just bad planning. The eager boy's mind. They'll certainly lock you up. How else could they set the prison alight? But when it's burning merrily, how can they get back to release you? You see, they hadn't thought of that. You can't blame them. They're only boys."

For years Bonomi had admired his friend's keen and logical mind, but just now his enthusiasm waned.

"Then there were some men at the door. They said the city is in revolt—some nonsense like that. Is that true?"

"The boys," said his friend, struggling with the suitcase lid, "started riots all over the place. The *scugnizzi.* The men are joining in. Scholl's frightened. I say, old friend, would you very much mind sitting on this case of mine? I think I can get it closed that way."

Bonomi sat on the lid while his friend pushed at the locks.

When the locks were closed, Bonomi still sat enthroned on the suitcase. He was too upset to think of getting down.

"But what am I to do? What am I to *do?*"

"I think the locks will hold if those damned Capri porters don't fling the thing about as they always do. Eh? My dear friend, it is I who should be asking you that question, and I would be if it weren't for my cousin with his villa. I've told you. The town's on the rampage. Just think what they would do to me if they found me. I've told you the gist of the thing—"

"You always have," said Bonomi gratefully. "But—"

"I've told you it's the *scugnizzi* who started this thing. Masaniello and all that. History repeating itself. You've read about it at school, eh?"

"Oh, yes."

"Well, then, use your head, dear friend. Supposing you'd been governor of a boys' jail under the Spaniards and there the other kids were, roaring through the streets. What would your wisest course have been?"

"Um," said Bonomi. "Er—well, open the doors, eh?"

"Exactly. *I'm* going to Capri to wait for the Allies. *You* open the doors and join the revolt. With your own faithful and friendly boys. Then, when the Allies come into Naples, as they will, there you are, a national hero."

"Why is it I can never think of things like that?" said Bonomi, getting up.

"Because you haven't lived as I have, for years, expecting to get a knife in your back every dark night. Now, I'm packed, and the car's due any minute. What about emptying the dregs of that bottle? No use leaving it for the bloodthirsty, murdering, raping etcetera and etcetera enemy, eh? Ah, I forgot. There's an English dictionary somewhere on the shelves. Be a good fellow and hold the lamp while I look for it, will you?"

The boys filed into the chapel at six the next morning, and Bonomi watched them. They were all much too wide awake. They were all too silent. And why didn't they look at him? From his long experience of boys, he knew that trouble was brewing. He had warned the priest to be quick, and he had told him why.

The priest now came in, vested for the Mass. The two acolytes took their places. The priest deposited the chalice on the altar and, quite outside the conventions of the liturgy, took a nervous look over his shoulder. When he said "Dominus vobiscum, the Lord be with you," the boys replied at the tops of their voices, "And with your spirit," in such a menacing manner that the priest got his place in the missal wrong and had to fumble.

But from then on the ceremony went without hitch. Indeed it went on so fast that the acolytes were positively hopping from position to position. Not since David danced in front of the ark of the Lord had an altar seen such animation. At last came the word, "Go, the Mass is ended," and the priest trotted off to safety.

"I've got a word to say to you all," said Bonomi, rising in his place. "Please remain seated." He went to the pulpit. He cleared his throat.

"You boys know that I am a well-informed man," and the boys

listened in silence to this beginning which was in its way as inevitable as the words of the Mass.

"The looters that I mentioned yesterday evening have been put down. And by whom? By boys—yes, boys. Your own friends and companions, the boys we call, not always as a compliment, *scugnizzi*. But believe me, and I am usually well informed, when at long last the Americans and the English and the French arrive in our beloved and much-tried city, those boys will be heroes. Because they fought against the Germans? Not entirely. But because they fought to defend their mothers and sisters and little brothers. Heroes, I say, to the forces of liberation."

He paused for breath. He surveyed the faces before him. They were without any expression whatever, in the way that only a boy in front of an elder can make his face a blank.

Bonomi resumed. "I see from your surprised expressions that you wonder how I can be so sure that the Americans and those others I mentioned will, in fact, come to our city. All I can tell you is that I have inside information that it will be so. Inside information that I have every reason to trust."

The boys still showed no signs. Bonomi wished he had a glass of water, but that is not a thing found in chapels. He went on manfully.

"Now, I wish to put a question to you, all of you collectively and each of you one by one. When those *scugnizzi* are being feted and put on the radio and given medals and all the things that go with being a hero, what will be *your* position? What will you say when people ask you, 'What did *you* do in the famous rising in Naples?' Will you say, 'I had the bad luck to be temporarily the guest of the government'? And years later, when you are married and you have boys of your own, what will you say when they ask, 'What did you do, papa, when the boys were fighting? I bet you were out in front, papa, weren't you?' "

This last touch, which Bonomi liked, again went for nothing. The boys' eyes never left his face, but they might have been images of stone. Bonomi's mouth became so dry he felt that he would have drunk the Communion wine if it had not been locked up. He braced himself for the climax.

"I do not wish these children of yours to be told that Colonel Bonomi blighted your lives. I shall be dead and gone by then, but

I wish to be remembered as a man who knew how to behave on a great, a historic, an unforgettable occasion. I myself am going to join those brave boys. I have spent the better part of my life with boys. If it will be my fate to stop a bullet, then let it be among them. Any of you"—and he threw away this last line with great art, even turning his head—"any of you who wish to follow me are welcome to do so."

There was, at last, a stirring and a whispering in his audience. He sat down on the priest's stool.

Then Andrea got to his feet. "Signor Governor."

"Yes?"

"The guns."

"What guns, boy?"

"You have eight rifles and ammunition in your office. We will go with you if you give us the guns."

"They are not my property. They are not mine to give."

"Then we shall go without them. We decided last night in the dormitory," Andrea went on in the calmest of voices, "that, as you say, we had to join our friends. We also decided to do something else." The calm voice had turned menacing on the last words, and the boys nodded.

Bonomi had an instant's vision of himself sitting at his desk, locked in his room, a fire raging outside, all for eight rather out-dated rifles. He came to a decision.

"It is true that your friends and companions will welcome any addition to their arsenal."

He had regained his self-confidence. "Arsenal" was a splendid word.

"You tell me there are eight rifles. I really cannot say. When, years and years ago, they were consigned to my care, I put the key to the cupboard behind the statue of the Madonna which you all know I keep in my office. I have never had occasion to take them out." He opened his two arms like a pope or a cardinal preparing to give a blessing, and he smiled a broad, slow smile.

In a second the chapel rang to a sound it had never before heard. The boys were standing on the benches, shouting and cheering. Then they scrambled down and made a rush for the door.

Bonomi had often marveled at the slowness of boys when it came to teaching them anything, such as woodwork or metalwork, or simply reading and writing. He was now amazed at the speed with which they learned to load, aim, and fire a gun. In less than an hour they were marching behind him up the Via Santa Teresa, the first four couples with rifles at the slope and bandoliers over the shoulders. He even ventured to say, "One two, one two, left, left, left," and the boys cheerfully obeyed. Bonomi was a happy man. He only wished he had a flag. But then, *which* flag? For a few hundred feet of the march, Bonomi's doubts came back. Was he, after all, doing the right thing? But then all doubts vanished because they heard the sound of firing.

The Via Santa Teresa ends in the Bridge of the Sanità. It is probably unique in the world, because it does not run over a river, or some similar uninhabited place, but over the roofs of houses, a great huddle of them, inhabited by some of the poorest people in Naples. There is a large church to serve their spiritual needs, with several tiled domes. The bridge is level with the base of the domes. Men with rifles were hiding behind the domes and, every so often, darting out, kneeling, and shooting at the bridge. At the end of the bridge, which Bonomi and his boys were now approaching, were some overturned carts and piles of paving stones. Sheltered by these were some *scugnizzi* and students. They, too, were firing. But most of the firing came from the windows of the houses that stood by the end of the bridge.

In the middle of the bridge a group of German soldiers were huddled behind two trucks. They were fighting back, but they were very frightened men. Very early in the morning they had come to blow up the bridge. It connected a hill behind Naples with the city itself, straddling the ravine that separated the city from the hill of Capodimonte. Their action was part of the plan to reduce Naples to mud and ashes, but it had been specially chosen for the spectacular result that would be produced when the mines went off. The bridge would collapse on the roofs of the houses below, killing or maiming all who lived in them. Moreover, the twisted iron girders of the bridge would stand up amid the shambles, an eloquent lesson to all who saw it.

A street boy had, however, seen the Germans in the gray light of the morning of the twenty-ninth. Instantly he spread the news.

Youths and boys and some men gathered in a side street. Arms and ammunition were distributed. The Germans, as soon as they became aware of what was happening, detailed some among them to keep up a protecting fire. But they soon gave up trying to lay any more sticks of dynamite; the firing of the Neapolitans was not very accurate, but, clearly, the bridge, or at least part of it, could be blown up with them on it.

Bonomi arrived with his boys, stopping just short of the fighting area. The moment lost some of the drama Bonomi had expected, because a mother ran out on a balcony and, waving her arms, frantically called, "Tatore! What are you doing here, you little devil? Go back to prison at once, at *once*, I say. Here was I thinking you were safe and sound behind bars and what do I see but you getting yourself into this mess. Go back, I say!"

Tatore was a thirteen-year-old. He was not one of those fortunate enough to have a rifle, but he had no intention of leaving the battle. He imagined he would be able to pick up a rifle from some fallen companion as was done in the comics he had seen. However, a mother is a mother, and so Tatore broke ranks and, looking up at the balcony, said, "It's all right, mamma. I can't go back to the prison because there isn't one anymore. The governor has let us all out because he wants us to help him fight the Germans."

"What with, your bare fists?" asked his mother at the top of her voice.

"Well, no. We've got guns. I mean, look there." He pointed to the leading boys who were now some distance away. "I mean *I* haven't got one yet, but as soon as one of those up there falls wounded or something, I'll get his gun and—"

"Wounded!" screamed his mother, now near hysteria. "You'll come right up here at once or I'll send your father after you!"

"All right. I'm coming," said Tatore. He saw that the boys were dispersing and disappearing into alleys. "I'll just have to report to the governor to tell him where to find me."

"You'll come right up here as I bid you."

"Sorry, mamma, prison rules. Home leave: you have to tell the governor where you are. Remember?" and he joined the other boys as fast as his legs would carry him.

His mother, leaning dangerously over the balcony to follow him, saw him speak to a group of youths, then disappear as though by magic. She sighed. She knew enough not to try to follow him. He was a *scugnizzo*, and not even the carabinieri could catch one of those when they chose to hide. "Wounded," she said, and shuddered. She went inside and said a quick prayer to the picture of San Gennaro. He looked cold and unhappy. The little red light that always burned before him had gone out days ago when the electricity had failed.

Her husband was shaving over a tin bowl, peering into the small mirror. "Was that Tatore I heard you shouting at?" he said.

"Yes."

"In trouble again?"

"He's gone to fight the Germans. I told him to come back."

"I don't suppose he will," said her husband. He ran a hand over his chin.

"No. The *scugnizzi* have gone right out of their minds," she said. "So has everybody else. The colonel's let all his boys out of jail, and that's why Tatore—oh, I don't understand anything anymore. I'm tired," she said, and sat heavily on a chair.

Her husband put on his jacket. "I'll see if I can find him," he said. Then he opened a cupboard and felt around inside. He brought out a revolver.

"What's that?" asked his wife.

"What's it look like? One of the kids gave it to me last night. They're handing them out everywhere. Well, I'll see you soon. I feel like doing a little fighting myself."

And like hundreds of other men of all ages on that Wednesday morning of September 29, he went to join the battle.

CHAPTER FIFTEEN

Scholl paced the lobby of the Hotel Parco, every so often going out onto the steps and looking up and down the road. Once he tripped over one of the elegant chairs with their spindly legs, and he kicked it so that it broke.

Then a motorcycle drove up, and, before it had properly stopped, an officer jumped out of the sidecar. He entered the hotel at a run, drew up, and saluted Scholl. Scholl did not return the salute, unless a more than usually violent twitch of his cheek could be thought to serve.

"Does it take you two hours to find out what a pack of street urchins is up to?" he said.

"No, sir."

"Then where in God's name have you been?"

"All over the city, sir. And it's not just urchins, sir, anymore. It's men. Armed men. I was shot at three times, sir."

"Where?" Scholl demanded. "Where? Tell me that and I'll have the whole street blasted sky-high."

"Very good, sir. May I consult the map, sir?"

"Yes, yes, yes. Go in, go in," and they went into the room with the green baize table, the two pictures, and the map on a stand. There were several more circles on it of the kind that the lieutenant hated so much, and as usual the names of the tiny streets and alleys were often obliterated.

"Well, sir," the observer said, pulling off his gloves, "the attacks took place around here," and he placed a finger on a piazza on the hill behind the hotel headquarters. "Piazza Vanvitelli."

Scholl seized a crayon and circled the place. "I'll burn those boys' backsides good and proper," he said.

"It wasn't a *scugnizzo*, sir. That's the Neapolitan word for a street urchin, sir," he explained politely.

Scholl roared at him: "In the last twenty-four hours, at least a dozen of my staff have explained that to me. Do they think I am an idiot?"

"No, sir."

"Then who *did* shoot at you?"

"A man, sir. About thirty years old. Armed with a rifle I judged to be a nineteen fourteen vintage and—"

"Did you shoot back?"

"No, sir. He was behind a barricade. It would have been difficult to hit him, and I was already late on my mission."

"You damned well were. Another barricade?"

"There are dozens all over the city. Nothing much to speak of, sir. A few upturned carts, rubble, old furniture. One of our tanks could go through it like paper."

"The tactics you will kindly leave to me," said Scholl, for he had detected something patronizing in the professional army man's voice. "Just now, confine yourself to information. Indicate on the map where these barricades are."

He put his finger in several places. "Those I have checked personally. There are reports of more."

"Is this just a rabble, or is it being organized?"

"I found this, sir," said the lieutenant, and he took a sheet of notepaper from his pocket. "I saw a respectable, well-dressed man pin it up on a tree with a thumbtack, so I stopped and sequestered it."

Scholl studied it. "Get me the interpreter."

The man went. In a few moments the interpreter came in.

"This may be important," said Scholl. "Tell me what it says."

The interpreter read silently, then raised his eyebrows.

"Well?" said Scholl impatiently.

"It says, '*I assume temporarily all powers, civil and military.*'"

Scholl's mouth fell open.

" '*Everyone will do his duty. Discipline must be absolute. All manifestations that will disturb public order are forbidden. All shops will remain open. Revolutionary action squads will ensure order in all food shops and establishments.*' It is headed," went on the interpreter, " 'the Single Revolutionary Front.'"

Scholl closed his mouth. "And who, may I ask," he said with heavy sarcasm, "has assumed full powers, civil and military?"

"Let me see. The rain has smudged it a bit," said the interpreter. "Yes. '*Signed for the Command, Antonino Tarsia in Curia.*'"

"Who is he?"

"The name goes back into history, I believe," said the interpreter cautiously.

"From the tone of that piece of paper, it goes back to Julius Caesar. I did not ask you that. I asked, 'Who is he?'"

"Then I must admit I do not know," said the interpreter.

Scholl took the paper back. He studied it as though he could understand it. Then, like a fortune-teller raising her gaze from her crystal ball, he said, "It is perfectly plain. We are dealing with a communist revolution. I knew it all along."

The interpreter remembered that Scholl had known all along that he was dealing with a pack of students. Had he not burned down the university to prove his point? Then, the interpreter had refrained from arguing. He did the same now.

"We shall nip it in the bud," said Scholl. "I have avoided any overt show of force until now. I have relied on the common sense of the Neapolitans. Communism is another matter."

He strode to the door. He looked out into the adjoining salon where the bar was and called to an officer who was drinking beer there. The officer, a major, came over to his superior with a graceful carriage and a respectful but by no means servile look. His uniform was elegant, his face long and perfectly shaved, and it had the required scar of the Regular Army officer. Scholl motioned him inside. He took him over to the map.

"I have evidence that we are fighting a communist uprising. It is well organized. It must be crushed immediately. I shall use tanks. They are still, I take it, parked here." He put his finger on the hill of Capodimonte.

"They are," said the major easily. "According to your orders. Away from the city to prevent sabotage, and poised for a sudden descent if needed. An excellent tactical decision, if I may say so."

"Thank you." Scholl's usually expressionless face showed a slight glow as if to indicate that the major might indeed say so, and more if he should wish.

"Now, we should strike right at the heart of the city. The Communists have barricaded this off," Scholl said, moving his finger down to the Piazza Plebiscito. "They have caused us some trouble, and they will now pay for it. There is a straight road right from Capodimonte to that piazza," and his finger traced a line down the road that led over the Bridge of the Sanità, Via Santa Teresa, and the Toledo. It was impressively straight. As his finger moved, it crossed a red circle.

"The attack must be sudden," Scholl continued. "A complete surprise. And our reaction to this communist challenge must be without mercy. Can I leave the details to you, Major?"

"Naturally, Herr Kommandant. But there is one difficulty."

"The thing seems straightforward enough to me, Major."

"It would be, but for that red circle. That is a bridge which it would have been essential for the tanks to cross. It no longer exists. You ordered it to be blown up."

Scholl stared at the red circle. All three men were silent.

The major coughed behind his hand. "A very good *strategical* decision," he said, and his hand served to cover a little smile while it lasted. "Its destruction must have had a profound effect on the morale of the citizens. Even perhaps on the organizers of the—er—communist revolution."

"I am glad you think so," said Scholl, as much put out as ever the interpreter had seen him. Then he recovered himself.

"So. Thus. It is clear," said Scholl briskly. "The tanks cannot go that way. So they go another way." He motioned to the interpreter to come to the map. "You know the city well. Be so good as to show us another way. The best for tanks."

"This," said the interpreter, and indicated a road going in the opposite direction. It did not turn back into the city until it went right off the map.

"That will do then," said Scholl, with a certain amount of relief in his voice.

"Scarcely," said the major. "I regret to say that while that would be a good *tactical* solution to our problem, *strategically* it has its drawbacks." This time he made no attempt to hide the fact that he was enjoying the two words to the hilt. "That road is the road to Capua. You can see that the name is there in small print, in the margin. Capua is well on the way to Rome. Thus if our striking force adopts that route, it will seem to every observer that our forces are in full retreat. Which is not, I take it, the impression we wish to give the population. It would only encourage the—ah—Communist rebels."

When your headquarters staff turn into a pack of obstructive buggers, get in touch with the officer on the spot. The words Scholl had heard in Rome from a friendly general came back to him. He had been nervous at being given the Naples command and, for once, he had sought advice. The general, well plied with wine from the Castelli, had obliged copiously.

"I shall get in touch with Capodimonte," he said, as decisively as he could manage in these very difficult circumstances.

"Certainly, Herr Kommandant," said the major. "He will no doubt have a solution. We can get him on the radio. May I have your message, sir? I will take it to the operations room myself immediately."

"No," said Scholl. "I'll go." If he had really made a fool of himself, the radio operator was too humble a person to risk a smirk. He left the room.

The major picked up the announcement of the Single Revolutionary Front. "Typewritten," he said. "Is there anything in this about a communist revolt? Nothing would seem to be less likely in Naples. Rome Intelligence assured us—"

"That there were practically no Communists in the city," said the interpreter. "And they were right. The Party rooted them out years ago. 'Tarsia in Curia,' " he said, reading the signature. "The name is ancient. Almost noble. I should think that this"—and he pointed at the sheet—"really *is* the work of one of those students that Scholl was so fond of talking about—until now, of course, when he's got Communists on the brain."

"Poor Scholl," said the major. "I almost hope there is another way out from Capodimonte—one, I mean, that doesn't mean we show the Neapolitans our tails."

"Not for tanks," said the interpreter. "Well, we seem to have been left by our commandant to our own devices. May I suggest a drink?"

"By all means. Scholl dragged me away from a beer. . . ."

The two men went to the bar.

Fifteen minutes later, Scholl came back. He had a message form in his hand which he was reading intently. He looked up, saw the major, and made a sign that he should follow him. When they were both inside the door, he closed it.

"I got through to Capodimonte. The unit that was to blow up the bridge has returned without completing its mission."

"Then the bridge is still there?"

"Yes."

"Excellent, but excellent," said the major. "Then your plan for a sudden and spectacular descent on the city will hold."

"Yes," said Scholl. "But the unit was driven back by"—he read from the message—" 'intense and sustained fire from civilians, apparently militia.' We have our hands full with these Communists, Major, we have our hands full."

Nobody, not even Lenin in exile on Capri, would start a revolution if he were the sort of person who faces facts. Revolutionaries turn their backs on them; they prefer their dreams of power, for themselves, or for a heaven on earth for everybody. So it was with Antonino Tarsia in Curia.

He returned to his wife, bloodstained and a shattered man. But only for a while. His wife cooked him a meal. He changed into his second-best suit. He went for a stroll. He went to bed. By the early morning, when he woke up, that boy's life, for Antonino, had not been lost in vain. The revolution was accomplished, at least in his mind. He, like Lenin, was its leader, its theoretician, its organizer. He sat down at his typewriter, still in the midst of his waking dream, and typed out his first proclamation.

He read it over several times, and once aloud. He was satisfied. It was sober, sensible, practical. He put on his hat and went to find a printer. Only when he was outside the local printer's shop did he realize that weeks ago the machinery had been looted by the Germans, and the proprietor had taken refuge in the country.

Never mind. Some disruption accompanied all historic changes; true leaders knew how to rise above it. He returned home, hung up his hat, and once more sat down at his typewriter. He opened the drawer of his desk to find carbon paper, and then remembered there had been none in Naples for months. Again, never mind. Slowly, with one finger, he typed out twelve clear copies. With a broad-nibbed pen he signed all twelve.

His wife peeped over his shoulder and was satisfied. That dreadful experience with the boy was no longer haunting her husband. He was back at his hobby.

She told him breakfast was ready, but she could scarcely persuade him to sit down and eat the slice of sausage and drink the glass of water that was all she could provide. He was soon out of the house, walking fast and determinedly.

He eyed his surroundings for likely trees, telegraph poles, or shuttered windows. Having found one, he pinned up his notice. He stepped back each time and surveyed it, or walked a little past it to see if it would catch his eye. It would do: it would do very well. The first action the Revolutionary Council (summoned by himself and chaired by himself) must take would be to set up a printing press and a newspaper. Then the declaration would reel off the machine in hundreds. Some would be jealously preserved, to appear under glass fifty years later in commemorative exhibitions, dominated by a huge portrait of Antonino Tarsia in Curia, chairman of the First Revolutionary Council. Or should he be the secretary? It would seem secretaries were the ones with the real power.

And thus, humming the "Internationale," he went his rounds. He was a little surprised to see a German in a motorcycle and sidecar pull up behind him. The Nazis should all be gone by now. But perhaps these were some belated soldiers on their way out. He went on his way happily.

There never was to be that committee. There was no organization, nor would the shops reopen or the population go quietly about their business—not, at least, till the Allies arrived. Antonino was never chairman or secretary. Years later, he died in his bed, poor and neglected. But Scholl was as convinced as he that a revolt had started, and both took their measures. Others, as a result, were not so fortunate as to die in their beds. But one of them is remembered, at least by anyone who stops to read the marble slab high up on a wall near the Piazza Plebiscito. He was Filippo Illuminato.

A man lay in the bedroom of a house that overlooked the Bridge of the Sanità. The left leg of his trousers had been split open, and blood oozed from a wound. His wife tightened the tourniquet once more.

"Pray God it hasn't reached the bone," said the man. "Another second and that man wouldn't have got me. Did you get any news of the doctor?"

"He says he'll come as soon as he can. There's lots more who got hit. Two were taken off to the hospital. There, that's as tight as it will go."

"Thanks. Maria, I'm sorry. I didn't mean to get shot."

"No. I've always known you were foolish, but I don't think you'd be as foolish as that." She laughed, and stroked his hair. "I'm not blaming you. You and the others saved the bridge. And think of all those people down below. Where would the poor souls be now if you and the boys hadn't fought? Those boys. I'll never forget them."

There was a knock at the door.

"That'll be the doctor." She went and brought the doctor in. He was bent and gray and grim with a lifetime of treating the poor, those who had an illness he knew he could never cure, their endless poverty.

He put down his bag, probed, moved the man's leg.

"The bone's safe. You're damned lucky. We must get you somewhere quick to get that bullet out. You'll have to wait your turn. The only transport we have is the butcher's wagon—he took the meat daily to those bastards who shot you. Well, you asked for it. Never have I seen men ask for it as you all did. Worse than the boys. But they were just boys."

And so, as he bathed and bandaged, he rambled on.

Then came a grinding noise and a roar of engines that grew louder and louder each minute.

"Maria—*ahh!*—no, doctor, it's not hurting—Maria, go to the window and see what that is. That noise."

She came back white-faced. "It's tanks. Four of them. They're coming down from Capodimonte. Coming quite fast."

The noise changed its tone to a thunderous drumming. Maria went back to the window.

"They're on the bridge. They're coming straight at us. They're . . ."

But her last words were drowned by the roar of the cannon.

"Get away from that window!" the doctor shouted, and both crouched on the floor. The cannon spoke steadily. The house shook, and there was the noise of falling masonry, and screams for help.

Then the windows stopped rattling and the house no longer trembled. The tanks had passed. But the screaming continued. Then they heard a man shouting a name.

"That's for me," said the doctor, packing his bag. "It looks as if our friends in those tanks have left plenty of work for me behind them. Now you lie still. Don't try to get up, and, Maria, give him only liquids for a bit. I'll be back as soon as the butcher's back. Well," he said to his patient, "I'll bet the Germans are grateful to you fellows for saving the bridge for them. They should give you a medal. *Arrivederci.*" And he went.

"Hear what the doctor said?" Maria asked the wounded man when she had closed the door. Her husband made no answer. "About the Germans being grateful. I mean, if you hadn't saved the bridge—I mean—I mean it wouldn't be there and the tanks wouldn't—I don't think I know *what* I mean."

"I don't understand either," said her husband.

The screaming started again.

"Still, there were those people under the bridge. Either them or—"

"Or that poor woman yelling her head off."

"Either them or us," said her husband. "No. It's no use. I don't understand. I just did my bit as seemed right at the time." He groaned as he moved his leg.

"Just don't try to think," said Maria consolingly. "You see," she said as he groaned again, "it makes your leg hurt."

The technique of cowing a civilian population in a city by means of tanks has been greatly improved since Scholl's day. But he and his forces had the rudiments. The successors of Antonino Tarsia in Curia's hero, Lenin, conquered, years later, Prague and Budapest with an operation that had the same fundamental aim: fright, a bowel-turning fright. Tanks, in this respect, save lives and to a certain extent property, when compared with aerial bombardment. You cannot see the bomb that is going to kill you: you do see the long cannon pointing straight at your head.

The tanks moved away from the Bridge of the Sanità and the

death and destruction they were leaving behind them. For the next three or four hundred yards of their progress, they would do nothing and nobody any harm. That method increased the uncertainty of the watchers, and saved ammunition. The long cannon, however, continued to gyrate with their armored turrets—first to the left, then straight ahead, then to the right, their muzzles slightly depressed so that they looked straight into ground-floor windows, or at anybody on the sidewalk. After this pacific interval, they would open fire, anywhere, and at no particular target. Then, once again, the respite. It was all as orderly and timed as a prison hanging.

Maria had not been the best of observers. Scholl had already lost one unprotected tank. Now two armored cars moved in step with the column, like the armed escorts that nowadays ride by the high and mighty. Tanks and cars moved slowly down the slope of Via Santa Teresa. At the crossroads by the great pink bulk of the Archaeological Museum, a machine gun opened fire on them from a rooftop. The tanks ignored it, the bullets bouncing off their thick plating. But the armored cars swung up their machine guns and spat briefly. A young man toppled from the roof and fell into the street. The procession moved on.

Piazza Dante was deserted. So was the Toledo. It seemed as though a mysterious plague had visited the city during the night and killed off its inhabitants. All the same, the cannon in the leading tank duly fired. It was a shot to be remembered, if not by the gunner, then by the Neapolitans. Hundreds of families live in small rooms known as *bassi* because they are on ground level. A wife, husband, children, and a baby in its mother's arms had gathered in one such modest home. The shell made short work of the *basso* and its contents, namely the entire family. The horror of putting the dismembered bodies of people of such varying ages together again so that the family could have a decent burial has lingered to this day in the minds of those who had the job. But the raw and bloody jigsaw was put together, at least approximately.

The tanks reached that part of the Toledo which was flanked by the narrow alleys and barricades of Montecalvario. Ahead could be seen the barricade that cut off the Piazza Plebiscito. Peering through his binoculars, the leader of the punitive expedition did not feel that the citizens had done a very good job. The barricades seemed flimsy and too low.

The night before, very few people in Montecalvario had slept more than an hour or two. The euphoria of the daytime was dissipated by the dark. Young men and boys gathered at street corners, holding their guns, and talked in the gloom. A lighted lantern would gather an audience as soon as it was seen, and everywhere the word was of Niello. He moved from group to group, talking, persuading. The tanks would come back to clear away the barricade. He wanted to be sure that everybody knew what to do.

"I've talked to a prisoner of war who knows about tanks," he said again and again. "When you've got one on its own—going back to its garage, or wherever it is they keep them—then our hand bombs and our gasoline bombs are fine. If you're quick, you can get near enough for aiming before they spot you. That's when the tank's on its own. But when they come back, they won't be. There'll be other tanks, one watching the other. And if the gunners are busy firing, there'll be armored cars on the alert. If you see that, hide. What we want is for them to go straight for the barricade. They'll go through it, and one or two will maybe get the mines we've laid. But let them find an empty piazza, or there'll be a massacre."

A middle-aged man, his sharp features emphasized by the light of a lamp, leaned on his shotgun and said, to all and sundry, "He's right, more or less. I've fought in tanks in Ethiopia, and you do like to feel you've got something behind you to back you up in case of trouble. Still . . ."

"Still what?" demanded a listening young man.

"Well, the niggers used to come right out at us and chuck their bombs. Yelling, some of them were. Just as Niello says, some of them didn't yell for long. We saw to that. But some of them got away. Nimble as bloody monkeys they were. You couldn't help admiring them. Of course they were the enemy. But you couldn't help admiring them," he repeated lamely.

Filippo Illuminato was just thirteen. He lived in a road next to the warren of Montecalvario. It is called Via Nardones and runs into an irregular piazza that is in itself part of Piazza Plebiscito, a sort of small and cozier antechamber to the vast square with its two bronze horses.

Via Nardones (called, invariably, "Nardone" by the people) is not the slum that makes up Montecalvario. The people who lived in it had certain standards. They sent their children to school, and Filippo duly went. He was a friendly boy, a little reserved and thoughtful at times, but one who, once he had chosen a friend, held that friend's affection.

One such friend was Lello. He was at school with Filippo. If you can persuade him to speak of Filippo today, he cannot do so without tears coming to his eyes. It is a strange place to see a man cry, for he is today the cheerful barman in the ruins of the ancient city of Pompeii. He is full of jokes. But when he speaks of Filippo, he does not joke for a long time afterward. He polishes the glasses in which he serves his drinks, polishes them when they are already gleaming. It helps him to forget and to be cheerful again as his job demands.

Filippo was not really a *scugnizzo*, except in the sense that any cheerful, active boy from the poorer quarters of Naples might be called that. He did not indulge in their tricks, nor their breaking of the law. But the true *scugnizzi* were his neighbors in Montecalvario, and thus his friends. Perhaps, like any thirteen-year-old who has to go to school, he admired and envied their freedom, especially after that first great day of triumph when they had held the Rinascente.

Just now he followed Niello around, drinking in what was said, but, boylike, not committing it to his memory. Besides, Niello's advice seemed rather dull. The man with the shotgun and his tale of niggers were more exciting. He went to bed very late and dreamed of tanks, and of fighting them.

He sought Niello and the *scugnizzi* the first thing next day. Some were busy making the barricade a less formidable object, while others were helping, with great caution, young army recruits to lay mines a few feet on the far side of the barricade. There was not enough to make anything like a minefield—it would be a matter of luck if they got a tank—but it was the best that could be done. Others were taking orders from Niello. He set up a string of messengers—boys of all conditions—whose task it was to keep him informed of any movement of the Germans. It was thus that news was relayed of the fighting at the Bridge of the Sanità, runner handing it on to runner as if in a sporting race.

For all that, it was the rumble of the tanks in Piazza Dante that first gave those at the barricades of Montecalvario and Piazza

Plebiscito warning that the German reaction that Niello had predicted was on its way. The tanks had outrun the legs of the boys, constrained as they were by the probing and swinging cannon to go by the back ways.

The commander of the leading tank spoke into his microphone: "All units, attention. You will check communications."

The replies crackled in from the other tanks and the armored cars. When all was proved in order, the leading tank grew chatty.

"I can't see hide or hair of anybody. They've turned tail at the mere sight of us. So much for the Naples version of the ten days that shook the world. He who fights and runs away lives to steal another day, eh? Attention, all units. Ignore the barricades on your right, I repeat, right. We don't want to get into that warren. Make for the barricade that stretches across this street, destroy it, and forgather in the square behind. The armored cars will keep us covered. Expect tricks. This is Naples—what the bloody hell is that?"

From behind the row of big buildings on the left of the tanks came the roar of an explosion.

"Hans," came a voice over the radio.

"Yes."

"I think it must be Hermann. He calved off to take the back way. As you ordered."

"God help him." He paused. "T one-four-five, come in."

An armored car responded. "Sir."

"Back up and go and see what happened. Keep in touch."

"Yessir."

One of the armored cars, with a great roar of engines, reversed rapidly up the Toledo and then swung into a turning. It was the same as that which Maddelena had taken on her way to find Corrado. The tanks in the main street waited for news.

It soon came.

"T one-four-five."

"I read you."

"The tank struck a mine, sir."

"Can it move?"

"No, sir. Left track ripped off."

Over the radio came the sound of a burst of fire from a machine gun.

"Was it attacked?"

"Yes, sir. About a dozen boys and a couple of adults. But they've fled. That was our machine gun showing them the way."

"The crew—any casualties?"

"Two, sir. The commander—"

"Poor Hermann," said a voice from one of the other tanks.

"And the gunner."

"Take them back to base."

"Yessir. Sir?"

"What is it?"

"The commander is dead, sir."

"I read you. Carry on."

There was a pause. Hidden behind shuttered windows, the inhabitants of Montecalvario watched and waited.

The commander of the leading tank swore softly and at length. "Gunner!"

"Sir."

"Put a couple of shells into that building on your right."

"Yessir."

The watchers saw the cannon nose around. There was a flash and a roar. A shopfront went up in a great burst of flame. Fragments flew into the air and fell onto the road. Watching through the slats of a shutter, Filippo saw that it was a shop that he had known since he was a child. It was next to Via Nardones and he had often been sent on errands there.

"Nobody in it," said the commander with disgust. "Two degrees to the left and let them have the other one, and let's hope we have better luck. Hermann was my friend."

The cannon moved. It fired again, this time at the front door of a house. There was a great cry from inside, and then silence.

Filippo felt the two hand grenades that hung from a belt at his waist. He waited for someone, some adult, to say or do something. He waited a minute. Nothing happened. Through the slats he saw the cannon move once again. This time it pointed straight at Via Nardones, the street in which he lived, *his* street. Suddenly a vision of what the cannon was going to do to the street came into his boy's mind. It was very vivid. He had dreamed of it the night before. He saw how the flames would burst from the windows, how the fronts of the buildings would crumble. Before he knew it, he was down the stairs and at the front door. A man was there beside it, peering through a hole in the wood.

"Open the door," said Filippo.

"You can't go out there," the man began, but Filippo said, "Do as I say," in such a tone that the man obeyed.

He ran a few steps into the street. He held the bombs hidden behind him as he had been taught to do by the *scugnizzi.*

Then the soldier behind the machine gun fired a warning burst. It went a few feet above Filippo's head. His eyes till now had been fixed on the cannon. It had raised its muzzle a few inches, and Filippo knew that at any moment it would fire into his street.

Another short burst came from the armored car. Filippo studied it for a moment. He took aim, and threw the first of his two bombs. It hit the car squarely, and for a few seconds the machine gunner was blinded by the smoke and flame.

Then Filippo took the second bomb. He aimed for the tank; but even as he swung back his arm, a searing pain tore into his side. The machine gunner had recovered. Staggering forward, Filippo threw his bomb. He never saw whether he had found his mark, because the machine gunner mowed him down. He fell onto the roadway. The machine gun continued to fire at him and a string of bullets cut off his leg from his dead body.

"Silly little devil," said the commander. "What did he have to do that for? Attention, all units—the barricade is probably a trap and mined. We'll come back with a detector squad and see. Meantime, back the way we came, till we get to Piazza Dante. We'll park there till I can get headquarters."

The Toledo filled with the roar of engines as the huge tanks turned and the armored cars protected their flanks, firing burst after burst from their machine guns at the windows of the houses as they passed them. It seemed that every one of the windows had a boy or man with a gun in it. Fire rained down on the convoy, most of it harmless. Gasoline bombs burst on the armor plating; but tanks and cars, with a din that split the eardrums, put on speed and got away.

When they were out of sight, the firing stopped. Filippo lay in his blood, alone. Then, one by one, boys and men came out onto the roadway. They stood around the body, shoulder to shoulder, to hide it from the women till a stretcher could be found.

Today there is a marble plaque high on a wall where Filippo died. It tells how he was awarded a gold medal for bravery. It tells of his thirteen years, and of how he went out to face the enemy alone. It speaks of the two bombs and how he fell.

The fumes from the traffic that thunders over the place where he lay have made the slab dirty. Nobody has thought of cleaning it. As the years pass, it grows more and more difficult to read.

PART FIVE

The Third Day

CHAPTER SIXTEEN

On the morning of the thirtieth, Professor Amadeo Maiuri rode up to his museum in one of the carabinieri's patrol cars. The sergeant helped him out carefully, for his foot was in plaster. Only when he was clear of the vehicle did he dare look at the vast pink building, once a cavalry barracks but turned by one of the more cultured kings of Naples into a place to keep the exciting discoveries being made almost daily in the ruins of Pompeii.

Professor Maiuri drew a deep breath. It was still there, intact. Every day during the Allied bombardments he had expected it to be destroyed, along with the greatest collection of antique sculpture in the world. But it had escaped.

Professor Maiuri was a mild, small man who wished well to everybody in the world except, perhaps, a workman who stuck a careless spade through some priceless relic in Pompeii. Only then could it be guessed by the uninitiated that he held the august position of superintendent of antiquities. Otherwise all Naples knew him simply as "the Professor." *The* Professor, par excellence, and he fitted what everybody thinks a professor should be.

The Professor liked to think that the Americans knew all about his famous museum and had spared it from their bombs. He was therefore much distressed and puzzled when planes came over the ruins of Pompeii day after day and dropped one hundred and thirty-six quite large bombs on what was, after all, already one huge ruin. Besides, a bomb splinter had entered his foot.

In the manner of Neapolitans, he continued what he had been saying in the car to the sergeant before he said his formal thanks and goodbyes, for it is considered impolite to break off a conversation too quickly.

"I simply could not understand it," he said, shaking his head. "Even from the air it looks like a ruin, and surely every American schoolboy has heard about Vesuvius and the eruption."

"Ah, *Professore*," said the sergeant sympathetically, "you are such a great scholar that you have no time to move among us simple folk. If you had, you'd have known why. Old women's gossip, Professor. They spread the tale in the markets that the Germans had mounted guns in your ruins, and that must have crossed the lines to the Americans."

The Professor looked dumbfounded. He was even more dumbfounded when, hobbling toward the entrance to his museum as he had done a hundred times, he was abruptly stopped by a boy with a gun. The boy stood, feet apart, in front of a pile of paving stones that blocked his path.

"Young man," said the Professor, "what are you doing playing with that gun? They're very dangerous. When I went to the hospital to have my foot attended to, there were two or three boys there with quite nasty wounds. They had been playing with unexploded bombs they had picked up somewhere and—oh, dear me, do please keep your finger away from that trigger. It might be loaded."

"It *is* loaded," said the boy with a broad grin. "But don't worry. We would not shoot our own Professor, would we?" he said to some passing boys. They were carrying boxes. "Now do be careful with that stuff."

"What is it?" asked the Professor.

"Dynamite," said the boy laconically.

"So near the museum!" the Professor wailed. "I must talk to someone responsible immediately. But immediately!"

He looked back to where the carabinieri's car had put him down, but it had gone.

"There's Niello," said the boy, pointing with the gun. "Every Tom, Dick, and Harry *says* they're in charge, now that we're winning, but most of them will waste your time. Niello!" he called. "The Professor wants to talk to you."

"*Buon giorno*," said Niello. He held out his hand and, as the Professor shook it, he gave a little respectful inclination of his head. "I am sorry to see you have hurt your foot."

"What are you doing with dynamite?" said the Professor, more abruptly than he could have wished with this polite boy. But it was his way when agitated, and just now he was very upset indeed.

"Well, we mean to throw it."

"But the museum—the museum—"

"Not at the museum, Professor. Heaven forbid. But at tanks. They'll stop at the barricade that you can see—just a bit of it—around the corner in Via Teresa, because they think it's mined. It should be, but we haven't got enough. Then we throw the dynamite."

"*Madonna mia!* Are the Americans that near to the city? I've been away for a week. The carabinieri very kindly drove me up from the excavations—I've got to get my foot treated again—and I didn't see a single American all the way."

"We're not fighting the Americans. This," said Niello, pointing to a hand grenade hanging from his belt, "is meant for Scholl and his Nazis."

"I see," said the Professor, but very dubiously. His feelings were mixed. He knew a great deal about politics, but only those of two thousand years ago. So when the Fascists had come to power, he had become a Fascist, at least in name. Memories flooded back. The Duce himself had come to visit the excavations, together with all the top Fascists, breeched and booted. The Professor had shown him around, marching breathlessly at the military pace that the Duce had set. The Duce had been quite knowledgeable about the Roman emperors. One little slip, perhaps: Nero was not Claudius's natural son. That was Britannicus. But, all in all . . .

A boy with a box of dynamite asking him to move brought his thoughts back sharply to the present. He looked at the part of the barricade that was visible. He saw a large number of young men working on it, all of them armed. There was a tremendous bustle everywhere.

Niello laid his hand gently on the Professor's shoulder. "We'll see that the museum isn't harmed. *We* will. I can't vouch for the Germans."

Maurizio came up and stood beside Niello, listening.

"You must be the boy who got up that procession with the dead soldier. I heard talk of that in the excavations," said the Professor.

"Yes, that was me."

"I was there, too," said Maurizio, who was a little piqued that the famous Professor had not even looked at him. "And a lot of good it did. Everybody just sat on their asses and shook their heads. And some of the men even grabbed their cocks as though we were bringing bad luck."

"Mind your language in front of the Professor," said Niello, though he, too, had noticed several men making the ritual gesture to ward off ill fortune.

"Sorry," said Maurizio swiftly, lest he be interrupted. "But you should see them *now*. The whole city fighting. And, Niello, I just got some news from Vomero. Piazza Vanvitelli. They're having a wonderful time. Shooting Fascists. Winkling them out and shooting them."

"Good God, how terrible," said the Professor. "You mean our own Fascists?"

"Our very own Blackshirts," said Maurizio complacently. "Of course, only if they shoot at us first."

"There's been a lot of trouble with snipers," Niello explained hastily. "Shall I accompany you to the museum, Professor? That way you won't be troubled by sentries."

"Thank you. Thank you. You are very kind. I confess guns make me nervous. Very nervous." He walked between Maurizio and Niello. "Dynamite," he muttered. "Dynamite."

He opened the door of the museum and the boys peered inside. It was very gloomy. All they could make out were great piles of sandbags. They had been put around the huge statues of Roman deities that had been too heavy to move.

The Professor thanked the boys again and was about to close the doors when Niello said, "Professor, we boys have never been inside your great museum."

"But you should see it, you should," said the Professor. "Someday when all this dreadful affair is over."

"When this affair is over, your guards will chase us out," Niello replied. "They always do whenever we go to places like this. They would never let us into the aquarium in the Villa Communale. Afraid we'd steal the crocodiles, I suppose. Professor, why can't we come in now? I'm sure Maurizio would like to see it, wouldn't you, Maurizio?"

"No," said Maurizio very determinedly. Then, at an almost imperceptible gesture from Niello, he said, "Oh, yes, ever so much."

The Professor was touched. "All the best pieces have been packed away," he said sadly. "Nobody has been in here since the bombardment began. If you would really like to . . . there's not enough light to see anything properly, but then there's little to see but—"

Niello cut him short. "Thank you, thank you, Professor, this is something we'll never forget. Fancy, two *scugnizzi* being taken around the museum by the Professor himself! Something to talk about, isn't it, Maurizio?"

The Professor, muttering that he always kept a powerful flashlight where the pay desk was, wandered off out of hearing to find it.

"Are you mad?" Maurizio whispered indignantly.

"Look at those sandbags," Niello whispered back.

Maurizio obeyed. "*Gesù*," he said, "just what we've been wanting for the machine guns."

"So the little brain is working, is it?" said Niello. "Now listen. This is what you have to do. . . ."

The Professor found his flashlight. He threw open a shutter or two and began taking the boys around the vast entrance hall. There was little that was not crated or sandbagged, but he was surprised and pleased at the rapt attention that Niello paid, even when he translated a Latin inscription on an altar. The younger boy, as was to be expected, grew quickly bored and, excusing himself, slipped away.

"There's—or so I've been told—" said Niello to the Professor, "a great hall with lots of tapestries."

"Up the stairs," said the Professor with enthusiasm. "We'll be able to see that *much* better because we couldn't cover up the very top windows."

The hall was very big, the tapestries very splendid.

"I never in my life would have believed that any room could be as *big* as this," said Niello in a hushed voice, craning his neck to see the distant ceiling like the most docile of tourists.

"Then there's the pictures. The Titians, and the Velázquez," said the Professor.

"I've always wanted to be an artist," said Niello humbly, "but it's not for the likes of a street boy."

"Never be sure," replied the Professor heartily. "Some of these great men," he said, waving a hand at the entrance to a gallery, "were just as poor as you. Come along."

Niello quickly discovered that the darkest and dullest paintings were the ones the Professor thought most of, and he duly admired them until his eyes watered. He was such a success that the Professor asked him to his office.

"I have some chocolate biscuits that I've been saving up," he said. Protesting that he would not dream of depriving the Professor of such a rare luxury, Niello allowed himself to be persuaded.

In the office was a photograph of Mussolini stalking through the ruins of Pompeii, the Professor at his side. The Professor looked at it, and then said, "I must confess I am most confused. Bombs, shooting Fascists, old wives' tales . . . It's all too much for me. Have a biscuit."

Considering that the operation was carried out by more than twenty boys, it went off in remarkable silence. Most of them, indeed, wore no shoes, which helped, and also Maurizio's dire warning that if anybody made a sound, Niello would kick them around the museum.

One boy clambered up the pile of sandbags around the giant statue of a Roman god. He detached a bag and threw it down, where it was caught by other boys standing in a circle. Two boys, taking it by the ears, then carried it out of the museum door and across the road. As the pile grew lower, the work grew easier, and soon two marble gods stood open and unprotected from all the assaults of war. Then the boys left, closing the museum doors quietly behind them.

Niello said that he must not keep the Professor from his vitally important work any longer, talking to an ignorant *scugnizzo*, and rose to go. The Professor made to accompany him out of the museum, but Niello would not hear of it—the Professor must get on with his studies. He even adjusted an acetylene lamp which was now spluttering and which had constantly baffled the Professor. He left.

It was about two hours later that the Professor was deafened by the sound of firing from outside the museum. Indeed, for intensity and duration, he had never heard the like. He ran upstairs to the top story, from which he could get an uninterrupted view. A ramshackle barrier stretched from one side of the street to the other. A posse of armored cars was drawn up in front of it. They were firing, but not at the barricade, which seemed to have nobody on it. Instead, they were directing their machine guns at the roof of the big entrance to the Gallery of the Prince, a shopping arcade opposite the museum. On the roof were machine-gun nests, and there were similar posts at half a dozen other places along the sides of the road. Each nest was snugly protected by piles of sandbags. Every so often amid the din, the Professor saw boys dart a few feet out of the doorways of shops and hurl a fire bomb or a hand grenade. The road was soon a sea of blazing gasoline. Slowly, still firing, the armored cars withdrew. To the Professor's horror, a body had pitched from the roof of the arcade and lay on the roadway.

It was only two days later, when the Professor was showing a very august personage around the museum, that he stopped almost before the tour had begun. He stood by the entrance. He looked up at the two giant statues of the Roman gods that made such an impressive beginning to any visit. They gleamed white in the sun that poured through the newly opened windows.

"I could have sworn they were protected—" he said, and stopped.

"Very fine," said the general. "Roman, I take it, or perhaps Greek?"

"Eh?" said the Professor. "Yes. I think my mind must be going."

"It must have been most trying for you, most trying," said the general. "I congratulate you on preserving this magnificent collection intact." And they passed on.

Professor Amadeo Maiuri had fully earned the general's praise. He had defended his collection at the risk of his life, not from the Germans, or the Americans, or the British, but from Italians. For now, on the third day of the four-day revolt, the adults began to take over from the boys.

Scholl had made short work of the barricade that protected Piazza Plebiscito. He had sent a squad during the night to defuse mines and to drive tanks through the piles of stones and old furniture. There was some firing, but it was desultory. The Neapolitans were tired. Niello had predicted the destruction of the barricades. The boys were overcome with the desire for sleep.

But very early the next morning, boys, students, and deserters from the army gathered outside the Church of the Conception, tucked away at the top of the rise of Montecalvario, where the revolt had taken its first steps: it was here that the defense of the Rinascente store had been organized.

The boys were rubbing their eyes and yawning broadly. When they had first met, the whole enterprise had seemed to their elders foolhardy; now women and girls moved among the boys and youths with baskets. In them were bread, hunks of cheese, and bottles of cordial to take away the damp of the September morning. The boys breakfasted on the jealously hoarded food of the whole quarter.

At that first gathering there had been newcomers, all boys or lads. Now there were many more new faces, among them grown men. Aldo brought Niello his breakfast and sat on the steps of the church beside him. Niello ate silently. He refused a drink from the bottle that Aldo held out to him.

"Thinking?" said Aldo at last, and made to get up and leave.

"Trying not to," said Niello. "No, don't go."

Aldo sat down again. Again there was silence.

"I want to say something, but I don't know what it is. It seems to have got stuck inside me," said Niello. "Ever get that feeling?"

"Sure. When my mother died."

"Did you ever find out what it was you wanted to say?"

"Bits. Not everything."

"Yes. Bits. That's it. Bits."

Then, eating a little, he pulled himself together. "I suppose you're wondering what I'm talking about."

"I think I can guess," said Aldo. Then, after a long pause, he said, "Illuminato."

"Yes. Filippo. Did you know him?"

"Not very well."

"I did," said Niello. "He used to like to talk to me about what he was going to do when he—when he—"

"Grew up?"

"Yes."

"What was it?"

Niello did not seem to hear him. He stared at the other boys, at the strangers in their midst, but there was no sign in his eyes that he saw them.

Aldo laid his hand gently upon Niello's arm. He spoke slowly and deliberately. "I said, 'What did Filippo Illuminato say he wanted to be when he grew up?' "

He could barely hear Niello's answer.

"It changed every week. He was only a boy. Captain of a ship, airman, famous scientist, circus proprietor once when the circus came by. And now there's nothing. Just nothing." Niello drew in his lower lip and bit hard upon it. Then he said, "But I told them to fight and—"

"And *run*," said Aldo. "He didn't. So it is not your fault."

"Yes. Fight and run. Fight and run," said Niello.

Then, as Aldo had wanted, the tears came.

Niello rose abruptly and hid himself in the narrow atrium of the church.

"Which of you is the famous Niello?" A brisk, confident voice was asking the question among the boys. Aldo saw it was a young man of some twenty-five years, with close-cropped hair and a military bearing.

Aldo got up and went into the atrium. Niello, he saw, had recovered his composure.

"There's a rather cocksure type asking for you outside," he said. "Soldier, from the look of him. He may be useful."

"I'll see him," said Niello.

A few moments later he was introduced to the newcomer with a word.

"The hero himself?" said the presumed soldier. He shook Niello's hand vigorously. "This is a great privilege. Lieutenant Marcello Martone," he said, and gave Niello a tremendous stamping salute.

The *scugnizzi* gathered round, deeply impressed. Martone was not in uniform, but it was an experience to see any member of the armed forces saluting a *scugnizzo* instead of chasing him.

"Anything I can do to help in this magnificent fight you are putting on will be a pleasure and a duty. I am at your service, sir."

Niello paid less attention than the boys expected, partly because he detected a note of irony in the soldier's voice, and partly because he saw Michele at the back of the crowd signaling to him. The boy was making the gesture of "Come here, I've something to say to you alone," a complicated and subtle movement of the hands, head, and eyes.

Niello thanked Martone, then left him abruptly. Martone looked offended, then shrugged his shoulders and gave everybody a broad smile.

Niello took Michele into a doorway. "What is it?"

"I've news about Scholl."

"Who gave it to you?"

"The barman up at their headquarters."

"Can you trust him? Working for the Germans, I mean."

"Well, *I* work for the Germans, don't I, at the brothel? And you trust me, don't you?" Michele was so anxious that Niello, for the first time that morning, laughed. "Of course I do," he said.

"Well, I *didn't*—the barman, I mean—didn't trust him further than I could throw him, because he worked up there. But the Germans have got him real mad. They shot someone in his family, I don't know which someone, I did an hour ago but I don't remember now and—"

"Never mind. What's the news he gave you?"

"Scholl's got through to his top brass. He's asked for re-in-something and he's got them. *Re-in-what?* I've forgotten again?"

"Reinforcements."

"That's the word. And they're on their way. Tanks and armored cars. The Germans are taking us seriously, aren't they? Isn't that great?"

"We'd better take *them* seriously," said Niello, "or they'll slaughter the lot of us."

There never was a commander who at one time or another during his active service did not bang the table in a rage because his communications were not functioning properly. Scholl, according to those who worked with him, suffered pitiably from the same cause.

The German forces were falling back from the Salerno front onto what are euphemistically known, always, as "prepared positions." But every commander knows that "prepared" is precisely what those positions are not. Scholl, obedient to his orders from Rome to reduce Naples to "mud and ashes," had destroyed the great communications center that Mussolini had set up in the city. The civilian network no longer functioned; he had to rely on the military. His nearest point where there was anything like a working system was Capua, thirty kilometers to the north. To reach that, he had to make use of shortwave radios, field telephones, and a series of—in Scholl's opinion—moronic operators especially chosen to frustrate him.

From Capua, things should have been better. The civilian line was working—or it was supposed to be working. After thirty-five years of peace following the end of the war, it still does not work very well. In Scholl's time, hollering at the top of the voice was the only solution. Rome headquarters hollered back, but without any enthusiasm. Naples, Scholl began to understand, was beginning to be considered a nuisance.

Scholl explained that he had a communist uprising on his hands. Rome, after an interval of atmospherics, crackles, and profound silence, said that this surprised them. Their information was that there was little danger, etc., etc., etc., and more crackles. Could he give details?

Scholl said he was losing men every hour in ambushes. He could not send a patrol into the suburbs and be sure they would return. There were gasoline bombs and sharpshooters. Rome asked for more details. Scholl reeled off a list of places where he had lost men. Rome asked him to give map references, on the military map, since they could not catch the outlandish names over the wire.

Thus it was (and it was a vital point in the revolution) that Scholl, bellowing, sweating, and finally resorting to Morse code, gave the six-figure references to actions the *scugnizzi* had taken in their alleys, dashing out, throwing a bomb, and running away. The barricades, Scholl replied to a query from Rome, were child's play. The loss of his men in ambushes was the demoralizing factor. That, in fact, was the real child's play, but neither Scholl nor Rome knew it.

The map in Rome grew dark with circles where Scholl had had either fatalities or serious casualties. Rome said it would consult the commander in chief.

Field Marshal Kesselring was rated, even by his opponents, as a master of his craft, though he had made one initial mistake: he did not think that the Allies would land down south, even though he had information that they would; he considered that they would land somewhere near Rome, possibly on the highly suitable beaches at Anzio, and attempt to take the capital city. After a long and bloody fight up the peninsula, the Allied commanders did precisely what Kesselring thought they should have done in the first place: they landed at Anzio, took Rome, and thus pass beyond the bounds of this narrative.

From Kesselring's point of view, if the Allies wanted to occupy Naples, he had little objection. If the city was in turmoil, all the better. It would give his adversaries something to keep them busy while he organized his defense in the North. He did not want Scholl to lose lives; but he did not want him to run away. That would make it too easy for the Allies. A spectacular withdrawal might persuade them that Naples was in the bag, and they could look elsewhere to give Kesselring trouble. Holding down an occupied city needed men, and provisions. Scholl was therefore instructed to react vigorously to the insurgents, but only just vigorously enough to deceive the Allies. He was to withdraw, but in a manner as confusing as he could make it. And he was to hang on to the last moment. He himself should come to Rome for further instructions, but at a time and in a manner at his own discretion.

It had not been difficult for the barman to gather his information. He had heard Scholl shouting for reinforcements. He, like everybody else in the Hotel Parco, had seen Scholl wiping his brow, but with an air of satisfaction. He had passed on the information to the boy who washed the glasses, who had passed it on to Michele.

Now is the moment to see what exactly the *scugnizzi* had done. In a sentence: *They had invented the technique of urban guerrilla warfare.* It was to be used in the coming years of peace all over the world. We may not agree with the aims of those who have subsequently used it—or we may applaud its victories as we hear them over the radio and television. That depends upon our political views. The *scugnizzi* had no political views whatsoever. But their device of pinpricking a heavily armed enemy, inflicting casualties, and then running away was the only answer that David could give Goliath, to whatever party Goliath might belong.

One story told by the *scugnizzi* later shows how unnerving the technique could be. A boy would see two soldiers standing some fifty feet away. He would wait until they noticed him. Then he would raise his arm and swing it wide in the gesture of throwing a bomb. He did not need to have a bomb: the soldiers, like sensible men, would bolt for safety. And so would he.

Michele, having conveyed his secret message to Niello, joined the other boys and had breakfast. The trouble was that many of his companions had seen him signal to Niello, and they gave him no peace until he told them what he knew. Secrets, among the *scugnizzi*, are not popular.

So Michele told them that the Germans were sending Scholl reinforcements and there was going to be one big glorious fight.

Marcello Martone listened. Marcello was a trained soldier. He knew what to do. He had never heard of urban guerrilla warfare, but he knew his manual of military instructions. He also knew Naples. He immediately buttonholed Niello. "I gather the Germans are sending reinforcements," he said.

Niello made no reply for such a long time that Martone began to feel awkward. Niello seemed to be looking right through him, and that was an experience new to him with the young. When he trained recruits, they looked him straight in the eye or he warned the sergeant to make a mental note that here was someone who might cause trouble.

"I don't want you to think I'm interfering," he said "but—"

"I wish someone *would* interfere," said Niello. Then he looked in the proper way at the lieutenant. "You're an army man?" he asked.

"Regular."

"Have you ever met a general?"

"Certainly," said Martone promptly. He had met half a dozen, in a manner of speaking, when they walked, all spit and polish, along the lines and eyed the men. "Of course. Why?"

"Nothing, really. Only, it's just occurred to me that they kill people."

"I suppose they do. In the line of duty."

"Duty. Yes," said Niello, and Martone began to feel he was dealing with one of those empty-headed boys. He was, Martone decided, thinking of his girl friend. Martone knew how to deal with that.

"I mean," said Niello, "they don't only kill the enemy, they kill their own—own—own—well, soldiers."

"There are casualties, yes. Why?"

"Casualties," said Niello. He repeated the word, almost savoring it: "Casualties."

So this dreamy, stuttering boy was the "hero" he had been hearing so much about, thought Martone. He had guessed as much.

"And these casualties—on your own side—what do you do about them?"

"Look after them," said Martone in his heartiest tone. "Get them to a hospital. Stretcher parties. Ambulance. Note down details: name, number, unit, time and place of incident. It's an officer's duty."

"And if the hospital is too far, or if it isn't—isn't any use because— What then?"

"Ah-ah," said Martone, comprehendingly. "I see you have the makings of a fine officer. Yes," he said confidentially, as one officer to another, "that's the worst part of it."

"What?"

"You know. Writing to the family. 'Fell gallantly in the line of duty. Mourned by his comrades in arms. His personal possessions will be sent to you in due course by the competent authorities. I, as his commanding officer, would like to add . . .' Yes, friend, that's the worst part of it."

Niello suddenly snapped at him so fiercely that Martone took a step backward. "You wanted to say something to me. What was it?"

"I've heard," said Martone, "that the Germans are sending reinforcements."

"You've got big ears."

"If you're going to be rude . . ."

Niello looked across to where Michele was munching his breakfast. To Martone's relief, the intense look on Niello's face gave way to a grin, the sort of grin he expected from a *scugnizzo*. "Well," Niello said, "what have you to say about these reinforcements?"

"Just this," said Martone, eagerly taking his opportunity. "There are only two roads by which Scholl can send tanks into the city. Down from Capodimonte along Via Santa Teresa, if he's using his own units. If they're coming from outside, it'll be the Via Foria. That's where the reinforcements will come."

"Yes," said Niello absently.

"Now, these two roads meet at right angles just by the museum. We're outnumbered and outgunned. What does the book say in those circumstances? I'll tell you," Martone swept on. "We need a redoubt."

"A redoubt?" said Niello wonderingly.

"I'll explain," said Martone swiftly. "A redoubt is a small, defensible position, well defended, in this case by substantial barricades. . . ."

Niello listened. He nodded his head often. But although he listened, he did not really hear. Running through his head were the words that had just been so lightly spoken: "I, as his commanding officer, would like to add . . . would like to add . . ."

It was thus that the adults took over the battle of the Four Days from the boys.

CHAPTER SEVENTEEN

Professor Maiuri had seen the result. There was no doubt that it was spectacular. The boys were given their part to play. They were all armed with bombs or rifles, and sentries were posted, as the Professor had found out. But their major role was to keep their elders supplied with ammunition. The elders were of all sorts: young men, mostly; deserters from the army; working men; and a handful of the better classes caught up in the fighting fever that the boys had provoked in the whole city.

The barricade of Via Santa Teresa presented a problem. The road was broad, and most of the available material had been used to construct an obstacle on Via Foria, the road along which the reinforcements were expected. The reinforcements duly came in the shape of the armored cars. That battle had been a triumph. The cars had been withdrawn. Martone was firmly established as the leader of men and boys alike.

He turned his attention to the barricade on Via Santa Teresa. At the top of the first rise of the road, a number of trams were parked. They had been out of use for days, since Scholl had blown up the power station that gave them the current to operate. The trams were big. They were on wheels. It occurred to one of the grown-ups that these could be made into a formidable barricade. The only trouble was that they were too far away from the redoubt.

Martone was consulted. Martone was enthusiastic. He summoned the boys around him and they listened with delight. In a moment they were running toward the trams. There was quite a scramble for the position of driver. The winners, with a shout, kicked at the various brakes until one of them found the way to release them. The tram he was on started rolling along its tracks.

It gathered speed amid the cheers of the boys. It ran down the hill, and men and boys scattered in front of it. For a moment it seemed as if it might career right down the road to Piazza Dante and beyond, but the boy at the controls stopped it in time.

It was a great moment. The tram was in the right place, though unfortunately it presented its rear compartment to the expected enemy, who would, of course, go around it.

Martone once more rallied the boys. "Turn her over," he commanded.

There was heaving and shouting and a general noise. Under the impulse of dozens of young arms, the tram fell on its side. It was then only a few minutes' work to drag the recumbent vehicle so that it lay in the correct position for a barricade.

Other trams followed. Boys and men clambered on the prone trams, cheering, aiming their rifles up the road, getting inside and smashing the windows to make loopholes.

The excitement was at its peak when the first tanks arrived. They were Scholl's last from Capodimonte. They ground down Via Santa Teresa, their cannons pointing straight ahead, not firing. Men and boys in and on the trams fell silent. Some boys ran to and fro, seeing that all were well supplied with ammunition. Others fiddled with their weapons, old soldiers giving them last-minute hints as to how to handle them.

A torrent of fire broke out from the barricade. Men and boys on the far side of the trams fired through the smashed windows. A machine-gun post, well protected by sandbags, opened fire. Niello was beside the gunner, seeing to it that the ammunition belt did not jam.

The tanks stopped several yards away from the barricade. A burst of fire from a heavy machine gun mounted on the leading tank sent men and boys crouching and hiding, but they still kept up their fire. Niello saw one lad roll over on the ground, wounded, but he was swiftly dragged to safety. The tanks were silent for a while, as though the machines themselves were assessing the situation. The fire from the barricades had done them no harm.

The tanks—or, to be accurate, the men inside the monsters—were indeed considering the situation. Conversation chattered over their communications system.

The commander, who was in the leading tank, said, "Ignore the fireworks. All they've got is peashooters. What we have to watch for is the mines."

"Yessir," said the radio. "How do we spot them?"

"They have little flagpoles with the Italian flag flying on them."

"Yessir. Sorry, sir."

"Driver!"

"Sir."

"At the end of that tram—look to your left—there is a stretch of pavement and then the wall of the garden of that big pink building, which, to add to the pleasures of this holiday tour, is a museum."

"I've marked the spot, sir."

"Drive exactly between the end of the tram and the wall. There aren't any mines there; they'd have had to dig up the paving, and they haven't done that. Other tanks follow. All clear?"

Assent came over the radios. The tanks made a tremendous din of changing gears and moved ponderously toward the gap. The first tank scraped the wall of the museum. The Professor, watching from a window, trembled. The tank passed on, doing little damage. All the tanks were soon behind the barricade. There were shots from the defenders, and a shower of hand bombs, but nothing penetrated the armor of the Tiger tanks.

The commander spoke once again, this time to his gunner. "I want you to scare the living daylights out of them. Use that popgun of yours, but don't shoot to kill."

"Yessir."

The cannon of the leading tank nosed around. A shot left it and crashed into a building on the other side of the street. Another followed.

Niello leaped to his feet. Standing on the sandbag barrier, he shouted with all the force of his *scugnizzo* lungs: "Run. Run for your lives! They're taking us in the rear!"

The Professor saw dozens of figures run across the open space between the barricades. So did the commander of the leading tank.

"All right," he said into his microphone. "Straight ahead through the second barrier. There can't be any mines in the way. If there were, they'd be hopping about like goats to avoid them."

The tanks, roaring and rocking, moved forward. The Professor saw boys, men, and lads run and hide in doorways or just disappear down narrow roads. He let out a long breath of relief. For the first time in his long and distinguished career, he saw how it was that the Roman legions had conquered the known world with their broad, slashing swords. In his mind's eye he had seen a massacre of the innocents.

The tanks moved in single file around the corner of the museum. They rolled over the crossing of the two roads. They crushed, with what can only be described as nonchalance, the barrier that had held up the armored cars. A mine went off beneath one of them, but it only served to ignite the dry wood of a piece of old furniture. It was an antipersonnel mine, as were the others that had been laid. The tanks fired two or three bursts of their machine guns, but without aiming, since there was no living thing to aim at. The gunner let off a round straight down the Via Foria. "Rome, here we come," he said into his microphone.

"What makes you say that?" said his commander.

"Wasn't that our orders?"

"The *road* to Rome. And this is it."

"Well?"

"We're stopping at Cassino."

"Cassino? That's Italian for a brothel, isn't it?"

"With one 's.' This is with two."

"I stand corrected, sir. Then what is it?"

"A monastery."

"Christ," said a voice from another tank. "Monks."

"Six months in Italy," said the gunner, "and I've never seen Saint Peter's. And me a good practicing Catholic."

"I'll tell the Pope," said his commander into his microphone. "He'll be worried. One more shot, straight down the road, to clear the air. We don't want to hurt any of these nice people."

"Not that I can see any. One round, sir, straight ahead."

"And make it straight. Don't hit that bloody great pink thing we're passing. Art treasures. They're on Goering's list, I'll be bound."

"If he can come and get them."

"He will. He will. We'll be back."

The tanks passed the Professor's view. The boys and men crept out of hiding. Martone appeared from behind a tram.

"Look to the wounded," he ordered in a loud voice, and several men and boys were carried off. The casual fire of the tanks had been more deadly than the Germans had intended.

Headquarters in Rome had done its measured best. Scholl had been sent his reinforcements, but in the shape of nothing heavier than armored cars. When these had got back to base, their news had redounded to Scholl's credit: there had been resistance as Scholl had warned. Some colonel yelled compliments down the line at him, but said that all the Tiger tanks that Scholl had were wanted and quickly; the Allies were making headway faster than had been expected; there was regrouping; could HQ have the tanks as quickly as possible? Other orders stood as before.

Scholl gave his orders to Capodimonte, and then, not entirely dissatisfied with the way things were going for him personally, climbed the stairs of the Parco Hotel to his apartment and began to pack his bag.

When it was quite clear that the tanks were not going to turn around and come back, the boys, the youths, and the men gathered around Martone. After all the excitement of turning over the trams, there was an air of flatness among them all.

Martone's training manual told him what to do. Explain, briefly, what had happened. Waste no time, but order action in order to maintain morale. "Morale" had been a very frequent word among his instructors, but, just at this juncture, there seemed very little of it about.

He climbed up on the overturned tram. "Our barricades were taken in the rear," he said.

"They bloody near took us in our asses, if that's what you mean," said one of the older *scugnizzi*.

"It is a maneuver that can happen in any action," said Martone; but another boy said, "Niello told us they'd be no bloody good. Barricades, I mean. Didn't you, Niello?"

"Listen to the officer," said Niello.

Martone said, "Thank you, Niello. Yes, we have had casualties, but we're still fighting—we shall go on fighting."

Some of the men raised a small cheer, but the *scugnizzi* were silent.

"The armored cars will come back, and maybe the tanks. We need new tactics. Up there"—and he pointed to the top floor of the museum—"is an ideal place for us to give them enfilading fire. That, with the machine-gun posts on the roof of the Gallery, which did such splendid work before, will give the enemy a thoroughly hot reception. We need ammunition, and I shall rely on you boys to find it and bring it to us." He looked around the *scugnizzi*, who in their turn looked to Niello for orders.

"We'll see to that," said Niello.

"Good. Don't just bring it one by one. That takes time. Form a human chain from the dump, up the stairs, and so to where we shall be. Human chain. Am I understood?"

"That'll be a fine target," said Niello. "A line of boys. We don't usually work in gangs."

"Target for whom?" said Martone, as though he were seeking information. "By the time the Germans come back, we'll have the job done. Then you boys can join us up there on the top story and give them hell."

The boys nodded eagerly.

"Then that's settled." He turned to the men standing around him. He said, in the best military manner, "I want *volunteers* for a party to go and tell the museum people what we're going to do. You, you, and you, and you and you . . ." he said, pointing out some good, stalwart men. He smiled broadly at the army joke he had made, and so did the chosen men. They, too, had done their military service, some of them in battle. Their blood pulsed happily to enjoy once more the authoritative voice, the air of confidence of the officers, and the little jokes.

The body of men (for that is what they now felt themselves) moved off to the museum entrance. The boys began to form their chain. The Professor, from his window, saw the men under Martone move toward the museum door. They rang the bell, at first gently, then with impatience.

"Coming, coming, coming," he said, although in the empty museum there was no one to hear him. The bell jangled, the Professor ran down the long flights of stairs, breathless and stumbling. At last he opened the door, not widely, but just enough to see Martone.

Martone saluted. "Commander of the Via Santa Teresa group of partisans," he said, bestowing the title on himself.

"Yes, I've been watching," said the Professor.

"In that case, you will have seen what happened."

"Yes. Very brave of you all. Very brave. I saw some wounded. How are they?"

"They are being well looked after, you may be assured."

"Good, good, good. These are terrible times, terrible."

"Professor, excuse me for being brief and to the point. We need a position for enfilading fire on the right flank of the Germans when they come back."

"Enfilading," said the Professor, mystified for the moment. "Ah, yes. You wish to take them in the—er—er—"

"Flank. Exactly. The best position will be from the top floor of this building."

"Here? *Here?*" said the Professor.

Martone pushed open the door with his foot in the approved manner of soldiers in a hurry. The heavy door swung out of the Professor's grip. "Yes, here," said Martone. "Come in," he said to his followers.

They came, carrying their rifles and submachine guns. The Professor walked backward in front of them. "But we must talk this over," he protested. "We must sit down together and talk this over."

It was a phrase he had used a dozen times: when there had been opposition in his faculty at the university; when colleagues at conferences had challenged his rulings; when bureaucrats had tried to put a spoke in his wheel while he was digging up Pompeii. It had always worked.

"Come to my office," he said, and, turning, led the way. But as he walked through the empty halls with their packing cases of treasures, he reflected that in those days his opponents had been armed only with pencils and fountain pens. These men had guns.

The men with guns followed the Professor willingly enough. They were men of the people; like the *scugnizzi*, they had never set foot in this famous place, and they were not a little awed as some of the unprotected masterpieces loomed at them in the uncertain light. A partisan nudged his companion as they passed the statue of a naked woman, and winked.

They crowded into the Professor's office. They declined to sit down, so the Professor stood too, but behind his desk, where he felt safer from the guns. He knew he was not really safer, but that was the way he always felt when he got a desk between him and trouble.

Martone said, "All we ask of you, Professor, is that you show us the way and"—pointing to a rack on the wall—"give us any keys that might be necessary. After that, I suggest you go somewhere safe down in the basement and don't give us another thought."

The Professor cleared his throat. "You are aware that I am the superintendent of antiquities."

"That's why we're here," said one of the men, growling and fiddling with his gun.

"You say you are partisans—*partigiani*—but I did not know there were any in Italy."

Some of the men shuffled their feet. They, too, did not know it. But they had heard rumors of Frenchmen who called themselves by that name and who had fought the Nazis, just as they were doing. They were not sure they liked the idea of being called by a Frenchified name, but they relied on Martone.

"There were not until the armistice. There are now. I am an officer of His Majesty's forces and I can assure you that there are thousands of them."

"Fighting whom?"

"The Germans."

"It is very confusing. You speak of His Majesty. I am also His Majesty's servant. I am a government employee. It is my duty to protect this museum. If it becomes the target of the Germans, there will be the same disaster as has happened at Pompeii. Bombs. Destruction. Irreparable damage. Irreparable."

"I appreciate your problem," said Martone. "Nevertheless—"

"But do you appreciate your own problem?" said the Professor. "Look," he said, and from force of habit picked up a ruler to act as a pointer. He indicated a large picture on the wall opposite to that on which hung the photograph of himself and the Duce marching through the ruins of Pompeii. The picture showed the Parthenon.

"You recognize that?"

"Of course, Professor. We military are not entirely ignorant."

All the newly baptized partisans nodded. In the propaganda buildup for the disastrous campaign in Greece, the Fascists had made the temple all too familiar.

"Then you will understand," the Professor went on, "that this is a priceless monument, like those in this building." His voice took on a new, authoritative tone. His hand with the pointer was firm and steady. Lecturing, the Professor was a different man.

"For centuries it stood almost unharmed. It was first a church, then a mosque, and lastly the Turks used it to store their gunpowder. During a war, someone fired a shot into it, knowing full well that it was a powder magazine. The result you can see for yourself. The man who fired that shot has gone down in history as The Bomber. You, sir," he said, pointing the ruler at Martone, "will be famous. You will win medals. You may well be given the freedom of this city. Your children will boast with your name. Maybe. Or maybe you will be known as the man who destroyed this museum and all that is within it." He laid the ruler down, carefully parallel with the inkstand.

"How will anyone know?" It was a young voice, and the Professor saw that it was a man of some twenty years or more, a student, the argumentative type. The Professor was used to dealing with the sort, except that this man held a long-barreled pistol.

"Because, young man, I shall record it in my diary, as will be my duty to posterity."

"Are you sure you'll have time?" said the man with the pistol. He raised the barrel. It pointed straight at the Professor's chest.

The Professor's lips trembled violently. He waited until he was in control of them again. Then he said, "I am quite sure." His voice was as firm as when he rebuked some impertinent student.

Martone saw the pointed pistol. He saw the excited look in the young man's eyes. Perhaps the man who destroyed these lumps of old stone all around him would not be too much blamed by the Neapolitans. But the man who allowed the Professor to be shot would be anathema until the third and fourth generations.

"You will kindly permit us to withdraw and consider the question in all its aspects, Professor," he said. "I shall return within a few minutes."

The Professor nodded his assent. As he led the way to the door, his knees shook.

Martone did not return. It was he who was shot, not the Professor. He stood in a small group on the ramp outside the museum which led up to the entrance. The *scugnizzi* broke the chain they had already formed and stood about, watching him. He was about to speak when a rifle shot cracked from nowhere. He grasped his side and, with a shout of pain, rolled on the ground.

The new partisans bent to help him.

"Some swine of a Fascist sharpshooter," said the young man who had pointed the pistol, and he and the others carried Martone to shelter. The boys scattered.

In spite of his agony, Martone gave orders to search out the sniper. It was soon apparent that there were many of them, all along the Via Foria, in the Via Santa Teresa, in the Toledo. They fired from a hundred vantage points, and their aim was often accurate. As the day waned, many of the new partisans lost their lives. As for the boys, they came into their own once again. A nimble *scugnizzo* was as good at dodging from cover to cover as any man—better, in fact, and harder to hit.

By nighttime, Martone's pain became unbearable. His companions put him aboard an open car and made for the hospital. But other groups of partisans had been formed. The military spirit had spread. At one point, in the dark, the men in the car were challenged in proper military style, as was taught to recruits in the Italian Army.

"Halt!"

The car stopped.

"Friend or foe?"

"Friend."

"Password."

There was silence. No one in the car knew it. Nobody had told them. The demand was repeated in a more threatening tone. Still there was no reply.

Someone from the barrier threw a hand grenade. It hit the car squarely. Martone died immediately, killed by men on his own side.

PART SIX

The Fourth Day

CHAPTER EIGHTEEN

The last of the Four Days was the shortest, and the bloodiest. It was all over by what the Neapolitans would have called lunchtime, had there been enough food to make a luncheon for anybody. By that time, bodies of men, women, and children were lying everywhere in the streets.

The insurgents were no longer fighting the foreigner—the German conqueror, the successor to the Spaniards whom Masaniello had challenged. They were fighting their own people.

Martone had been cut down by a sniper in one of the central points of the city. But the fight now passed to Vomero. The Parco Hotel is on the edge of Vomero. It is an area that rises above the museum, above Santa Lucia, like the dress circle of a vast theater. In those days of the uprising, it was occupied by the rich, who lived in fine houses separated by spacious streets.

Those who lived in the fine houses had no reason to look forward to the success of the insurgents. Their money had come—honestly if possible, dishonestly if not—from the regime that had just collapsed. There had been black shirts and breeches and champagne at many a happy reception in the days gone by. And when some onetime guest now turned up, boldly wearing his black shirt, carrying a rifle with a telescopic sight, and asking for the use of a window, it would have been inhospitable to deny him what he wanted. Vomero, then, was the last stand of the Fascists. History regards such diehards as either fanatics, or fools, or models for the young. It depends on how history rolls along.

Niello and his boys moved to Vomero, for it was quite clear that it was there the issue would be decided. The engagements were much to the taste of Niello and the *scugnizzi*. You were on your own—hiding, leaping out to shoot, ducking back (if you were lucky). But just shooting at windows, as the adults were doing, was not very productive. You had to take the sharpshooter from behind, as the boys and men at the museum had been taken by the tanks. To do that, it was necessary to climb roofs, shin up drainpipes at the back of the sumptuous mansions, and drop down into a house like a thief. There was many a Fascist patriot who met his end with the insurgents suddenly opening a door behind him and pressing a trigger. One Fascist lived to tell the tale—perhaps to explain his comrades. He owed his life to Antonino Tarsia in Curia.

Antonino's wife had turned him out creditably, in spite of the fact that his best trousers were ruined with blood and would have to go to the cleaners—when, if ever, there were cleaners again. But he went out to do battle for his revolution dressed as a Neapolitan gentleman of the old school: neat, pressed, and spotless from head to foot. Nor was that as absurd as it might seem to us, in our sloppier days. He moved about among the fighters; he was cheerful; he was a reminder to both boys and men of more elegant days. He was a reminder, too, that the better classes could be on the side of the hoi polloi—the street boys, the poor. In the sweat and death of a revolt, it is strange how cooling and reassuring such a figure can be.

It was in Piazza Vanvitelli that he saved a life. The insurgents had taken possession of all the angles of the square. They were well armed. The boys, when not actually beside them shooting, kept all amply supplied with ammunition. All weapons were aimed at one barricaded window. From this, at intervals, came accurate fire from someone who clearly knew how to shoot. It was sure death or mutilation to expose oneself. Yet the man behind the window had no hope.

Somebody produced a bullhorn used by the stallholders at local fairs to advertise their goods. An officer of the town police had joined the revolt and had experience in using it in flushing out recalcitrant criminals. He told the man behind the window that he hadn't a chance: boys and men had surrounded the building in which he was firing; the roof was covered; the back and front entrances were covered; if worse came to worst, they had bombs that could set the building on fire. Why did he not surrender?

The man surrendered. He came out of the front door, but his hands were not over his head. He still held his rifle, while his left hand was on his hip, and his chin was flung up, the arrogant pose made famous by his hero, the Duce. Instantly there was a howl of anger from men and boys alike. He was recognized as one of the informers who had told the Germans where Neapolitans were hiding from the trucks collecting them for forced labor. His rifle was snatched away from him and his arms were held. An enraged *scugnizzo* made a loop of rope and put it around his neck. He was dragged across the piazza, men and boys aiming blows at him with sticks and rifle butts.

Antonino Tarsia in Curia was there. In his dream of the revolution, beating and dragging a man about and spitting on him had no part. He drew himself up and, in a calm voice, told the insurgents to behave themselves. The man—the halter around his neck, his face red and swelling from blows—stood in front of him.

Antonino asked him why he had gone on fighting. The Fascist looked about him at the boys and men with a look of utter contempt. "Because," he said, "I want to die."

"Then," said Antonino, "you shall not."

Nor did he. At that moment, firing broke out from another quarter. A German motorcyclist had been stopped and was defending himself. The men and boys left the Fascist alone with Antonino. Tarsia in Curia was as noble as his name. He signaled the man to go, and, with the halter still around his neck, the Fascist ran.

The German motorcyclist was an unfortunate man. The insurgents shot him. He had a dispatch case with him, which one of the boys seized. An elder took it from him and opened it. There were only sheets of paper, some handwritten, some typed, and all in German. At that moment, another sniper began to fire on the assembled boys and men. They ran for cover, and the bag and its contents were left lying in the roadway. It was a pity that no interpreter was among the insurgents at Vomero. The bag contained the news that they had won everything they were fighting for. The messenger had spent all night traveling between the various German posts with Scholl's orders for a measured and discreet withdrawal.

During that night, a strange encounter had taken place. For the first time, Scholl came face-to-face with a Neapolitan who had risen against him. He was Vincenzo Stimolo, and he was very Neapolitan indeed.

Antonino Tarsia in Curia had convinced himself that he was the Lenin of Italy, and once he had thrown himself into that role, nothing would deter him, neither facts nor ridicule. It is a great gift for those who possess it; a sort of magic emanates from it. A singer like Caruso or Gigli could convince himself he was a young lover despite a paunch and a double chin. He could sing Pinkerton in *Madame Butterfly* and make thousands believe he was twenty-five instead of forty-five. That was because he believed it, at that moment, himself. It is a gift that can carry a Neapolitan to the peak of success in the world, or plunge him into the direst of disasters. Often, it does both, the one after the other. The true Neapolitan knows it, recognizes it when he meets it in his fellow citizens, and goes along with it. Watching it is a form of entertainment.

When the revolt broke out, Vincenzo Stimolo decided he was two things: he was a captain in the Italian Army, and he was an invincible hero. To be the first (because he was not a military man at all) only needed a little playacting; nobody would expect a "deserter" to produce his papers or his epaulettes. To be the second needed a wild, improbable courage, a little like that which had led Januzzi to his death in the bayonet charge. But Vincenzo was a grown man.

Scholl was burning papers in a terra-cotta stove in the middle of the night when the duty officer entered the room and saluted.

"Well?"

"One of the rebels wishes to see you, sir."

Scholl said absently, "Where is he?"

"Just outside the door, sir."

Scholl stared at the officer. The officer looked at the wall. Scholl's cheek twitched several times, then he swore because a paper he was holding burned his fingers.

"You mean one of those dirty Communists is here, in my headquarters?"

"Yessir."

"How did he get in?"

"He gave the password, sir."

"He *what?*"

"Password, sir. I think Major Sakau had given it to him."

"Has Major Sakau gone out of his mind?"

"I wouldn't like to say, sir. But he is outside, too. He came with the—er—Communist individual, sir."

"Why?"

"I gather, sir, under correction if I have misunderstood, that they wish to make a deal with you."

Scholl carefully fed some more paper into the fire. His cheek stopped twitching. He thought about his orders from Rome while he watched the flames consume those he had issued himself in his brief reign over Naples. He had been told to leave the city quietly after creating as big a state of confusion as possible, in order to give trouble to the occupying enemy. What could be better than to leave the Americans a Red revolution to deal with? It would be a comic-opera revolution, no doubt: these were Neapolitans. But there are lots of complications in comic opera.

"I will see them. Take them to the conference room. Oh, and wake up the interpreter and tell him I need him."

Vincenzo Stimolo looked around the room with its green table. He smiled at the picture of the woman with the bare breasts. He was perfectly at his ease; or, to be more accurate, he was playing the part of a man perfectly at his ease. Had he dropped the role for a minute, he would have fainted with terror.

Major Sakau looked like a very, very nervous man, and he was not playing the role at all. He had to tell the commandant that this short man with the black hair and the shabby suit had got the better of him. He wished that the man had not brought his two fighter companions into the room. They looked even more disreputable.

There was a long wait. Scholl firmly believed in finishing one job before he took up another. Unhurriedly, he burned the last papers, thinking deeply all the while. Meanwhile, in the conference room, a sleepy interpreter entered, buttoning his uniform. He yawned broadly; then, seeing the major, stifled it.

"My dear Major, what are you doing here at this hour?"

The major made a hesitant gesture toward the three Italians. The interpreter surveyed them. All three badly needed a shave. But then, so did the major.

The interpreter said lightly, in Italian, "This is most irregular, gentlemen. If you are going to be shot, it should be done at dawn, after a good breakfast, not at this unearthly hour."

One of the Italians went white to his lips. Stimolo merely smiled.

At that moment, Scholl came in. The Germans exchanged salutes.

"You wished to see me, Major?"

"Yes, sir."

Scholl ran his eye over the three insurgents and then ignored them.

"Please explain."

It was a difficult thing to do, but the major, clearing his throat, plunged in manfully. Scholl listened and, from time to time, glanced at the map.

The major had been in charge of forty-seven Neapolitan prisoners. They had been kept in the Campo Sportivo, a complex of football fields, locker rooms, and an open-air arena. Unexpectedly, said the major, he had found himself surrounded by insurgents.

Scholl studied the map. "Surrounded? Surrounded, Major?" Scholl ran a finger around the layout of the sports center. "I should have said that it would need several battalions to do that." He turned to the interpreter. "Ask this man how many men he had."

Stimolo rubbed his blue chin in an admirably cool gesture. "Two hundred of my own men, I should say, Commandant. I cannot give you an exact figure for the civilian auxiliaries, but it must be near a thousand."

It was a magnificent lie. Stimolo had never seen more than two or three dozen men and boys. But he had sent the boys running from point to point, keeping up a sporadic fire all around the arena.

"Well, Major. Continue. You presumably radioed for reinforcements from me."

"Yes, sir."

"Good. But I don't remember having seen the message."

"No, sir. We radioed, but the apparatus did not work. A corporal had dropped it."

"Such things happen," said Scholl. "You sent a messenger?"

"Yessir."

"Again," said Scholl, "I do not seem to—"

"No, sir. He was met with such intensive fire that he returned."

"Forgive my interrupting," said Stimolo to the interpreter, "but since I am not, as you hastily assumed, a prisoner, but here under safe-conduct, would it not be proper if you translated what is being said?"

The interpreter repeated the request to Scholl.

"The insolent little bugger," said Scholl, but not angrily. Then, to the major: "Is this business of safe-conduct true?"

"Yes, sir. I considered the situation and informed this man here through a sergeant who spoke a little Italian that I proposed to shoot the hostages, one by one."

"Correct," said Scholl. "And then?"

"The reply came that this man here and his supporters would shoot us one by one, too, as we came out."

"Could he do this?"

"I considered the situation, sir. He could."

By this time the interpreter was thoroughly enjoying himself; he religiously translated every phrase. By this time, too, Stimolo was feeling splendid. His gaggle of running boys and youths had become for him an iron circle of hardened warriors, supported by an armed and dedicated citizenry. And after all, the major had believed him.

There was a silence in the room for a while. Then Scholl said, "So you have brought him here. What for?"

The interpreter did his duty.

"To offer you terms," said Stimolo. "I have ordered my forces to take the Campo Sportivo by storm at dawn. Alternatively, we can agree that the hostages are to be released, and I, on my part, will assure the safety of your soldiers in transit to whatever reception point you may indicate."

"And," said Scholl, "if I have you taken out and shot in the courtyard, what then?"

"That has been provided for. The assault will still take place, whether I am there or not. I have set a time for my return."

Stimolo wished he had really thought of that. He wished he had enough men to make the assault. He wished he had not got himself into the whole affair. But he had cast himself into the role of a hero, and it had taken hold of him. To his own astonishment, he found that he was not afraid to die.

Scholl studied Stimolo for a long minute. By dawn his own men would be out of the city, for their orders had been to begin the evacuation at 3 A.M. He, too, would be out of Naples, on his way to Rome. This disheveled and unshaven man in front of him was a troublemaker, a nuisance, a rabble-rouser, he was sure. He would probably dislike the new invaders of his city as much as he disliked the old. But he had courage. He would be Scholl's parting gift to the Americans.

"Your terms are accepted," he said abruptly. "You may all dismiss."

The moment was a little diminished in its drama by a long, noisy sigh of relief from one of Stimolo's companions. It was Antonio Russo. But then, we owe the record of the encounter to him. He was a transparently honest man. He admits, frankly, he was very much afraid to die.

Scholl had been defeated. The boys had won. It should have been a night of triumph, a Neapolitan *festa*, with people pouring into the streets, singing, dancing, embracing one another, weeping, laughing, and getting tipsy on whatever wine could be looted from hidden stores, the sort of *festa* so celebrated in histories of the past, so often portrayed in engravings of men in breeches dancing the tarantella.

But this was 1943. Scholl was no Spanish viceroy ready to welcome Masaniello with Latin abandon. Scholl was a German. The boys had won, but he was much too clever to let them know it.

There are many pretty legends about the way that Scholl left Naples. One of the least likely is that he asked for a safe-conduct from the rebels, who (so goes the story), with operatic gallantry, agreed to give him one. Surrounded by armed young men, followed by exulting lads, his car drove through streets lined with observers, silent for the most part, save for some imprecation that some onlooker could not suppress. Had any such thing really happened, Scholl would have been dragged from his motorcar and torn to pieces before he had got two hundred yards, safe-conduct or no safe-conduct. He had, after all, killed a lot of citizens.

And, indeed, Scholl must go down in history as a tyrant. But history plays strange tricks upon those it picks up for a moment, then puts back into its box of puppets. Scholl, in flesh and blood and heart, was nothing more or less than a middle-class German businessman, a respecter of rules, a believer in order, method, and bureaucracy. He was now the chief civil officer in the city, since the Prefect Soprano had disappeared. He therefore picked up a telephone, contacted the police, and asked for the usual car and the usual small motorcycle escort due to such a person. He did not state the reason for his journey, and, according to the rules, he did not have to. His order was obeyed.

He left at three in the morning, in a closed car with an official Italian number plate, accompanied by two motorcyclists.

Thus we lose sight of him forever, on the road to Rome, and oblivion. Did the headlights of his official car pick out the ghosts of dead boys watching his departure? If there were any, they were wasting their time. The government cars of prominent Fascists were very comfortable. Scholl, we may safely guess, was asleep. It had been a long evening.

Such celebration as the boys got took place in the damp hours of the early morning. It was then that the word spread, hesitantly, unbelievingly, that they were the victors.

All night the trucks and armored cars of the Germans had left the city, going along the Via Foria, but in small groups, with dimmed headlights in order not to draw too much attention to themselves. But they were noticed. A few tanks and armored cars had always used this exit, but now, secretive as it was, there was an endless column.

By seven in the morning the streets were full of people swapping news. Was it a retreat? Was it a trick? Were they coming back as they had done before, with all the horrors and disasters that had followed in their wake? No. It would seem that they had really gone. News trickled through from the German headquarters of officers packing their bags, taking down family photographs, leaving notes for prostitutes of the town.

The women lined up for bread at the few shops that had any, and at the fountains that still worked. Here, in whispers, the boys had their tribute.

Scholl had known that this would happen, and he left the Neapolitans a parting present. He gave explicit orders to Capodimonte. On that hill was a cannon that dominated the whole of Naples. The crew that served it were commanded to begin a steady cannonade of the city at seven precisely, and to continue until the enemy (that is to say the Allies) were sighted at the borders of the town. These, too, like most of the main roads and the bigger piazzas, were visible from the hill.

The cannonade was to take place at irregular intervals. There was to be not less than five minutes between each shot, and not more than fifteen. The targets were to be anywhere in the heart of the city, at the choice of the gunners. Each target was to have one round only. On the entry of the Allies, the gunners were to remove the breechblock, put it aboard a truck that would be standing by, and then leave by the road to Capua, where they would rejoin their regiment.

The first shell fell in the crowded area around the cathedral where San Gennaro's blood liquefied to tell the Neapolitans of their fate for the coming year. The fate of a dozen women and girls was settled without the intervention of the saint, for the shell fell squarely on a breadline. Bodies and limbs were scattered on the tiny piazza.

The gunners on Capodimonte, in obedience to their orders, shifted their sights. A second shot fell, killing still sleeping people in Ottocalli. And thus it went on, the gunners choosing their targets at whim. A tall bell tower of a church would tempt them to fire at one area; an apartment block another. Piazza Garibaldi, with its statue of the hero, had its share. The hero, could his bronze eyes have seen, would have witnessed blood and death once more.

Niello and Maurizio were in Vomero that morning. They were both on the first floor of a shop, and Niello was firing regularly at a building down the road. The last of the snipers was there, and he was proving very hard to get, even though men and boys aplenty were trying to hit him.

Niello ran out of ammunition and asked Maurizio to go and fetch some. Maurizio went willingly. The route to where the ammunition could be obtained was behind the houses and safe from the sniper. Maurizio, sketching a salute, went.

The shell from Capodimonte burst as he was turning a corner. A fragment hit him in the back. He staggered a few steps, and then fell.

A few moments later, Aldo ran up the stairs of the shop, shouting, "It's Maurizio! A shell has got him! Follow me!"

When Niello arrived, a priest was kneeling beside Maurizio. He had been lifted onto the sidewalk, and the priest was muttering prayers.

Maurizio opened his eyes. He saw the priest. "Am I going to die?" he asked.

The priest continued to pray, but tears were streaming down his cheeks.

"Yes. I see I am," said Maurizio. "I must confess, mustn't I?"

The priest nodded.

Maurizio said, "Where's Niello?"

Niello knelt beside him. Maurizio turned to the priest and said, "If I confess to Niello, is it the same?"

The priest nodded.

Maurizio turned his gaze full upon Niello. "Tell the commendatore it wasn't the butler who stole the gun. It was me, and I am sorry."

His gaze clouded over. He turned his head away, and died.

It was ten o'clock in the morning. At two in the afternoon, the first of the Allied tanks rolled into the city.

During the Four Days, the custom had grown up of covering with flowers the place where someone had been killed. On the evening of that day, Niello picked a bunch of flowers and took it to the heap that now marked where Maurizio had fallen.

It was already growing dark. Niello laid down his flowers. When he straightened up, he saw through the evening light that the commendatore was coming along the road. He waited.

The commendatore approached the heap of flowers. He stood with head bent, his hands behind him, looking at it, in the pose that Maurizio had so often imitated.

When he raised his head, he saw Niello. "Niello," he said.
"Commendatore."
They both fell silent.
"Did he suffer?" said the commendatore.
"No. It was quick. He had a message for you."
"Yes?"
"He said that it wasn't the butler who stole the gun, it was—"
"Yes," said the commendatore gently. "I knew."
"I thought you might."
They walked away together.
"And you, Niello," said the commendatore, "I suppose you'll be the most famous boy in Naples."
"Except that I shan't be here."
"Where will you be?"
"Don't know. America. England. I'll talk to the troops, and then I'll decide. Somewhere far away, at any rate."
"For good?"
"Yes." Niello paused. "At least until I've forgotten." They walked a little further. "If I ever do."
They arrived at a crossroads. As they shook hands, the commendatore said, "If you're going away to another country, you'll need money. Your fare. A nest egg to start you off."
"I daresay."
"Then come to me. You know where I live?"
"Yes. Maurizio showed me."
With that, they went their separate ways.

Notes

NAPLES   One of the oldest cities in Europe, Naples was founded by Greek immigrants in the seventh century B.C. and subsequently came under the rule of Rome, Byzantium, the Normans, the French, the Spaniards, and (briefly) the Germans, Americans, and British. During the later Dark Ages, parts of the surrounding territory were held by Arabs.

Its topography can best be understood by seeing it as a vast Roman open-air theater. There is a flat area around the port resembling the space in front of the stage. Above this, the city rises in tiers till it meets the hills on its periphery. The Bay of Naples takes the place of the stage.

THE BAY OF NAPLES   Celebrated for its beauty, the bay embraces the Sorrento peninsula and the islands of Capri and Ischia. It gave rise to the saying "See Naples and die." It is frequently mentioned in this narrative, but the view has since been obscured by pollution from industrial development along its shores. It can still be seen in its original glory, but only about forty days in the year, when the winds blow away the smog.

NEAPOLITANS   A highly individualistic citizenry, they are a puzzle to the rest of the Italians, and often a despair. They pride themselves on surviving the worst disasters and the most corrupt and inefficient governments. The process of survival is known as "arranging oneself" (*si arrangia*), and it takes myriad forms—some legal, some not.

The picture that the rest of the world has of the Italians does not fit the Neapolitan. He is not vivacious, artistic, smiling, or a great lover. He is usually melancholy, with a strong dash of cutting irony that is masked by his dialect, which is a mixture of Italian, Spanish, French, and perhaps even of more ancient languages. It is robust and earthy, particularly among the lower classes, and has given rise to some exquisite, if sad, poetry. As for the visual arts, Bernini, the architect of the baldachino over the papal altar in Saint Peter's, Rome, and the famous colonnade of Saint Peter's Square, was a Neapolitan, but, like a great number of his fellow citizens, an emigrant from the city.

The Neapolitan must not be confused with the Sicilian (portrayed in popular romances such as *The Godfather*).

THE GERMAN HEADQUARTERS   Situated in the Hotel Parco, in the higher area of Naples. Originally it was the Hotel Parker, because an eccentric English resident, Mr. Parker, not wishing to be disturbed when the hotel was threatened with bankruptcy, bought the place on the spot. The Fascists, disliking the English name, changed it to Parco (meaning park). It has now reverted to its original name, and although the surrounding area has been changed out of all recognition by development, the hotel remains much the same.

SANTA LUCIA   This, too, is largely unchanged, having been rebuilt after the war. The swimming boys still operate.

MUSSOLINI, BENITO (1883–1945)   The inventor of fascism. At a meeting in Naples in faraway 1922 (October 24), he decided to send his squads of bullyboys on a march on Rome to overthrow the feeble democratic government. The march (on October 28) was a complete success; Mussolini entered the historic capital in triumph, having gone, himself, cautiously by train. One would like to think that it was in commemoration of his history-making journey that efficient stationmasters for the next twenty-one years adopted the phrase that will forever be associated with his name: "Mussolini made the trains run on time." (See also below: Mussolini, Fall of.)

Fascism   In reading this narrative of events in Naples, it is important for anybody who is not an Italian to rid his mind, at least for a while, of the nefarious meanings that have become attached to the word "fascism." The word itself was an invention spawned from Mussolini's daydream of reviving the glories of Ancient Rome.

Consuls—the heads of state in republican Rome—had, within limitations, the power of life and death over the citizen. To symbolize this, they went about with *lictors*—"gorillas," or bodyguards (as all heads of state do). The *lictor* carried a bundle of rods in which was bound an ax. The rods were for flogging the citizens, the ax for cutting off their heads. The word for a bundle in Italian is *fascio*. Hence "fascism."

But in Mussolini's Italy there were no floggings and no chopping off of heads. True, in the very early days the black-shirted supporters of the dictator gave his opponents heavy doses of castor oil —a mild form of political repression compared with what the world was to know later. But murders were almost unknown: the one exception, a politician called Matteoti, shocked the country. There were also no concentration camps or psychiatric prisons for dissidents. Nobody was deported to inhospitable places like Siberia. Opponents *were* sent to remote places to live under surveillance, but one of them, the island of Giglio, is now a popular summer tourist resort. It was, however, dangerous to hold Communist views.

To the Neapolitan, fascism was a form of government no worse —albeit equally corrupt—than all the others in its long history. It was Mussolini's misfortune that two of his theatrical devices were copied by Hitler (who despised Italians)—the Roman salute of the raised arm, and the fancy Party uniforms.

Mussolini, Fall of   Mussolini entered World War II on Hitler's side, but he was completely unready to do so because Hitler, deceiving him with the same ease with which he had deceived the British prime minister (Neville Chamberlain), had told him that he would start the battle three months later than he actually did.

Mussolini's armies never recovered from that mistake. They suffered crushing defeats in Africa and Greece, and were involved in the German debacle outside Stalingrad. As a result, he lost prestige and influence. At a meeting of the Fascist Grand Council in Rome, his right to rule was put to the vote, and he lost, 19 to 8. He went to see the king in order to resign. The king, an old friend and supporter, was extremely gracious: he accepted the resignation; expressed his regret; and in a courtly gesture accompanied Mussolini to the threshold of his palace, where, as he knew, the Duce would be promptly arrested.

An ambulance was waiting. The Duce was hustled into it and taken off to prison. Later he was sent to a place of confinement in the Apennines, called, with the irony of history, the Field of the Emperor. A party of ninety German parachute troops rescued him from his prison, and he set up, with German help, a new government at Salò, in northern Italy. This was overthrown by victorious American and British troops. Mussolini was shot by partisan fighters.

Mussolini was a many-sided man. He wrote, in his youth, a novel with the splendid title for a paperback *The Cardinal's Mistress.* He was a family man who raised six children. He was faithful to the end to his mistress, Clara Petracci, and she was faithful to him. Her body was hung upside down at the gasoline station beside his. A passing Samaritan pinned her skirt together with a safety pin so that the gaping crowds should not see her panties.

Ceramic plaques, suitable for hanging on the wall and carrying some of Mussolini's sayings, are still on sale in shops in Naples. He has a warm corner in the memory of the citizens of Naples for many things, among them the fact that he made his favorite politicians jump through flaming hoops to prove they were not cowards. The sudden fall of the dictator was utterly confusing to the Neapolitans, and this accounts for their long delay in taking up arms against the Germans.

Hitler and his entourage were equally taken aback. Communications had failed and they had not an inkling that it was going to happen. This would be unbelievable if we did not have the diary of Josef Goebbels to tell us about it. He was, of course, Hitler's propaganda minister and a magnificent liar, but he is clearly telling the truth here:

The news is almost incredible. It seems that the Duce has resigned and that Badoglio has assumed power in his place. The whole situation as far as I have been told is, at the moment, obscure. The news that we have came by radio through Reuters Agency. . . .

There have been violent contrasts in the Fascist Grand Council. Various members have declared themselves contrary to Mussolini's policies and to his conduct of the war. The principal figures in the conflict are Ciano and Grandi.

Then, having admitted so frankly that the whole affair had taken the Nazis completely by surprise, Goebbels comes up with a full explanation: it was all the work of the Masons and the Vatican.

The fall of Mussolini has been as thoroughly investigated as any event in history, and there is no more reason to think that the Masons or the priests of Rome were the cause of it than there is to believe, say, that they poisoned Goebbels. He was to take that final dose when Berlin fell, for the good reason that he thought it was the best thing to do in the circumstances. Mussolini resigned in much the same way.

For Goebbels, there remained the king, but he did not look on him with any great reverence. "The King of Italy," he wrote, "is too stupid and too short-sighted to understand this maneuver."

The king was no Charlemagne or Louis XIV, it was true. He was too concerned with his collection of coins, medals, and other solid pieces of pectoral decoration to be a great monarch. But it is only fair to say that he did not understand the conspiracy because it never existed. Goebbels, however, once away from hunting witches either in aprons or soutanes, resumed his strange, evil, but fascinating brilliance of mind. With something of the penetration of an Edward Gibbon or a Thucydides, he goes on to say: "It is always true that as soon as a dictator falls, the man in the street makes himself heard. I think, therefore, that we will not have to wait long before that happens in Italy."

It was not the man in the street but the boy in the alley.

BADOGLIO, PIETRO (1871–1956)   Duke of Addis Ababa and victorious commander in chief in Mussolini's war against Ethiopia, Badoglio had fallen into bad odor with the Duce because of his opposition to the Greek adventure. With the fall of Mussolini, the king made Badoglio prime minister, a post he held from July 1943 to June 1944.

THE ARMISTICE   Badoglio was convinced that he could come to terms with the Allies and join them against Hitler. He had sent an envoy, Castellano, to Lisbon—a neutral city and a spy center of wartime Europe—to negotiate. At first there seemed to be some hope. Roosevelt had gone on record at a press conference with a highly pragmatic speech suggesting that he would work with the Fascists— or ex-Fascists, as they now preferred to be called. Roosevelt had said:

> The first thing to do for a victorious army is to obtain the end of armed opposition. The second is that when that armed opposition comes to an end, to avoid anarchy. In a country that gets into a state of anarchy, it is a pretty difficult thing to deal with, because it would take an awful lot of troops. . . . I don't care with whom we deal in Italy, as long as it isn't a definite member of the Fascist government, as long as they get them to lay down their arms, and so long as we don't have anarchy. Now he may be a king, or a present prime minister, or a mayor of a town or village.

But this aroused the ire of every liberal American, who pertinently asked, if that was so, what was the war all about? Churchill, re-membering the success of the campaign in Britain to "Hang the Kaiser" after the First World War, now demanded unconditional surrender. Roosevelt gave way, and, having announced in a fire-side chat, "We will have no truck with fascism in any way, in any shape," agreed to an unconditional surrender that was signed by the Italians in an olive grove in Sicily, an island now completely in the hands of the Allies.

The surrender signed, Roosevelt issued a declaration to the Italian people telling them that nothing now remained except for them to rid their country of the German Army. The call never reached the Italian people. It was effectively censored.

On September 9, 1943, in their newspapers and on the radio, the Neapolitans read and heard the following announcement:

> The Italian government, recognizing the impossibility of continuing the unequal fight against the overwhelming su-periority of the adversary, in the intention of saving the nation from further disasters, has asked General Eisenhower for an armistice.

The request has been granted.

Consequently every hostile act against the Anglo-American forces on the part of Italian forces must cease.

They, however, will react to any possible attack coming from any other quarter.

BACKGROUND TO THE SALERNO LANDING   It should be emphasized that the Neapolitans knew nothing of the strategic and tactical reasons for the sudden invasion of nearby Salerno. But they may be of interest to American and British readers since they involved the conflict of wills of three powerful personalities—Churchill, Roosevelt, and Eisenhower.

In the First World War, Churchill had conceived the strategy of attacking Germany from below—that is, up from the South instead of down from the North, where the war was going badly. He therefore ordered a landing at Gallipoli, a place in European Turkey, on the west shore of the Dardanelles. The idea was to bowl over Germany's Turkish ally and to proceed thence, by stages, to Berlin.

The Turks bowled over Churchill's troops instead, so the war was back to square one—Flanders, the most blood-soaked in history. Churchill, the war over, put this right in sonorous English prose, but it was not quite sonorous enough to convince everybody. Gallipoli hung over him like a cloud and kept him from the prime ministry until, with the Second World War, his hour struck.

He revived his strategy. Germany was to be attacked, not from across the English Channel but on its "soft underbelly," the Mediterranean. Some islands were first to be taken (*which* islands was a mere detail) and Italy invaded. The Allied troops would sweep up the peninsula and, surmounting the barrier of the Alps, conquer central Europe, Romania, and so forth. Then, on to Berlin, as before.

The American Chiefs of Staff could not see this at all, including Eisenhower. He, orthodox in everything except his grammar, thought that the Germans should be met head-on by a massive landing on the coasts of France. The Chiefs of Staff pointed out that it would have to be a very massive landing indeed and there would be no troops to spare for sideshows.

Franklin D. Roosevelt supported first one view and then the other. He finally decided to adopt both plans. The island to be invaded was Sicily, and then Italy itself at two points. The first was right on the heel of Italy at Taranto, a task left to the British. The major landing was to be on the beaches at Salerno.

The landing met with fierce opposition from the Germans, and at one stage the Allied generals considered withdrawal. The operation, however, was finally successful. General Mark Clark was in command of the Fifth Army (American), and General Bernard Montgomery was in command of the Eighth Army (British). The commander of all the German forces in Italy was Field Marshal Albert Kesselring, who remained in Rome.

THE BARRICADE OF SANTA TERESA   There are many claimants for the title of originator of the idea of using the trams. It may well have come from a bystander, who subsequently joined the revolt—Alfredo Parente.

PARTISANS   It is agreed by all observers, including declared Communists, that there was no partisan group in Naples until the Four Days, when, as with Martone, they were formed on the spot. In the north of Italy, they were very active. It was these northern partisans who captured and executed Mussolini.

STIMOLO, VINCENZO   A legend grew up around Stimolo after the war. It was said that he went north and died in a daring parachute engagement, but this cannot be sustained. He was certainly not a "captain," nor was he a member of the Communist party.

EXPLETIVES   The swearing of the *scugnizzi* is untranslatable since it needs a knowledge of the Neapolitan way of life to be understood. Thus, the most commonly heard expression is *Gia marronne*, a shortening of *Managgia' la Madonna*, which one *scugnizzo* delicately explained to the author as "not letting the Madonna sleep peacefully in her bed." I have used English and American equivalents that bear a similar weight in discourse as those used by the boys.

THE INTERPRETER   The interpreter was Ugo Berti, who subsequently ran a beauty parlor in Udine. He wrote about his experiences with both the Italians and the Germans in an extremely ironical tone.

MAIURI, AMADEO   After the war, the Professor made extensive excavations in Pompeii that greatly extended the known area of the city. He recorded his experiences during the Four Days. He died in 1963.

THIRTY YEARS ON: WHAT HAPPENED TO THE *scugnizzi?*   The writer of this narrative greatly envies those other authors who, investigating an event in modern history some years after it has happened, send a team of assistants, armed with tape recorders, to find out the truth. That does not do for Naples. Faced with a microphone and the promise of a fee, the Neapolitan will tell the researcher exactly what he most wants to hear. Good manners demand no less.

I had heard the story from the boys themselves, just after the war, and hot off the hob. Going back some thirty years later to check, I had to face problems not usually found elsewhere.

The principal difficulty has been put very well by one of the finest, most sensitive writers Naples has produced: Giuseppe Marotta. The Neapolitan, he has said, has a negative pride. Ask him to tell you of something much to his credit, and he will diminish it in its telling until there seems little left. The revolt of the boys and the young men was an act of heroism. A Neapolitan will boast unashamedly of the most improbable conquests of women, but he is uncomfortable when you call him a hero to his face.

The second difficulty lay in the *scugnizzo* himself. The qualities of sheer survival in a hostile environment stand him in good stead in later life. He does not remain a barefoot boy; very often he succeeds in life where boys brought up in more comfortable circumstances wilt and fail. One of the highest paid and most admired among pop singers and film stars in Italy is Massimo Ranieri. He was a street boy. He admits it, and with the money and applause he earns he can afford to. But boys who have made a more modest success in life—opened a shop, brought up a family, gone into the profitable tourist industry—have no particular wish to be reminded too publicly that they were once pickpockets and thieves. And when, in their cups, they do reminisce, it infuriates their wives and their in-laws.

The last and most formidable obstacle was (as it always is in Italy) politics. When the boys first told me their story, it seemed reasonably certain that Fascism had gone forever. That is not the way it has turned out. While I tried to reconstruct the story, gangs of neo-Fascists were roving the streets, beating up opponents. It was all on a small scale. It will probably remain that way. But it does no good to advertise the fact that when you were a boy you shot somebody's grandfather dead, especially if that man's grandson has a knife, a gun, or a cudgel. Thus there was no enthusiastic rush to gain publicity, as seems to greet interviewers for television and such in less cautious or, perhaps, less experienced cities in the world. But the story was there. To find it needed time and patience. I had to walk the streets and frequent the bars or idle in the piazzas until the citizens grew familiar with my face. I had to convince them that I really did speak Italian as easily as I did my native tongue. Above all, I had to convince them that I was no journalist, looking for a tale to tell: I had discovered a good deal of the truth many years before.

In the beginning I had known the boys who appear in these pages by their first names only. (You do not throw your surname about when the police may well be after you.) Some had taken me to their homes. These I could trace. But very often their parents, now old and gray and full of years, were not necessarily very happy that the misdeeds of their children should be blazoned to the world. Many of them had thoroughly disagreed with the young scamps, some with very good cause, for the young scamps had died, and all that was left of them was a fading photograph. "And what," I was asked, "did they give their lives for?" Looking round at the chaos of Italy today and the continuing poverty of Naples, I had no answer.

Some boys had made good. It took time to convince them (in their little restaurants, shops, garages, and, in one instance, a prosperous boutique) that I really admired what they had done during the revolt. Admiration for anything is rare in Naples, except for footballers. But it could be managed. I have preserved their anonymity so far as their surnames are concerned, except in those cases where they have passed into recorded history.

Concerning these records: in addition to the documents in the archives, Mario Orbitello, Giacomo de Antonellis, Aldo de Jaco, Mario Schettini, and Giovanni Artieri have published their researches on the Four Days in the form of pamphlets or collections of reminiscences from eyewitnesses. In the course of my own inquiries I was told, of course, many tall tales, particularly when following mistaken tracks by which I was led to a person who, it turned out, had often not been in Naples at all. (That was considered good Neapolitan fun.) But my measuring stick was, throughout, this: the incidents included in this book were mentioned (if not always in full detail) by at least two of the writers or editors I have listed.

So much for the difficulties. What was easy and pleasant was to urge the participants to reconstruct for me their way of talking or thinking and the tricks they had played in their daily life as boys. Nor have things changed much. The *scugnizzi* of today, with whom I checked, have shoes and decent clothes, but they still swear the same way, and they have not lost the art of picking a pocket.

Niello went to England. The commendatore helped him to do so, and so did I. He married an English girl, an excellent person very much in love with him, but with the sturdy common sense of a Yorkshire woman. Before she finally married him, she wrote to me to ask what he was really like as a boy. I am happy to say that when I told her, it made her more in love with him than ever. He brought his wife and two young sons to see me. They have a great deal of their father in them. The family visits Italy for holidays, for he has a British government job in the tourist business, and is moderately prosperous. But, however much the family pleads, he will never stay for more than a few hours in Naples.